# Don't Knock,
# He's Dead

# Don't Knock, He's Dead

## A Longshot Candidate Gets Schooled in the Unseemly Underbelly of American Campaign Politics

ADAM GORDON SACHS

*"In a democracy, someone who fails to get elected to office can always console himself with the thought that there was something not quite fair about it."*
Thucydides, Athenian general, *History of the Peloponnesian War,* 400 BC

*"In a society governed passively by free markets and free elections, organized greed always defeats disorganized democracy."*
Matt Taibbi, *Griftopia: Bubble Machines, Vampire Squids, and the Long Con That Is Breaking America,* on the 2008 Wall Street financial crisis

All the events depicted in this book are true, facts are based on public documents and sources, and places are real. Though aliases have been used for some candidates and politicians, all people depicted in this book are real and descriptions are true. Some dialog has been recreated to the best of my recollection, but the essence of all conversations is accurate. In other words, this book is true to life and contains no fiction.

**Also by Adam Gordon Sachs under Sirenian Publishing**
*Three Yards and a Plate of Mullet*

ISBN: 1533357749
ISBN 13: 9781533357748

# Contents

# Prologue: Don't Knock, He's Dead

On a frigid late December day, I parked my mountain bike with the attached kids' bike trailer adorned on its three sides with bright blue "Sachs for Delegate" lettering on yellow lawn signs on the sidewalk and bounded down the stairs to the two ground-floor units of an eight-unit condo building. In condos, a candidate can knock on lots of doors fast; the drawback, however, is that condo dwellers are more transient and less likely voters.

An older couple was unloading bags from their car and followed me down the stairs. I was planning to knock on the door of a Mr. Jacobson, whose name and address I had recorded on my "walking list," or in my case, "bicycling list," culled from the Democratic voter registration for my election district. My analysis showed Jacobson had a pattern of voting in gubernatorial primary elections, my primary targets. I thought the people trailing me were the Jacobsons, so I waited in the stairwell to greet them. The woman obviously had noticed the Sachs for Delegate BikeMobile on the sidewalk.

Before I could greet her, she accosted me.

"Are you soliciting? You're not allowed to solicit here, didn't you see the sign?"

I was taken aback by her unconcealed hostility.

"I'm running for state delegate in this district and I'm campaigning," I answered. "Do you consider that soliciting?"

"Yes," she nodded. "Do you?"

*Lady, do you see me lugging a vacuum cleaner?*

"No," I responded. "I'm here for an election. I consider soliciting when you're trying to sell something. I'm not selling anything. I'm here because I want to represent you in the Maryland legislature. I want to know if you have any concerns."

"I'm concerned about your soliciting. We're tired of salesmen."

"I'm a candidate," I repeated.

"What's the difference?"

The woman motioned to the condo on the right, my destination address. The people before me weren't the Jacobsons after all.

"Don't bother knocking. That man's dead. And we don't want any," she said, entering the adjacent unit and shutting the door in my face.

That doorstep rejection was a metaphor for my longshot run for a Maryland state delegate seat representing portions of two dichotomous suburban counties in one of the nation's highest-educated, wealthiest and largest metropolitan areas, the Washington-Baltimore megalopolis: enduring petty slights, suffering campaign poverty, struggling to "sell" myself, persevering despite disrespect and disappointments, calling attention to a "progressive" platform considered politically impractical, trying all the while to figure out this corrupt, depraved and vicious yet exhilarating, flamboyant, rewarding and, yes, potentially even honorable game called "politics."

## Primary Night: Keepin' Hope Alive

*"Despite what the pundits want you to think, contested
primaries aren't civil war, they are democracy at
work, and that's beautiful... I tip my hat to anyone
with the courage to throw theirs in the ring and
may the best ideas and candidates win."*

Sarah Palin, former Republican vice presidential
nominee, to the 2010 Tea Party Convention

**"I** *got nowhere else to go!"*
Zack Mayo to Sergeant Foley, trying to break Mayo into quitting
the Navy in *An Officer and a Gentleman*

Primary election night, June 24, 2014, and I had nowhere to go.
Ordinarily this wouldn't have been a big deal, except that I was a candidate, and candidates always have somewhere they are supposed to be, somewhere their supporters and admirers are waiting for them to shake their hand, share a good luck wish and, if lucky, to celebrate. The world revolves around them. The most organized candidates show up after a long day of election poll hopping to an event planned and executed by their campaign manager and volunteer staff, paid for by their surplus of campaign funds and in-kind donations from businesses that support them. I had nowhere. I was Zack Mayo.

3

In the galaxy of campaign politics, I was always the ring, never the Saturn. I didn't have a big team of volunteers to invite to my house to watch the election returns, like Zelig, the high-achieving, hard-working young physician whose purple- and yellow-clad squad adjourned to his house for pizza. I didn't have the dedicated family members as campaign workers or the lifetime roots in the community, like Ballerina, whose father, known as "Soft Shoes," was a legendary Baltimore politician, and who hosted followers at a Main Street eatery.

There was no communal Democratic Party lovefest, like there would be for the General Election. So I went where the action would be, the election night party for the hottest gubernatorial candidate in Maryland, Heather Mizeur, a progressive, dynamic Maryland state delegate who had risen from obscurity and less than 5 percent in the polls to the mid-20s with momentum against two Establishment power brokers, Maryland's attorney general and lieutenant governor.

As the most "liberal" candidate in my field for one of three open District 12 delegate seats in the Maryland General Assembly, I latched onto Mizeur's progressive campaign early.

Mizeur was openly gay with a spouse, and promoted such causes as legalization and decriminalization of marijuana, universal pre-kindergarten education and a hefty minimum wage hike. She had an undeniable authenticity, honesty and transparency on the campaign trail that inspired passion in legions who were disgusted with manipulative, disingenuous politicians, dictatorial party machines and corrupt politics as usual. I identified with the Mizeur campaign's status as the underdog, underfinanced outsider fighting The Establishment, given little chance to prevail but plowing ahead doggedly.

With no other options, my wife Amy and I headed for energy, diversity and karma at the Mizeur "victory" celebration. It was an eclectic gathering of the LGBT community, hipsters, liberals, artists, tree-huggers, activists, college students, feminists, idealists and others enamored with the anti-politician politician. Fittingly, one of our tablemates for pizza and wine was Transvestite Ed, a sultry blonde with a raspy voice and burly build.

The event in the Baltimore Historical Society's courtyard, which seemed buoyant under clouds of blue and orange balloons, was festive with a palpable sense of anticipation because of the momentum Mizeur had generated. The bright lights of TV news crews illuminated the gathering of supporters absorbed in anticipatory conversation.

By 9 p.m., an hour after polls closed, Amy was itching to check for early District 12 election returns on her cell phone. I urged her not to check yet. I wanted to stave off the potential disappointment, and not prematurely dash dreams of an upset and top three finish. I wanted to extend the feeling of the quest, of doing something consequential and challenging and even miraculous. And I was afraid of failure, of rejection and disapproval, of having to accept a conclusion that I wasn't popular and didn't measure up, regardless the reasons. Amy put the phone away. Fifteen minutes later, she got her phone out again and started scrolling through returns from Maryland's 47 legislative districts.

"Put it away, it's too early," I told her. "Let's not ruin the suspense."

"Relax, I'm just checking on Ted's race," Amy said.

Amy's Uncle Ted Levin was a seasoned politician who already had served five terms in the Maryland General Assembly until he lost an election in a redrawn district. But he couldn't get the thrill of politics and the hunt of the campaign out of his system. For the second time in four years, he was running for a public office comeback, this time to regain his old seat in District 11, just before my District 12 in the online results. Amy promised she wouldn't scroll down to District 12. I gave in to temptation, and steeled myself to learn my preliminary standing.

"OK, go ahead and check," I said, feeling queasy.

"Who do you think is in first?" Amy asked.

"Anointed One."

"Right. And then?"

"Zelig"

"Yes. Next?"

Third place was a tougher call. Anointed One and Zelig, who entered the race early and built political "relationships" and strong fundraising operations, had established themselves as favorites from the start. Popular wisdom was that the other eight candidates would be competing for the third and final spot to advance to the general election. It was up for grabs.

The huge bonus was that whichever three Democrats advanced to the general election would be heavily favored to sweep the corruptly gerrymandered district designed to protect the Democratic Party and secure seats in the Annapolis State House.

The only candidate who I believed did not have a chance at a top three spot was the 80-year-old attorney Spare-A-Dime, who approximated a Tea Party Democrat with his conservative views. I clung to the belief I had a chance to squeeze into third through the perfect storm of divided-vote circumstances.

"OK, enough predictions. Purse the phone. I don't want to know any more."

I wanted to keep hope alive. Even if I couldn't ascend into the trifecta, I wanted respectability, a showing that would affirm that my nine months as an outspoken candidate had resonated, that my messages had penetrated the consciousness of the small sliver of the electorate that was paying attention, despite my campaign's lack of money to distribute those ideas broadly through traditional campaign methods.

The problem was, even though I believed I worked hard, I knew deep down I didn't want it enough, didn't have that burning desire in my gut, that ruthless drive and all-consuming passion to work around the clock, to do all that was necessary and then some to win.

In many ways, I was not a good candidate, meaning not good at the game and machinations of campaign politics. I didn't have the basic political ingredients that all successful campaigns possess: a campaign infrastructure, a "ground game," a financial "war chest," or the politicians' stock-in-trade called "relationships," code for mutual and reciprocal agreements between political players to enhance each other's power and political access.

To my detriment, I didn't much care about all that, and abhorred the thought of spending much of my time as a candidate trying to create such a machine. Moreover, I just didn't know how to, didn't have the connections, didn't pre-pour the concrete. So I avoided the nuts-and-bolts of a campaign without which the whole beast suffers from self-starvation. It was akin to a general going into battle without his army—or even a tank—a fine plan for getting slaughtered. In this way, I was a masochistic candidate.

As an unknown emerging from nowhere, I had run for public office once before, eight years earlier, for a seat on the County Council in Howard County, Maryland, an affluent, fast-growing suburban jurisdiction of 275,000 whose main population center is the nation's most famous planned city, Columbia, a 1960s utopia of racial and economic integration and community-oriented villages. But that race was different. I was the only challenger taking on a favored incumbent. Now I was trying to stand out among 10 contenders in what one political commenter referred to as "a three-ring circus."

It was a race reminiscent of Agatha Christie's novel *And Then There Were None* about 10 nefarious individuals invited to a deserted island, who arrive full of hope and excitement but soon realize their fate will not be so pleasant: They are killed off one-by-one, which would also be the destiny of seven of the 10 candidates tonight.

Early on primary night, I felt I may lose the war. But I knew I would wake up June 25, no matter how I placed, feeling like I had won a battle by giving this torturous, maniacal American democratic process all I personally could give, running an ethical race, and being true to myself. On that Wednesday morning, I would either start strategizing anew on how to beat the three District 12 Republicans in the general election, or retire from candidacy in electoral politics, this time for good, with no regrets.

# An Unlikely Politician

*"Usually the amateur is defined as an immature
state of the artist: someone who cannot—or will
not—achieve the mastery of a profession."*

ROLAND BARTHES, FRENCH LITERARY
THEORIST AND PHILOSOPHER

In this book, you won't find advice on how to win an election. I would like to dispense expertise on how to trounce political foes by raising gobs of cash; building a vast volunteer network; organizing an elite "ground game;" piling up endorsements; maximizing social media; generating media coverage; inundating a district with strategically placed signs; converting phone banking into surefire votes; mastering data analytics to parse and target voter registration lists; deluging a district with direct mail; polling for effective messaging;  conducting opposition research; and attacking opponents' weaknesses.

I couldn't tell you, at least not with any authority based on proven success.

What you will find, if you've ever had the aspiration to run for public office, or even wondered what a political candidate must endure, is what it's like to spend every weekend and many weeknights until dusk knocking on doors of strangers; to be ignored by political organizations supposedly responsible for fairly evaluating candidates to make endorsements;

to feel poor and unsuccessful among more financially-connected candidates; to be targeted for barbs by highly opinionated, unfiltered bloggers. You'll know the struggle of waging uphill battle against advantaged candidates with political resume-builders who, among others, snared insider endorsements from all four sitting incumbents, self-funded a campaign with nearly $100,000 in personal wealth, claimed a legendary state senator for a father, and served as speechwriter for the sitting governor.

In other words, you'll get a vicarious glimpse into the experiences of an amateur politico trying to fit his round personality and sensibilities and lack of political chops into the square hole of American campaign politics.

I was an unlikely politician—an introvert in an extrovert's playground, one who enjoys individual pursuits more than massive team efforts and is generally uncomfortable at schmooze-fests that characterize successful politicians and campaigns.

Yet I had a desire to have an influence, to make a mark, to do something significant, and, plain and simple, to *be somebody* important, a big factor for anybody who runs for political office yet never admitted, always shrouded in high-minded political Pablum such as the burning desire to "serve the public," "get things done," and, above all, "fight for you."

In *First Person Political: Legislative Life and the Meaning of Public Service,* Grant Reeher explained that the power to achieve results and challenge themselves intellectually through the complex process of crafting policy motivated people to run for public office. Reeher drew his conclusions from a survey and interviews with state legislators. His findings closely mirrored my reasons for running.

"Legislative life offers the potential for a great sense of personal efficacy as well as the ego gratification of fame," Reeher said. "[Legislators] liked feeling effective and being important in people's lives."

I didn't want to join the madding crowd of lockstep candidates saying what they thought each audience wanted to hear, but to champion bold positions of change in which some politicians may have believed but wouldn't dare consider supporting for fear of the political or financial fallout or party disapproval for breaking encumbrances, such as: a transformed health care system guaranteeing access to essential health care for all and eliminating the stranglehold of private health insurers; a reformed campaign finance system to eradicate the pervasive and undue influence of political action committee (PAC), corporate and union money on politics; income tax relief for the middle- and working-class; and removal of politicians from a parochial, corrupt redistricting process.

I had no particular base to disappoint or funding source to protect, so I felt independent and free to speak my mind. I wouldn't have wanted to run for Maryland state delegate any other way.

No matter whether you owe allegiances to legions who pledge to help you get into and retain public office, or run as a renegade like I did, being a candidate is unquestionably an unappreciated grind.

The emcee at our candidates' forum at a retirement community of 2,000 residents outside Baltimore captured what it's like to be a candidate and how little the all-consuming endeavor is understood or respected:

"In today's political climate, elected officials are not always received positively," said the emcee. "And that attitude makes it difficult for anyone to decide to run for office. It takes a huge amount of time, enormous energy and strong dedication to follow through on that decision, especially because doing so has an impact on each one individually as well as on their job and family."

Amen, my Brother! I never felt I could do enough, or meet the prolific expectations everybody seems to have of a candidate; there just weren't enough hours in the day. The process was overwhelming and exhausting, all-consuming mentally, physically, emotionally and spiritually—and simultaneously enlivening. I have never felt as inspired, engaged in life and engrossed in a noble pursuit as when I was a candidate. I wasn't just trudging through life, waiting to collect my bi-weekly paycheck and get off the hamster wheel for a two-day respite. I was doing something important to which I had committed my mind, heart and soul, and I felt that to my core. Execution was another story.

## Worthy of the Public's (Dis)Trust

The word *candidate* originated from the Ancient Romans who sought high public office while dressed in white togas—in Latin, *candidatus*, or clothed in white. How the mighty have fallen! Now the public looks upon candidates not as pure as holiness but as base as sin, so much so that candidates might as well trade in the archetypal toga and run in the black-and-white, horizontal-striped uniform of jailbirds, or in all red carrying a devil's pitchfork.

The public holds politicians in "low esteem," Reeher said in *First Person Political*, causing a snowball effect on civic life. The public's distrust of politicians—64 percent of respondents to a 2015 Gallup poll on honesty and ethics in professions ranked members of Congress "low" or "very low"— has contributed to a "decline in the democratic health of our political system." That decline has reduced interconnectedness and trust among citizens, which has correlated to a decrease in civic engagement. I felt the political alienation and cynicism—some citizens, like the "Don't Knock" woman, treated me like a derelict scam-artist or a menace to society. The only statistic you need to know about citizen disengagement is that only 1 in 5 registered voters in my home county bothered to vote in my primary.

But Reeher's research on legislators also painted a picture counter to commonly held ideas about politicians' selfish motivations and duplicitous, corrupt natures. Many politicians, he found, have altruistic motives and intentions: Candidates "look a lot like the Ancient Roman idealized version. Contrary to what most people think, most candidates pursue office, and once elected serve in office, primarily out of a motivation to advance the public good," Reeher found. And for that devotion, Reeher added, "many pay dearly for their efforts."

I was not as sanctified as an Ancient Roman, and neither were my competitors, but for the most part, I believed we were running largely for the altruistic reason Reeher cited, not primarily for personal aggrandizement, though I know I couldn't have denied the ego boost an election win and state delegate position would have brought me. No doubt, I wanted to *be somebody,* feel good about myself and make my life more meaningful, but I also wanted to have a positive impact on other people's lives and society on the whole. There are few more powerful ways to do that on a grand scale than changing a policy that could affect everyone statewide, like enacting universal health care.

Traveling to countless meet-the-candidate events and forums; pounding the pavement door-to-door; making fundraising requests and volunteer recruitment pitches; writing speeches; designing websites; producing videos; creating promotional materials; working with printers and direct-mail houses; building a social media presence; researching a myriad of high-profile and obscure issues; responding to innumerable questionnaires and interviewing for treasured endorsements as if applying for jobs—the tasks were endless and demanded time, planning, strategizing and energy.

## A 100-Year Political Storm

But I had an opportunity that was like the proverbial 100-year storm to fuel motivation. All three sitting delegates from my District 12 had decided to retire, including two who had become virtual institutions after serving for 20 years each. Such turnover in the Maryland General Assembly—and probably anywhere in the U.S. lacking term limits—is unheard of in an industry dominated by "career politicians" who can control and manipulate the game's mechanisms to keep outsiders at bay. The Maryland delegate turnover rate was about 1 in every 8 representatives in 2010. In my district, it was a miraculous 1 in 1 in 2014!

The unanticipated "Help Wanted" situation prompted the entry of an unprecedented number of contenders for a Democratic primary.

The District 12 field was packed with 10 candidates, with no slouches or unaccomplished pretenders. It was a powerhouse group of contenders: Ivy League graduates, doctors, lawyers; business owners, state government insiders, and former candidates, judges and politicians.

There was **Man of the People**, a cancer survivor and working-class community activist,  fighter for the blue-collar worker, the oppressed and downtrodden, the youngest-ever chairman of the Baltimore County Democratic Party; **Spare-A-Dime**, attorney and former judge; **Gadfly**, business owner and relentless opponent of a controversial mega-commercial development; **Erik Energy**, Maryland's Outstanding Mathematics Teacher of the Year; **Joker**, a State House lobbyist and disbarred attorney, former Maryland delegate and consummate insider tied into the Old Boy Network of developers, Realtors and financiers; **Anointed One**, a physician from a pioneering, high-achieving African-American family; **Zelig**, seemingly everywhere, a Johns Hopkins University physician and community leader with legislative experience at the state and national levels; **Ballerina**, a state education official and daughter of a legendary former Maryland senator; and **Next Big Thing**, the sitting Maryland governor's former speechwriter and a lawyer with a prestigious firm.

The two doctors, Anointed One and Zelig, were the first to enter the race and were considered frontrunners from the outset. As physicians, they were a rare breed on the campaign trail. Since 1990, only three physicians had served in the Maryland legislature.

Never mind the others, in Anointed One and Zelig, I was going up against two candidates from my home turf, Columbia, Howard County, who probably qualified as brilliant—I mean, likely in the ballpark of Mensa, the world's largest high IQ society. As Mensa allows admission only to those who score in the top two percent on certain intelligence tests, I would put my money on Anointed One and Zelig gaining entry any day over a George W. Bush, John Boehner, Nancy Pelosi, Joe Biden, or Donald Trump for that matter.

I would have to be a quick study on subjects about which I knew little—the decriminalization or legalization of marijuana; hydraulic fracturing, or fracking; the economics of a minimum wage increase; taxes; retirees' concerns; offshore wind energy; and the new national Common Core educational standards, to name a few.

But I wasn't deterred. The race was wide open—well, at least on paper. I believed I had a chance, maybe slim and unlikely, but a chance nonetheless. If I didn't believe that, I would have been tempted to quit; a supporter even suggested dropping out to throw my votes to a "more viable" candidate to prevent Joker from winning.

Robert Sarvis, a Libertarian candidate for Virginia governor in 2013, expressed what it's like for candidates like me who persuade ourselves that we have a chance to win as substantial underdogs, a mind game to protect ourselves from possibly admitting we are committing tremendous effort to a futile cause.

"You suffer a lot of indignities," Sarvis said in the *Washington Post*. "You introduce yourself to people and you see in their face that they're thinking 'I don't need to pay attention to this guy.'"

Candidates must have a "thick skin" and "endure the emotional challenge of standing for election," wrote Reeher in *First Person Political*, by placing themselves "on a stage of maximum personal exposure."

"Putting yourself before an anonymous vote of your fellow citizens is psychologically daunting," Reeher said. "When a candidate loses, the defeat cannot help but feel to some degree like a personal negative judgment."

Judgement Day was an intimidating thought, but I wouldn't be a quitter, I decided, no matter if I felt overwhelmed by the money, resources and connections of other candidates, no matter if my effort was cast as hopeless by political observers and insiders. I was in it for the long haul. I daydreamed of the moment during primary night at some local Democratic hangout, when returns from major precincts posted, showing Sachs in the top three and among those who would advance to the general election, with looks of surprise on insiders' faces, suddenly becoming more viable and popular, like the prototypical high school stud, confidently accepting handshakes and back slaps from sycophants who suddenly wanted to be around me.

## Dreaming Big

Yes, it could happen, I convinced myself, if the stars aligned just right and a complex equation of votes from two disparate counties shook out just right to allow me to make an end run around enough other political novices and carpetbaggers who faced their own questions about viability or preparedness for political office. Of course I had a chance. You know, like the gospel all elementary school children hear and are led to believe before reality sets in and you realize your limitations and that the world doesn't particularly care about you: "You can be anything you want to be. You too can be president, if you just believe in yourself and work hard enough." That's The American Dream. That's American democracy at work, right?

For anyone who's ever wondered what it's like to be a candidate in a major, high-stakes political race; who's ever considered subjecting himself to scrutiny and the whims of uncensored public opinion; who's ever debated whether it would be worth the time and effort to run for public office; who's ever stepped to the precipice of throwing a hat in the ring and then backed off with either regret or relief; or who still has a dream to make a difference in people's lives by entering politics—you know, *someday*, when everything is perfectly aligned and your finances are in supreme order, and your employer gives you essential flexibility and full backing, and your family has attained impeccable stability, and the moon eclipses the sun, cicadas emerge after 17 years underground and the Chicago Cubs win the World Series and the time is right to run, *someday*—here's my account of what it's like in the trenches of an election as an amateur, entourage-less, DIY, working-stiff candidate.

My race encompassed the particular character and personality attributes and flaws of 10 self-selecting participants in a large swath of Maryland suburbia along the I-95 corridor. It was local, and at the same time global: Elements of the political game I experienced—the subterfuge, unfettered ambition, unabashed self-promotion, all-consuming pursuit, power plays, overzealousness, braggadocio, greed, blindness, opportunism, coattail-riding, favor-courting, brick-throwing and more—could be practiced by any candidate running in any political jurisdiction in the U.S. I was Candidate X, Anywhere, USA.

Democracy isn't pretty. Neither is the sight of lions eating their young. It's a brutal world, survival of the fittest, the quest to establish territorial dominance, husband resources, travel in packs, create alliances and ward off attackers. I would have to summon my inner caveman to have any chance of success in this hunt.

# An Introvert Playing an Extrovert's Game

> *"Tocqueville saw that the life of constant action and decision which was entailed by the democratic and businesslike character of American life put a premium upon rough and ready habits of mind, quick decision, and the prompt seizure of opportunities—and that all this activity was not propitious for deliberation, elaboration, or precision in thought."*

> RICHARD HOFSTADTER, *ANTI-INTELLECTUALISM IN AMERICAN LIFE*

If I had asked the 16-year-old me if I would ever run for public office, the answer would have been a resounding *no.* I would have gotten no votes in the Most Likely to Become a Politician popularity contest. I was not a student government leader, or an organizer of any kind. I was and always have been an introvert, more energized by individual aims than group endeavors, which is how I ran my campaign, in contrast to the more stereotypical extroverted politicians. Extroverts are viewed as leaders high in charisma, desire for power and sociability, traits that would fill a job description for "politician."

I can behave more like an extrovert when the situation calls for it, something I've learned to do through years of attending frat parties, working as a reporter, networking, starting new jobs, returning to graduate school, campaigning for office and other life events. But it's not my comfort zone, which means the fundamentals of productive

17

campaigning—glad-handing, meet-and-greets, working a room, fund-raising events—that ignite the energy of extroverted candidates like steroids for body builders can be draining for me.

As an introvert, I struggled with confidence growing up. I suffered from fear and anxiety that made public speaking difficult and nerve-racking. The fear of being fearful made me want to do anything to avoid being put in that spotlight. If I had told that 16-year-old me that one day I would be fielding unpredictable questions from a candidates' forum moderator to which I would have to respond extemporaneously with a coherent, two-minute answer in front of an audience of 200, I would have been anxiously plotting excuses to leave the room. With intentional effort and experience over the years, the fear all but disappeared, replaced with confidence, or at least, a sense of competency.

## Planting the Seed

But just because public speaking no longer was my Achilles heel didn't mean I was eyeing a run at politics. I credit my mother Sandra Sachs, a diehard liberal Democrat from Boston who had a fascination with the Massachusetts Kennedy clan, a devotion to other charismatic pols and a penchant for volunteering for campaigns, for getting me interested in politics. My mother's passion for politics eventually led her to jobs on Capitol Hill for Democratic Senators Bill Bradley of New Jersey and Daniel Moynihan of New York.

Through nepotism, I landed a job in Senator Bradley's mailroom after my freshman year of college, working for the man I had rooted against in the 1970s when he played for the great New York Knicks championship teams and I cheered for their rivals. Seventeen years later, I stepped foot in the political waters again, when Bradley ran for the Democratic nomination for president in 2000 against Al Gore and I traveled to frigid Iowa City in January to volunteer for his campaign in the bellwether Iowa caucus.

It was the first time I had ever gone door-to-door for any political candidate, experiencing the graciousness and inquisitiveness of most door-openers and the annoyance of a minority. I stood outside the University of Iowa basketball arena one 10-degree night to pass out Bradley literature to game-goers who were most interested in getting to warmth and seeing their beloved Hawkeyes. I quit passing out fliers too early, not eager to be working when others were heading for fun, a harbinger that I likely wasn't doggedly determined enough to succeed in this 24-7 game.

As a reporter for the *Baltimore Sun* in the 1990s, I worked my way up from the agriculture and business beat in a largely rural county to cover the county's Maryland General Assembly delegation. It was my first glimpse of citizen legislators up close. The lawmakers were provincial men, long-established and well-respected in their tight-knit, small communities—a tire shop owner, a World War II pilot/dairy farmer/ banker, a pharmacist, a Realtor, a stock broker. Covering them gave me a glimpse that it was possible for regular folk to ascend to political office and become bedrock representatives. I wondered if I could do what they did. Anyway, journalism and political careers could not be intertwined, so the hypothesis was null.

It wasn't until I transitioned into public relations that the light bulb came on. As community affairs director for a social services agency, I organized political forums for state candidates. Observing the forums, I thought that I could perform as well as many of the inexperienced, run-of-the-mill candidates, and a seed was planted.

After a job layoff, I entered the Baltimore City Teacher program for career changers, and taught elementary school in low-income communities. I struggled to survive. I met with the principal, who emphasized if I didn't give it my all, , I would drown. The next day, I submitted my resignation, jumping ship from my fledgling teaching career with no life preserver.

Only four months earlier, I had separated from my wife, headed for divorce, with two young kids. I was both free and free-falling.

## Opportunity Knocks the First Time

It was just short of a year before the next election cycle, and the dormant thought of running for political office surfaced. *Maybe I'll have time to campaign while I look for a job*, I thought. I didn't know if it was a life raft to cling to or a bold dream to fulfill, or both. I discovered that my county council member had fallen out of favor with the Democratic Party. It seemed possible the party would welcome a challenger. I began gathering intelligence.

Meanwhile, I obtained a communications position at a health insurance giant—far from a dream job, but a consistent paycheck. But by then, the idea of running for council was firmly embedded.

Soon after I filed to run, the unpopular incumbent council member resigned, leaving it up to a county Democratic Committee to interview applicants for appointment to complete the term.

It was almost a great break—except that the one other officially registered candidate had run and lost against the departing councilman in the previous election and since had become an insider. The insider with a track record was selected.

## One and Done?

In the 2006 Democratic primary, I ran a bare-bones campaign against the newly appointed councilman with party backing. I lost, garnering 34 percent of the vote—respectable for a late-arriving political no-name who couldn't check the prerequisite boxes as stepping stones. I had not "paid my dues" or built my political network.

I received compliments during the campaign from insiders about my potential and encouragement to stay involved and build upon my effort. I didn't. Life intervened: a new girlfriend, young kids, aging parents, a stressful job. I figured the new council member would become entrenched, and he did. The desire didn't burn intensely enough, and I faded from the political stage.

I was satisfied to have given electoral politics one shot, so I wouldn't spend the rest of my life wondering whether I had the courage to run and what it would be like to put myself into the court of public opinion, to expose myself for all to judge and render a verdict. I had closed that chapter and had no plans to return. I'd sworn it off, closed the door—but left it unlocked. I was occasionally reminded by friends about my run and was asked if I was going to run again, as if I really was a dyed-in-the-wool politician. My answer was no...followed by the caveat that allowed for a sliver of possibility: *But I never say never.*

Seven years later, the perfect storm conspired to compel me to open the door again.

# Falling Dominoes

*"Not knowing when the dawn will come, I open every door."*

Emily Dickinson, writer/poet

In September 2012, the reigning dignitary of progressive, liberal politics in my idealistic planned community of Columbia, Maryland, a five-term delegate who marched to a different drummer, announced that she would retire from the Maryland General Assembly in 2014 when her term expired.

I didn't even notice. I was paying no attention to politics, and had no thoughts about pursuing state political office. I had just started in a graduate program part-time in counseling, and was looking at a six-year grind while working full-time to complete it. Four months before the delegate's retirement announcement, I broke my leg in a recreational league soccer game. Much of my physical and mental energy went into rehabbing, slogging through the days.

## Marching to Her Own Drummer

Delegate Drummer was known as a principled, progressive politician who wasn't afraid to speak her mind and take a stand. Her constituents loved her for her independent streak in a legislature bound by the tradition of "follow the leader," where horse-trading and allegiance leads to increased prestige and advancement. Drummer made a living standing up to political leadership and special interests. She railed against big-moneyed interests and opposed initiatives popular with the Democratic governor and legislative leaders, such as using taxpayer money to build a stadium for football's Baltimore Ravens and expanding casino gambling.

Drummer was aided immensely by the way the three-member district was drawn and structured. Drummer ran in a single-member sub-district (District 12B), which concentrated the liberal, progressive, affluent, highly educated base of Columbia as a consolidated voting bloc. As a progressive-minded lawyer, Drummer represented the sub-district well demographically.

## The Blue Dogs

Two other delegates represented the 12A sub-district, a more blue-collar, less transient region comprised largely of older, multi-generational communities, more an extension of Baltimore than was Columbia. Just as Drummer fit the profile for her white-collar area, Fireman and Cop were the perfect archetypes for their more working-class, Baltimore County region; both had lifelong roots in their community and were similarly popular and entrenched.

Fireman, who joined his small town's volunteer fire department as a teenager and became a career firefighter, was the son of a former Baltimore County sheriff and state delegate.

Cop served as a Baltimore County police officer and detective. While Cop seemed reserved, Fireman appeared the prototypical, outgoing "good-time Charlie" politician. He knew everybody, a result of growing up, living and working in the same community all his life. Fireman was quick with a funny quip, a pat on the back or a hug and a greeting of "Hey Buddy" or "Hey Beautiful." His campaign slogan—I don't know if he coined it or someone else made it up to suit him—was, "You're never alone with Fireman Petrone." Fireman prided himself on his high standards for "constituent service," which guided his approach to the job far more than crafting far-reaching, intricate legislation that the policy wonks among him relished. Coincidentally, my wife Amy once rented a room in Fireman's house through a mutual connection. Little did I know when I attended a Christmas party at Fireman's house in December 2012 that I would be running for his seat a year later.

## Zaching Makes an Impact

The 12A/12B sub-districts illustrated gerrymandering—the practice of drawing district lines to favor one political party, individual or constituency over another. Drummer and the Baltimore County delegates were well-protected in their respective spheres of influence in an elongated district that inexplicably stretched about equally over two largely disparate counties with vastly different roots. By law, sub-districts are intended for sparsely populated, expansive areas—not dense, metropolitan areas like mine.

Maryland's constitutionally required once-per-decade redistricting plan that took effect in February 2012 changed everything, and ultimately planted the seed that germinated into my unlikely entry into a free-for-all political race. The plan eliminated the 12A and 12B sub-districts, and their tribal fiefdoms. All three delegates now would have to campaign for votes district-wide in a unified District 12 to preserve their seats.

Drummer, whose act wouldn't play so well in more conservative Baltimore County, apparently had had enough anyway. She would have been 71 at the start of a sixth term, and she was more interested in her next stage of life. She had observed her grandson Zach Lederer battle brain cancer for years. Zach became a social media sensation when, after surgery to remove a tumor, he had a photo taken of himself in bed in his hospital gown, with tubes hooked up to his body, with his biceps flexed and fists raised and a look of steely determination. The image spread across the Internet and the pose became known as "Zaching." He died in March 2014 at age 20.

Drummer's e-mail to constituents announcing her pending retirement was quoted in a September 4, 2012 *Baltimore Sun* story: "The way our grandson, Zach, is living his life with such joy, courage, generosity and gratitude in the face of brain cancer has had a profound impact on me. This has led me to take a close look at how I want to live the remainder of my own life, and I now know…my work in public office will be finished."

## Should I Stay or Should I Go?

The decisions on whether to stay or go for the conservative Democrats, Fireman and Cop, were not so simple and non-political. But as soon as the 2013 Maryland General Assembly ended, the pair announced they would not seek re-election after their terms expired in 2014. Speculation was that neither relished running in the new territory that embraced the progressive Drummer, where they weren't regarded as homegrown sons and pillars of the community, but as little-known, parochial lawmakers.

# HEAL: A Reason to Run

When the 2013 legislative session concluded in April, the fact of all three delegates declining to run again hadn't registered with me. Still, out of habitual restlessness for a goal to pursue, I began chewing on the idea of another run for office. I let my mind wander on bicycle training rides in preparation for the May 2013 Columbia Triathlon, the big goal that motivated my rehab for my broken leg a year earlier. It was just dreaming while pedaling past farm fields. I couldn't come up with a compelling reason to put myself through the arduous ordeal of a campaign.

But on each ride, I came back to it. Then I landed on health care. As a public relations representative for a health care association, I had worked for several years to support President Obama's Affordable Care Act (ACA) —known as Obamacare. While Obamacare helped make health insurance more accessible and affordable, it also made a complicated health care system even more convoluted and strengthened the dominance of profit-hungry private health insurance companies. I came to view Obamacare as a gift to health insurers that did little to reduce health care costs, restore choice of health care providers, eliminate bureaucratic red tape, or provide equitable health care to all citizens. In other words, Obamacare was legislative lard, a classic Rube Goldberg scheme—a deliberately over-engineered law attempting to appease too many competing interests and ideologies in addressing a fundamental and crucial problem that requires understandable and fundamental solutions, not pretzel logic.

My health care association advocated for "health care for all," meaning nobody going without access to basic health care. Essentially, that would mean a "single-payer" health care system, like Medicare for seniors, only for everybody. However, my association was too cowardly politically to argue that Obamacare was insufficient and to take a stand for "universal health care." I wasn't.

I came to believe that a publicly financed, not-for-profit health care system that provided essential health care services to all citizens, regardless of employment status or ability to pay, was most equitable and humane. It would separate the illogical connection between health care insurance and employer, which left so many people in the lurch, even those who were employed. It is the model used in various forms by other developed nations, including Canada, Australia and throughout Europe, at a per capita cost about half or less than that of the U.S. And by many common health measures, those nations' citizens are healthier. Less costly, more efficient, more transparent, greater access and better health—what could be the arguments against that? In America, plenty, because of entrenched capitalistic business interests, unpliable political ideologies, ill-conceived fears of socialism, and the unshakable belief that America does everything better, regardless of clear evidence that suggests otherwise.

The idea of being the candidate who represented a significant change in Maryland's health care system to guarantee accessible, affordable health care for *every resident* inspired me about the prospect of running for state office.

I discovered that Vermont had undertaken this advocacy process and had become the first state to pass legislation authorizing establishment of a single-payer system in 2011. It wasn't unprecedented; it was possible. Vermont's leading example gave my universal health care idea more weight. With that cornerstone, I believed a Sachs candidacy—still just an amorphous possibility—would have a reason for existence.

One day driving home from work, I was thinking about a slogan with a catchy acronym that could represent the idea, and hit upon Healthcare for Everyone All Lifelong, or HEAL. I scribbled it down, and embraced it from the beginning of the campaign, incorporating the slogan in my registered campaign name—Adam Sachs for Delegate – HEAL.

I thought about all the usual questions that deter many people from running. Would I have enough time? Did I have the energy? Did I want to expose myself to public scrutiny? Could I withstand the stress? Could I raise enough—scratch that—any money? Would my employer allow flexibility? Would I have to quit my job? How would it affect my marriage? Was it even remotely practical?

And, of course, the $64,000 question: Who was I to even think about being a state delegate?

There was no better place to explore how to go about being a state delegate than the annual fundraiser for the Rock God of Howard County politics.

# June 13, 2013 - Learning from the Rock God

A can't miss event for county Democratic politicos was the annual Rock God Pizza Party fundraiser, which I had attended several years previously because I knew Rock God and supported him. Rock God usually held the event at his house. I would have to park several blocks away because the residential streets were so crowded with supporters—a crush of friends, politicians, Democratic activists, and civic and business leaders. Backers would be overflowing throughout his front and back yards, driveway and garage, stacked with pizza boxes.

But because of a severe storm warning, Rock God moved his 2013 event a day in advance to a drab community center, putting out the notice by social media and e-mail. The dire weather forecast and sudden change of venue might have doomed a less popular candidate's fundraiser to failure, but the looming squall didn't hurt Rock God's turnout. In fact, my arrival was similar to Rock God's past events—the center's main parking and overflow lots were full, so I parked far away.

I first met Rock God in the early 1990s when he was a relative nobody, testifying as a board member of one of Columbia's villages at a meeting I was covering for the *Baltimore Sun*. I later learned that Rock God was not the typical village board member without political aspirations beyond the architectural merits of fences. Rock God was a born public servant and political devotee, an Eagle Scout who proudly displayed his boyhood scouting achievements in a photo on his website. By age 26, Rock God had already worked for a congressman on Capitol Hill and run unsuccessfully for Maryland delegate. He kept plugging away, working as a legislative assistant to a Howard County Council member before being elected to the post himself in 1998, and ascending to state delegate in 2006.

As usual, Rock God's Pizza Party fundraiser attracted a mob. Since Rock God had been serving Howard County residents as an elected official for 15 years and as a legislative assistant for another half-dozen years before that, he had taken full advantage to meet and assist as many constituents as he could, and it showed at events like this. His political website photos featured a microcosm of his public service: Rock God reading to elementary school students; planting trees and leading a trash clean-up crew for a commercial district revitalization; eating a Nutty Buddy cone and celebrating Dreyer's Grand Ice Cream plant's ground-breaking ceremony, helmeted with a shovel perched on his shoulder in an open field.

People showed up for the event because they felt they owed it to Rock God for his diligence and dedication in office, and if they had any personal interactions with him, for his responsiveness.

I also owed a debt of gratitude to Rock God. I often ran into him around town and talked to him about his political activities. During Rock God's run for Howard County Council, I posted his election sign on my lawn. When I told Rock God I was curious about running for office, Rock God graciously agreed to join me for dinner, where we discussed what it's like to campaign and to be an accountable, responsive public official. That meeting stuck with me for years, until I finally took my first election plunge for Howard County Council.

## Undercover

This time, I wasn't attending Rock God's event just out of support for Rock God; I was exploring. I was seeking to get into the political frame of mind and immerse myself in the machinations of local politics by attending events held by popular, seasoned and victorious politicians. I was taking a whiff of what my life could be like for the next year, and seeing if the aroma smelled of honeysuckles or manure.

I observed the crowd to see what the politicians and candidates did and how the attendees reacted. I noticed how attendees hobnobbed and socialized and attempted to talk to the "right people"—those who, by position, wielded influence. The politicians were never alone, never without people who wanted to talk with them. Just like in high school, they were the popular clique—people swarmed them like bees to honey. The politicians stood in place, and people would approach them one at a time while others several deep cued in line for their turn. The politicians, of course, were happy to see and greet each and every one of them, although sometimes their gaze left their greeter to scan the room for more important arrivals.

I knew several politicians at the event from my 2006 County Council candidacy; we traveled the circuit of forums and fundraisers together. They were always engaged in conversation. I thought how nice it must feel, what a head rush to be so popular, fawned over, admired. It wasn't so different than the frat parties I attended in college as an unaffiliated Independent; the Greeks always had more pull, more of an orbit around them, while the Independents drifted from constellation to constellation, searching for their place in the hierarchy. The Greeks were comfortable right where they were, they knew they belonged; the Independents were uneasy.

With no political cache to offer, people weren't naturally going to approach to talk to me, so I milled around, starting up conversations with familiar faces and strangers to look occupied, knowing full well that if an opportunity to converse with someone with more influence or stature came along for my companion, my conversation would likely be over. I ran into a reporter acquaintance who had recently retired from covering government at the *Baltimore Sun*.

"You've written a lot about this stuff. You've probably seen it all. Now that you're retired, you can get into this game yourself," I said. "Have you thought about it?"

"You kidding? I'd never want to run. It's not for me," he replied. I kept my thoughts under wraps.

As in the past at the Rock God event, I got in line for the obligatory handshake and chit-chat with Rock God. It had been about a decade since my "mentorship" dinner with Rock God, and seven years since we traveled in the same circles during a campaign season, so we were not tightly acquainted. As usual, our greeting lasted about 15 seconds of benign pleasantries. I shook Rock God's hand, congratulated him and wished him good luck. Rock God appeared happy to see me, but people were waiting in line, and Rock God was equally happy to greet them; I stepped aside, next person up. I don't blame Rock God for the perfunctory greeting; that's part of the role of the popular politician. The more hands shaken, the better.

The bottom line is that I was an outsider. I was in no one's inner circle. The Rock God event made it clear that if I were to join the fray, I would have to work hard at making connections, or I would go it largely alone, which is not a formula for winning in politics.

If I could only find a way to skip all those time-consuming, arduous, painstaking, deliberate and, dare I say, boring baby steps—what politicos call "paying your dues" like serving on the Library Improvement Commission or Downtown Beautification Partnership—and jump right to being Rock God. Wasn't there a political consultant somewhere who could make that happen for me? *(Oh, yeah, forgot, that would take big money.)* OK, first a fundraising consultant, *then* a political consultant to transform me into the Rock God ...or even just the sidekick Robin to Rock God's Batman?

## Forget 'I Want to Be Like Mike;' I Want to Be Like Rock God

Rock God's event was atwitter with the buzz of an anticipated announcement. Two months earlier, public service giant, Jerry Ruley, who had served Howard County for five decades as police chief, county executive and state senator, announced he would retire from the Maryland Senate in 2014.

Rock God's announcement became anticlimactic when Thomas V. "Mike" Miller Jr., a kingmaker if there ever was one in Maryland, showed up. Miller is a true lion of the Maryland Senate. He was first elected to the Maryland House in 1970 and to the Senate in 1974, and was installed as Senate president in 1987, commencing an unprecedented dynastic run of power. When I covered the Maryland General Assembly beginning in 1990, the proverbial "Lion of the Senate" had a great mane of wavy, sandy brown hair. In 2013, Miller still had the flowing mane, only silver.

How it went down this way, only the insiders know. Rock God's colleagues who represented District 13 in the Maryland House—20-year Delegates George Mercer and Susan Pendleton, Rock God's one-time mentor and employer, both of whom had been in their positions 12 years longer than Rock God—peculiarly decided to run for re-election to the House, forgoing the opportunity to grab the Senate brass ring. Apparently, Mercer and Pendleton, Rock God's elders by about 15 years, either deferred to him in a backroom negotiation or, less likely, weren't interested in the more prestigious office. Or possibly, the local and/or state Democratic Party machine determined that the younger Rock God would be the strongest candidate with the brightest future and dissuaded either of the others from running against him so the "Team 13" power structure would remain intact and the triumvirate would retain hegemony.

Regardless, Rock God announced he would be stepping up to run for state Senate, to enthusiastic applause.

## Politician vs. Public Servant

In his introduction, Ken Ulman, a longtime Rock God ally and youthful Howard County executive, made a particular point to say, "Rock God is not a politician; he's a public servant."

For his part, Rock God said he used only one measure to decide what office to pursue: "Where can I do the most good for Howard County?"

Sounded good, but I didn't completely buy it; nothing wrong with being ambitious. Go ahead, wear your aspirations proudly. That's politics—ambitious go-getters climbing past each other to scale the mountain for more prestige and influence. Why get lost in a crowd of 141 delegates when you can stand out among 47 senators, with the Moses of the Senate, Miller the Lion, parting the political seas for you?

Rock God gave an earnest, reflective and humble speech, devoid of rah-rah, recounting his father's working-class roots as a Baltimore steelworker and his mother's role as a homemaker. Indeed, Rock God was an American success story, a self-made politician…err, public servant, who was ascending due to sheer force of his desire, diligence, hard work and shrewdness. After all, a steelworker does not a political scion make.

Rock God paid his dues, and then some. His list of service on legislative and civic committees, task forces, workgroups, panels, blue ribbon commissions, councils, and advisory boards, was as long as the Torah.

To be sure, Rock God was an exemplary "public servant." But I believe "public servant" and "politician" are two sides of the same coin. You can't be the former without mastering the skills of the latter. And Rock God, to be sure, is far down the road toward being a "career politician," and there would appear to be no railroad crossings on the horizon.

Rock God was in the *practice* of serving, legislating and policy making, but he most assuredly was in the *business* of politics, as all politicians must be if they want to protect their turf and establish a stranglehold on their position.

All it takes to know that politics, and thus being a "politician," is serious business for Rock God that goes far beyond the syrupy designation of selfless "public servant," is to look at his money-raising and spending activities.

For someone heralded as a "public servant" and "not a politician," Rock God had a fat campaign bank account at his disposal. At the end of 2013, Rock God had more than $400,000 on hand from a broad array of individuals, businesses, PACs and unions for a local race where Democrats outnumbered Republicans by 2-to-1, where Rock God would have no Democratic primary challenge and where no Republican candidate was even on the radar. It begs the question: Why would someone who is merely a loyal public servant need that much money? The answer: to scare away, or overwhelm, any would-be contenders for the mantle. Like a lion, the practiced politician with well-honed survival instincts protects his lair.

Rock God's political operation was veritably a business unto itself. Far from using campaign cash only for traditional electioneering purposes such as creating literature, distributing mailings and buying signs, Rock God used his funds the way a business or entrepreneur would to pay for all manner of services, products, technology, business trips, consulting fees, event tickets, salaries and investments in other candidates. It's big business, big money.

Rock God trounced his underfunded, politically inexperienced, little-known Republican opponent and became the district's new senator.

Rock God crushed his opponent in an avalanche of dollar bills. During the 2011 to 2014 election cycle, Rock God spent about $550,000; his opponent, $30,000.

Rock God raised nearly a quarter of his funds from the political power base of special interests and political cronies including political clubs, political and candidate committees, political slates and PACs. Demonstrating his ever-strengthening political muscle, in the two-month period after he was elected to Senate, Rock God received contributions from 22 PACs from anesthesiologists to firefighters to nursing homes to car and truck dealerships.

Rock God spent nearly $100,000 on salary and compensation for campaign staff and consulting during the election cycle, including about $50,000 in the election year, an average of $1,000 per week. One has to wonder: How much strategic or fundraising advice could consultants offer that would make a difference with voter registration numbers in Rock God's district tilted so heavily in the Democrats' favor, and Rock God out-spending his opponent by an 18-to-1 margin? Let's face it: The only way Rock God could have lost was to be caught in the vortex of another 1994 Newt Gingrich "Contract with America"-style Republican revolution. And if such a historical repeat was to have happened and the electorate unpredictably went rogue, no amount of consulting would have stopped the tornado.

## Political Incest?

For some of those consulting payments, I can't help but think of the word "incestuous," though I know how ugly that sounds. But hey, let's call a spade a spade: Politics *is incestuous*, rife with all manner of convenient, sycophantic, symbiotic and synergetic bedfellows. Of course, many walks of life and business are governed by the "you scratch my back, I'll scratch yours" ethos and relationships. It's just that in politics, sometimes it may be more detectable because of its public nature.

In both 2013 and 2014, Rock God made a one-time payment for "consulting fees" of $10,000 to his paid staff legislative assistant, who had worked for him for 16 years at both the county council and state delegate levels. I can't say what exactly the assistant did to earn the $10,000 each year, in addition to her regular state government salary, but whatever the advice or recommended strategy or research or grunt work was, on the face of it, it had to have been quite valuable.

In turn, Rock God served as the campaign treasurer for his legislative assistant's own campaign committee for a spot on the party-cheerleader Howard County Democratic Central Committee. Rock God transferred $800 from his campaign to his assistant's committee fund. The assistant collected $700 more in contributions from Rock God's two District 13 delegate colleagues, then transferred the money to a newly established "team slate," which included the assistant and six other Central Committee candidates.

What does all that wheeling-and-dealing mean, in the big scheme? Not much. What it illustrates in microcosm, however, is the intricate, interconnected web of political relationships and the shell game that is played with money among the web's weavers to parlay influence, bolster insiders and obscure sources of money and power.

## Political Robin Hood

Another thing effective politicians like Rock God do is spread their influence. Rock God acted as something of a political Robin Hood: collecting money from supporters and redistributing it to aid political allies. Rock God transferred $250,000 of his funds to other candidates and to political slates over the four-year election cycle, with $208,025 transferred in the 2014 election year alone. All told, Rock God shared his largesse with more than 40 slates, committees and candidates, ranging from school board, clerk of court, and register of wills to county councils to General Assembly candidates all the way to state attorney general, lieutenant governor and governor.

Those in power protect their own. It's a tight club, wagons circled, ranks closed, fortified against would-be intruders and gate-crashers. It's strength in numbers, with cash the Popeye's spinach to make the whole lot stronger. Money is redistributed from entrenched, well-heeled politician to entrenched, well-heeled politician like wafers and wine to Christian congregants; everyone properly devoted to the cause and the flock is blessed. Rock God certainly didn't stand apart as a generous soul (with other people's and corporations' money). The powerful chairman of the Maryland Senate Judicial Proceedings Committee, Marcus Zeitzer, who represented my Uncle Ted's suburban Baltimore district, was another case in point, raining nearly $150,000 in 22 candidate account transfers in 2014 alone upon Senate colleagues and candidates and other politicians, including $58,000 for the Maryland Democratic Senatorial Committee Slate.

The shocking statistic: Of all the money Zeitzer spent on his campaign in 2014, *85 percent* was in transfers to other candidates, slates and political PACs and committees. Perhaps not an altruist in the mold of Bill Gates, Zeitzer still could afford to be a philanthropist for political cronies with the one-third of a million dollars he raised during the election cycle because his stronghold on his seat and his loyal corporate, union and PAC contributors' support was so stout that he had no challengers for either the 2014 primary or general elections, rendering his political wealth all but useless save for a shield against any future sword-wavers on a kamikaze campaign mission. *(To see the anatomy of a $100,000 political fundraiser, see Appendix 1 detailing Zeitzer's political benefactors.)*

During that 2011 to 2014 election cycle, Rock God finessed campaign funds like an entrepreneur managing a business, investing to upgrade his technology, computer equipment and software; further his political connections; employ staff; hire consultants; travel to political conferences and the Democratic National Convention; buy tickets to philanthropic events; attend President Obama's inauguration; send feel-good marketing mailers; donate gifts to schools; and wine-and-dine supporters.

Rock God was running a multi-national conglomerate, a Walmart; I was operating a sole proprietorship, a Kwickie-Mart. You can be a candidate, but if you aren't a quick study in and devotee of the business of politics, your venture likely will go belly up, or you'll be more successful being a cashier, getting your fix of politics around the edges of campaigns, to a CEO like Rock God.

# July 11, 2013 – Health Reform in
# Vermont: It Can Be Done

I took my first real action toward entering the District 12 race when I searched for the groups that inspired the Vermont single-payer health care initiative and found Dr. Deborah Richter, a physician in Montpelier, Vermont and president of Vermont Health Care for All. I e-mailed her and received a response inviting a call. I talked to the doctor about how the Vermont advocates had managed to push a concept regarded nationally as politically unviable through the Vermont State House and how the state would implement the new program with an Obamacare waiver.

"How did you get health care providers on board and convince the legislature?" I asked.

"Insurance is a bad way to pay for health care. Insurance is about maximizing revenues and avoiding sick people," Dr. Richter replied. "Health care is a public good. It should be publicly funded. Most costs in health care are fixed. We're going to pay one way or another."

"How have you countered the argument that a single-payer system is a government takeover of health care or socialized medicine?" I asked.

"Now decisions are made by insurance companies. There's not a need for that," Dr. Richter said. "We're talking about socialized financing, not socialized medicine. It would be like Medicare. When you have a system, you can design it to emphasize more prevention, primary care and wellness."

It sounded logical and one state had already bought in. Why not Maryland?

I also found a couple of Maryland organizations involved in health care reform efforts, and discovered that Health Care is a Human Right Maryland was striving to achieve exactly what I was considering as a cornerstone of my campaign: health care for all. I found a chapter of the group scheduled to meet in Baltimore, and marked the date as an opportunity to make contacts and learn about representing the group's mission in a campaign.

## July 12, 2013 – Doctor Makes a House Call: The Anointed One

I knew who she was, but hadn't formally met The Anointed One until she came to my door nearly a year before the primary, wearing an "Anointed One for Delegate" t-shirt. I was still exploring my own run for delegate and gleaning intelligence about the contenders, but didn't let on. Ironically, I was dressed politically incorrectly when I answered the door, wearing an "It's All Good in the Hood" t-shirt featuring Mr. Fred Rogers of Mister Rogers' Neighborhood, given to me by African-American friends.

Anointed One impressed me with her low-key, down-to-earth, friendly approach. She had bright eyes, fanciful, auburn-orange curly hair that indicated a playful streak and an easy, radiant smile that exuded warmth. I discussed health care issues with her, knowing she was a doctor, a plastic surgeon. She said she wanted to ensure that Maryland did a good job implementing Obamacare. When I asked about her core issues, she focused on human trafficking, which surprised me. I recognized this as a plague to eradicate in Third World nations, but in Maryland? Anointed One said it was happening here, for example with illegal immigrants forced to subjugate themselves.

## Anointed One

Anointed One was practically knighted as a successor to the retiring delegates when the field was empty, before candidates could even officially file to run. Anointed One garnered early endorsements from all three of the sitting delegates—Drummer, Fireman and Cop—and the state senator representing District 12, Career Pol.

Less than three weeks after registration for candidates officially opened, 14 months before the primary, Anointed One held a fundraiser, emceed by Fireman, at which the three sitting delegates, Senator Career Pol, and even nine-term U.S. Congressman Elijah Cummings of Baltimore endorsed the Columbia plastic surgeon, giving her campaign the feeling of inevitability and providing a financial godsend from the start.

In *Becoming a Candidate*, author Lawless found that political recruitment by party leaders served as the key ingredient in fueling candidates' interest and willingness to run for office. For Anointed One, support from entrenched politicians must have been a potent elixir whetting her appetite for candidacy.

Potential candidates are reluctant to run without establishment backing, Lawless noted. "You need to have the party's support in order to have a viable run for any office," said one potential candidate. "I'm not politically connected...Without party support, there's nothing to consider," echoed another. Anointed One did not have that concern.

Lawless said the potential candidates recognized the "legitimacy" and "political viability conveyed by [political] gatekeepers' suggestions to run. Party support brings the promise of an organization that will work on behalf of a candidate." On the contrary, for individuals who receive no support or encouragement from political gatekeepers, like me, "a political candidacy feels far less feasible."

The strongest and most influential endorsement for Anointed One came from the popular, retiring Drummer, who essentially gave Anointed One the Good Housekeeping Seal of Approval to take up her progressive mantle. An endorsement from Drummer, with her three decades in politics representing Anointed One's home base of progressive, liberal, idealistic Columbia, was worth its weight in gold. Drummer described Anointed One in the *Maryland Reporter* as having "a passion for social justice, economic justice and environmental justice," exactly the traits for which Drummer was known and admired. The testimonial sounded as if Drummer had cloned her own political version of *Austin Powers'* Mini-Me.

Anointed One and Drummer weren't only closely affiliated in their political views; they also lived on the same street. And Drummer had a longtime relationship with Anointed One's mother, a community and political activist and former state delegate candidate, who once lost election to Drummer. When Drummer was Howard County executive in 1982, she appointed Anointed One's mother as the first African-American to serve on the county board of appeals.

Upon Drummer's retirement announcement, Anointed One's mother declared that whoever was elected to replace Drummer would "have a giant to follow."

As Drummer made her political retirement intentions known in 2012, Anointed One was already emerging from the giant's shadow, identified by the *Baltimore Sun* and political insiders as a possible candidate. Less than a week after Drummer's retirement announcement in August 2012, Anointed One said in the *Baltimore Sun*, "It just seems that it's time to be part of the team that's actually in the game, rather than on the bench," all but announcing her candidacy, more than a year before I registered to run.

## Pole Position

The political blog *HoCo Rising*, authored by a Democratic candidate for delegate in an adjoining district, reported that Drummer "handpicked Anointed One and recruited her to run." Indeed, Anointed One's statement about getting "in the game" just days after Drummer publicly announced her retirement strongly suggests that the two neighbors had been in discussions about succession plans for some time. Someone who hadn't already deliberately thought about such an opportunity, weighed pros and cons and started planning wouldn't offer a nearly ironclad statement of candidacy cavalierly or spur-of-the-moment.

*HoCoRising* said Anointed One's endorsements from the District 12 retiring delegates and Career Pol and their support at her fundraiser were significant because they instantly raised her profile and name recognition and likely came with campaign cash attached.

"I think we can expect to see a near max-out contribution from Drummer," he wrote, "and substantial contributions" from other District 12 office-holders.

The prediction was dead-on. Anointed One received $4,000 from Drummer in 2012. In June 2014, three weeks before the primary, Career Pol donated $6,000 to Anointed One's cause, the maximum under law. *HoCoRising* concluded 14 months before the primary that Anointed One had already filled "the pole position" by virtue of her clean sweep of District 12 legislators' endorsements.

Even though Fireman and Cop's political leanings were discernibly more conservative than Anointed One's to match their more working-class communities, they reserved advance seats on the Anointed One Bandwagon anyway. Cop explained his premature endorsement by saying that electing people who were "good," "honest," "decent" and "hard-working" trumped political ideology. "We're going to do everything to get Anointed One elected," Cop declared, echoing Fireman's sentiment.

Anointed One was an impressive candidate. Still, I was disgusted to observe the way politics worked. It's easy to shrug and dismiss the gamesmanship, power plays, backroom deal-making, back-scratching, influence-peddling, the insiders' dance—all the things you know play out in politics—from a detached distance. It's like sausage—you can accept, and even approve of the final product, but you certainly don't want to see or smell it being made. Hell, much of what happens *in life*—success or failure, winning or losing, opportunity or stagnation, prestige or obscurity—is based on these dynamics of who you know, where they are stationed, who they are surrounded by, what they are willing to do for you and what you can do for them in return. In this way, politics is like the Titanic: Some will receive priority and be aided by the arms of many in authority positions onto the seaworthy boat, destined for survival; many others, left aimlessly at sea to their own devices, will go down with the ship. Anointed One sailed first class, dining with the elite, handpicked apprentice to Captains Drummer, Fireman and Cop; I was in steerage, cueing up for porridge and a life vest.

## Pioneering Achievers

Anointed One came from an inspiring and high-achieving family. Anointed One's family was among the African-American pioneers to move in 1969 to Columbia's idyllic first "village," planned as a community of racial harmony and diversity where blacks and whites would live in the same neighborhoods, attend school together and participate in creating the future.

Anointed One's mother was inducted into the Howard County Women's Hall of Fame for her volunteer civic and government service. She earned a law degree at age 54, focusing her practice on child abuse and neglect.

Anointed One's sister, a Princeton University graduate, served as a judge for the Howard County Circuit Court upon appointment by the Maryland governor, and later as a Maryland deputy attorney general and Maryland Board of Education member.

Anointed One, 55, fit the mold of her older sister and mother, an academic standout, from high school class president to a Harvard University degree in bioelectric engineering to a medical degree from the Columbia University College of Physicians and Surgeons to establishing her surgical practice in Columbia in 1991.

Anointed One not only was as smart as her credentials reflected; she was personable, charming, passionate, serious and committed; whatever faint hopes I had that Anointed One was merely a paper tiger were irrevocably dashed when she showed up at my doorstep.

## July 14, 2013 - The Moment of Truth with My No. 1 Constituent

The momentum toward registering as an official candidate was growing in my own mind, yet I still hadn't talked to anybody about my intentions, other than Dr. Richter in Vermont. I knew the time had come for a Come-to-Jesus moment with my wife Amy.

"I'm thinking of running for state delegate," I blurted over dinner, and braced for a catapult of mashed potatoes.

"What? Are you serious? Where did *that* come from? When did you decide *that?*"

"I'm just thinking about it, checking it out. I haven't decided."

"When were you going to tell me?"

"Tonight. I just did."

"I've supported you in a lot of things before, when you quit your teaching job and when you ran for council and when you went back to school. I don't know if I can support this."

My proposition had landed like a *Biggest Loser* contestant's balance beam dismount.

"How will you have the time?" Amy asked. "You complain about not having enough time to do things you want to do now."

"I'll just use whatever time I have. Maybe it won't be *enough time,* just *some time.*"

She had a good point, but I didn't care about such logic or practicality. The idea had taken root, and it had grown hardy, and I couldn't prevent its development. Like a cocaine addict, I knew I was too far gone to stop.

My council run in 2006 was an easier sell. Since our relationship was new, I had decided I was going to run for county council no matter Amy's opinion, and Amy would have to adapt—or leave if she really didn't like it. It was an early test of our relationship, whether we could support each other's goals. Seven years later, it was harder to take such an uncompromising position since we were married. I didn't feel I could be as cavalier—and maybe self-centered—anymore. *There's no 'I' in 'Team' mister,* Amy would rib me cornily when I was all about me, which was often.

Still, I countered Amy's reflexive dismay at the idea by expressing concern about being controlled and giving up dreams for my life. Amy and I were fundamentally different. She valued safety, security and predictability. I felt restless and stifled without risk, ambition, challenging goals and freedom.

## I Want *The Real Life*

At 50 years old, I wanted the freedom to live life my way, like Sinatra crooned, the freedom to make my own choices and to live with the consequences of success or failure. A midlife crisis? No. I didn't give a crap about a red Porsche or Botox injections. But I did feel the clock ticking on the time I had to do meaningful things with my life. What was I going to wait around for? A heart attack? Dementia? Retirement? I don't even play golf. I had the nagging sense, as John Cougar Mellencamp sang in *The Real Life*, that opportunities to grab the "gold ring"—hell, even bronze—would be continually dwindling:

> *My whole life*
> *I've done what I'm supposed to do*
> *Now I'd like to maybe do something for myself…*
> *I guess it boils down to what we did with our lives*
> *And how we deal with our own destinies*
> *But something happens*

*When you reach a certain age*
*Particularly to those ones that are young at heart*
*It's a lonely proposition when you realize*
*That's there's less days in front of the horse*
*Than riding in the back of this cart*

# Yolo

As I pondered launching a campaign, my sense of urgency about life heightened. A month after my 50th at my daughter Rebecca's high school graduation, the student commencement speakers referenced the new buzzword "YOLO" —You Only Live Once. They were right, of course, but what can a teenager realistically know about YOLO? It's not until we've had dreams dashed, experienced bad luck and bad timing, suffered life's tragedies, disappointments, cruelties and failures, come to terms with our own limitations, and battled against becoming stultified or buried in mediocrity and tedium that some of us truly embrace the YOLO creed. Much more than failure, I feared regret. I subscribed wholeheartedly to the saying that you will not regret the things you did, you will regret the things you didn't do.

I had some cajoling to do with Amy, and I was thinking it would take some finesse. I let things cool down, allowing the idea of a state delegate run to percolate without mentioning it again. Finally, I couldn't avoid revisiting it any longer.

# July 16, 2013 – Another Candidate in the Pool: Man of the People

I went to my neighborhood pool party for a swim and pizza, and discovered what is truly meant by the saying, "All politics is local." I recognized Man of the People from his newspaper photo, the only one, except for another candidate from a different race, dressed formally. You can't get any more serious about meeting voters than shaking their hands dripping wet and nearly buck naked, while getting splashed by a cannonball.

At 28, Man of the People was the youngest candidate. But despite his youth, in no way was he the least accomplished or worthy. Man of the People stated in his candidacy announcement that he wanted to devote his life to public service. Unlike many candidates, when Man of the People said that, I believed it.

Man of the People was the first candidate with whom I communicated after officially entering the race.

Man of the People wrote an e-mail to all the candidates expressing his concern and making us aware that one candidate, Gadfly, was displaying information about other candidates on her website.

"Instead of staying positive," Man of the People wrote, "[Gadfly] is attempting to go negative and malign certain individuals by sharing each of our bios instead of focusing on her own campaign." Man of the People was upset specifically because Gadfly highlighted that he had left Baltimore County for a job in Arizona, claiming it was a dig that he wasn't loyal to the district.

The missive was foreboding. Man of the People and Gadfly had run-ins three years previously when both competed unsuccessfully for a Baltimore County Council seat. Now they were aiming higher, and apparently neither had forgotten whatever slights or campaign transgressions had taken place. The result of their clash would see one of them charged criminally with a violation of election law just weeks before the primary and battling futilely to right a sinking ship.

In an e-mail reply, I asked Man of the People about his health, knowing that he had suffered from cancer, which brought him back from Arizona to Baltimore for treatment. "I battled and defeated a rare, life-threatening cancer—I think that's an accomplishment," he responded.

I had a favorable impression of Man of the People from this initial exchange, and knew from his community activism that he'd have a strong following. The more I encountered Man of the People at events, the more I found him personable and down-to-earth.

I met Man of the People at the first candidates' forum. Before we all got seated to make our pitch, I heard Man of the People make an off-hand comment to the only other candidate younger than 30, Next Big Thing, joking with his rival that it was an unfortunate challenge to run against such a tall, handsome guy. Man of the People may have realized that attractiveness and votes go hand-in-hand.

## Achilles Heel

If Man of the People had an Achilles heel, this was it. Man of the People did not have "the look"—entirely superficial, but nonetheless a big factor in electoral politics, where people make an immediate impression of a candidate based on appearance.

Man of the People would not be plucked straight out of Central Casting for the role of the fetching young candidate on the rise. He was large, roundish, bespectacled, and prematurely balding, not exactly assets for a young man entering politics, where the image of a trim, good-looking, wavy-haired Kennedy or the confident, debonair, coiffed presence of a Mitt Romney is the standard. Besides an unremarkable physical appearance, Man of the People also had the uncontrollable condition of profusely sweating. The sweat stains could be interpreted as strength by showing that he was working his ass off. Voters could interpret the hyperperspiration the way they wanted, though Man of the People couldn't project the image of the cool, calm, unflappable candidate.

The prototypical image of the refined, suave politician was antithetical to Man of the People's strength anyway. Man of the People was unquestionably the most powerful and passionate candidate at our appearances. He had blue-collar, working-class roots and deep ties to his community. He was born and bred in Lansdowne, one of the red-headed step-children of the Baltimore County side of the district. Lansdowne and other similar working-class communities played second fiddle to Catonsville, the more affluent, Norman Rockwell-esque community that had monopolized the region's seat in government for 50 years. During his 2010 council run, Man of the People had said he wanted to change the "Catonsville complex" that focused attention on Catonsville at the expense of neighboring, more downtrodden communities such as Lansdowne, which were experiencing blight and in danger of being "left behind."

## Early Grooming

He was a community and Democratic Party activist from youth and had earned political stripes that other candidates could not equal, the boy with an activist spirit and sense of right and wrong who follows his passion to public servant.

Man of the People was the youngest person in Maryland to head a county Democratic Party, having been elected to the Baltimore County Democratic Central Committee at 21 and to the chairmanship at 23.

He was also chairman of a public schools advisory council and president of Lansdowne's Improvement Association, heady achievements for someone barely out of college.

At the University of Maryland-Baltimore County (UMBC), a stone's throw from his boyhood home, Man of the People started his grooming as a candidate. While at UMBC, when most students are deciding which bar to patronize and playing the latest video game, Man of the People ran for the student's seat on the University of Maryland System's board, having been nominated by a UMBC selection committee. "He has the kind of sophistication and presence of one much older than his years," said the selection committee leader.

## Fighter and Survivor

Man of the People had the compelling story about battling cancer, a struggle that stoked his fire for life and for fighting for others. He gave impassioned speeches about standing up for the rights of the poor and working-class, veterans, the disabled and the elderly. It came across as heartfelt and genuine. Man of the People connected with those groups that lacked a voice and lobbying influence.

From the outset, I believed Man of the People was the strongest candidate for the large working-class portion of the district. As proof, Man of the People scored a contribution from the roughneck Teamsters PAC—once America's largest union.

But as the campaign wore on, Man of the People became more inconsistent. In contrast to his most fervent speeches, sometimes he was uncharacteristically bland and dispassionate when talking about the same issues that seemed to fuel him early on. Sometimes, the energy he harnessed to fight for his blue-collar neighbors seemed to dissipate, detracting from his message and appeal. When he failed to manifest his heartfelt passion, Man of the People was reduced to the "everyman," not attractive enough to woo the average shallow and unknowledgeable voter.

# 'You Look Mahvelous'

*"It is amazing how complete is the delusion
that beauty is goodness."*

Leo Tolstoy, Russian author

There's no way around it for Man of the People and the rest of us who can't pull off the debonair regality of a chisel-faced Romney or the aw-shucks, boyish good looks and charm of a Bill Clinton. Hey, I'm only 5-foot-9; I would need six-inch elevator shoes to look statesman-like. Never mind positions on controversial issues or evaluations of past performance; more attractive candidates have an advantage before they even utter a word.

The American public all but validated this theory in the first televised presidential debate in 1960. Richard Nixon was deemed the winner by Americans listening on the radio. But John F. Kennedy, the handsome politician who looked younger, fresher and friendlier than a sweating, stern-faced Nixon with his receding hairline, was preferred by those watching TV.

Tim Judge, University of Notre Dame management professor, has conducted studies that found that taller people earn significantly more than shorter people, especially men, and that "beautiful people" earn more. The traits of height and beauty translate to politics, Judge said, noting that taller people are viewed as having more leadership qualities.

In this dimension, Next Big Thing had an advantage over the District 12 field.

In a 2013 article in *Notre Dame Magazine*, Judge rattled off "debits" for a male politician: facial hair, eye glasses, baldness, and being "ugly. "We all know that if you were ugly, deemed that way by others, you wouldn't have a chance," Judge said.

"We like to think we're a deep society, but sometimes these superficial characteristics have a big impact," Judge said. "We're dominated a lot of times by these instant impressions."

Several studies on voters in democracies suggest that physically attractive politicians who "look the part" enjoy greater electoral success, according to a 2010 article in *World Politics Journal.* Research found that snap judgments by research subjects about a candidate's appearance—perceptions formed by looking only briefly at images of candidates' faces—correlate with candidates' actual performance in elections. These findings are consistent with psychological research indicating that people often judge unfamiliar individuals based on their appearance, inferring personality traits such as charisma, competence, intelligence, honesty, leadership, likeability and trustworthiness from facial features alone. This phenomenon is known as the "halo effect"—the assumption that attractive people must have holy characteristics.

Another study by researchers at the University of Helsinki determined that "evaluations of beauty explain success in real elections better than evaluations of competence, intelligence, likability, or trustworthiness." The study found that for every small increase in attractiveness there was a much larger jump in perception of the candidates' personal qualities. "If good-looking people are more persuasive, are treated better in social interaction and achieve higher occupational success they might also do better in politics," researchers concluded. Adding a new twist to the attractiveness theory, researchers at Arizona State University connected political choices to evolutionary and primal survival instincts. The study found that citizens were more likely to select physically attractive leaders to avoid disease threats. The study determined that voters in congressional districts with higher levels of disease threat tended to cast a higher percentage of votes for more attractive politicians. Politicians who were rated significantly more attractive than average—a quality equated with wellness—had nearly double the odds of winning.

Armed with that knowledge, all I wanted to know was: Would I be attractive enough to convince the public that a vote for me would be a vote against contracting bubonic plague?

# July 22, 2013 – Rapprochement: Taking a Cue from The Columbia Bike Guy

A my was more amenable to talking about my potential candidacy the second time. I felt no choice but to talk about it again, unless I wanted to be deceitful, as if sneaking around to hotels with another woman in true politician fashion, because in three days I was planning to make my first public outing as a prospective candidate at the Health Care is a Human Right-Baltimore Chapter meeting.

## The Columbia Bike Guy

I elaborated about my desire to run, about running on the platform of changing the health care system to provide essential care and coverage for all. I also presented my idea to raise the visibility of the campaign through a low-cost advertising tactic inspired by The Columbia Bike Guy, the ubiquitous cyclist who traversed Columbia on his small-wheeled bikes with bags hanging from the handlebars, wearing stylish helmets with feathered mohawks, who often got off his bike on busy thorough-fares to pick up litter, who was so widely recognized he had his own Facebook page with 5,000 Likes under the name "The Columbia Bike Guy" with people posing with him for pictures at the mall food court and posting about locations of "Bike Guy" sightings and affectionate cau-tions to the Bike Guy about dangerous areas to ride and riding against traffic, which he often did.

I believe cycling and cleaning up trash on his beloved roads served as therapy for The Columbia Bike Guy. It was obvious he loved nothing more than being on his bike in all weather. If The Columbia Bike Guy could become widely recognized and embraced unintentionally by riding his bike, I figured it might work for me as an intentional ploy in a political campaign. Amy embraced that strategy as quirky and unique—except, of course, for her fear that I'd get killed.

For a candidate who is married to be successful—or at least whose campaign doesn't end in divorce—it's essential to gain the acceptance of the spouse. Even better is to win complete buy-in, and if the family includes kids, their eager participation, making it a full family effort. That establishes the core of a strong team. Energy benefited from that advantage, with his kids running his campaign. Gadfly had a kindred rabble-rouser in husband Pest.

I was glad I had earned Amy's acceptance, if not complete buy-in, freeing me up to go public at the upcoming Health Care is a Human Right meeting.

I had no formal "exploratory committee" to test my candidacy. No method to measure name recognition, popularity, money-raising capability or the resonance of campaign messages. Health Care is a Human Right-Baltimore would become my de facto committee. That would be the first place I would test the feasibility of a campaign built around Healthcare for Everyone All Lifelong (HEAL).

# July 25, 2013 – Beta Test with a
# Few Old White-Haired Guys

**E**leven months before the June 2014 primary election, I attended the Health Care Is a Human Right (HCHR)-Baltimore meeting at a cavernous church. I expected to encounter at least 50 passionate activists in an ornate sanctuary and planned to blend into the audience to listen and learn. Instead, I entered a cramped room in an office wing with five men squeezed around a table, all elderly with white hair and beards except for the youthful state director. This was my introduction to the reality of a campaign built upon an idealistic concept such as health care for all: Though proponents came from all backgrounds, the most avid advocates were retirees who had the time to indulge intellectually, and their ranks were thin. Younger people who believed in the ideal generally were too busy working jobs, raising families, or trying to survive day-to-day to have the time for intense advocacy needed to create change.

I introduced myself as a potential state candidate to Sergio, the state director, and the erudite elders Rich, Dick, Bernie and Rod. They were smart and committed to the cause; one was a physician. But where were the legions to make it happen? Maybe it would be my job to produce them.

By virtue of uttering my latent candidacy for the first time publicly, that night essentially reinforced my decision to run. I had crossed a threshold, and even though it still would have been easy to turn back—the elders weren't going to hold my feet to the fire, and they were outside my district anyway—breaking that barrier also made it easier to go forward.

## August 13, 2013 – Becoming a True Believer

Seeking to make local connections with universal health care advocates, I attended the Howard County HCHR chapter meeting at the home of retired pediatrician David Glickstein. Nine activists, mostly retirees and state director Sergio, informally gathered around Glickstein's dining room table to discuss the daunting task of spreading the message of a more equitable way to provide health care and turning a small insurgency into a statewide grassroots movement. I introduced myself as a potential candidate who wanted to make the group's mission a primary tenet of my campaign.

The group discussed a march and rally uniting Maryland's HCHR chapters with workers' rights groups in Baltimore. The rally would employ "street theater" along the route, acting out the discrepancies in the American health care system through a symbolic play, and would end at the headquarters building of health insurer giant CareFirst BlueCross BlueShield, my former employer. Essentially, I would be marching to eliminate my one-time employer's corporate reason for existence, and I would have been fine with that.

I decided to participate in the rally. It would be my coming-out party to stand for something in my campaign. I would discover it was much harder to gain support as a candidate than by simply showing up and saying you were down for a cause, especially if I might have been considered Johnny-come-lately. And just a few days after the rally, a couple of Howard County HCHR activists would disavow me of the notion that you could come to the party late and expect to be accepted just the same as the grizzled organizers.

# September 17, 2013 – To Tell or Not to Tell, That Was the Question

Before making a decision to run, one issue faced by every Maryland candidate who has to make a living beyond a part-time legislators' $43,500 salary is how to arrange a career to fit into nine months while leaving the three months between January and April available for General Assembly business.

As a longshot to get through the primary, I debated whether even to mention my plans for candidacy to my employer, a health care professional association, where I worked in the communications department. If I avoided interrupting my work life for the campaign, there would be no disruptions to my job and no reason to involve my employer in my outside activities if I should lose in the primary.

On the other hand, I knew taking that pessimistic view was a loser's approach, a sure path to a self-fulfilling prophecy of failure. It would make it harder to commit to going all out to advance through the primary without knowing I had my employer's blessing. With the district tilting overwhelmingly Democratic, a primary win would equate to better than even odds for winning in the general election and becoming a delegate. And that would have major repercussions on my job, necessitating the support and flexibility of my employer.

Since my Uncle-in-law Ted Levin had run for the General Assembly six times and had served for 20 years, I asked for his advice on whether to broach the topic with my employer so early in the game. As a lawyer with his own practice, I knew Uncle Ted's situation was different than mine; he could adjust his schedule and work life as he pleased, nobody was standing over his shoulder, except maybe Aunt Barb. Uncle Ted advised talking to my employer far in advance of a hypothetical scenario actually coming to pass. He had known plenty of legislators who had worked out arrangements with their employers, including leaves of absence and other ways to fill in for their three-month hiatus. Some employers, he noted, liked to tout that one of their employees also served as a state legislator as a sign to their clients that they employ important, influential and successful people.

I called a meeting with my boss and told her I was considering running for Maryland state delegate. I approached the conversation with trepidation. My boss looked at me quizzically. I knew immediately it would be a hard sell. Let's just say she had never been my Number One Fan, and she liked to keep her employees corralled like bleating sheep. She offered no indications of support or enthusiasm for my pending ambitious endeavor. Not a good sign. I could tell the only gears turning in her brain were notched on how my possible run would affect her. And secondarily, on some version of this: *Just who the hell does this guy think he is, running for state delegate?*

"I'm still just considering running for delegate. I haven't officially registered yet," I told my boss, staring back at me grimly and disapprovingly.

"If I do decide to run, it won't have any impact on my job unless I actually do get elected, and that wouldn't be for almost a year and a half until the 2015 legislative session," I said, trying to cushion the landing. "How about if we meet with HR and see if we could figure out an arrangement that could work for all of us?"

"How long would you be gone?" my boss asked, unpersuaded that my individual pursuit would yield an iota of value for our health care association.

"Three months."

I reached for the only trick in my pocket, courtesy of my employee union's contract.

"If I get that far, maybe I could apply for a leave of absence for the first session to see what the job would be like, and we can both see what kind of arrangement may work out for the future."

"Have you read the contract?" my boss asked. "Aren't leaves of absence are only for illness?"

"No, the leave of absence provision doesn't say anything about being limited to health reasons. It just says it's for a maximum of six months and shouldn't be denied unreasonably."

My boss hated the union and willfully ignored or misinterpreted provisions of the contract regularly. Finally, my boss got down to brass tacks.

"If you're successful, you may have to be ready to resign," she told me.

That wasn't what I wanted to hear; I was hoping after five years on the job my employer would be interested in working with me on a solution that could benefit both parties. After all, I thought, my employer potentially could benefit from having an employee who knew about the organization's top-priority legislative issues serving in a state legislature, a platform where he could call attention to and advocate on such matters *from the inside*, rather than chirping for the faintest bit of attention from the outside.

"Could you talk with HR to see if any alternative work arrangements would be possible?" I asked. I was certain such a scenario had never been addressed by my employer; no employee had ever run for public office.

"When do you need a response?"

"Within two weeks would be great," I said, as I was aiming to officially file my candidacy with Maryland soon thereafter.

Two weeks passed and I heard nothing from my boss or the HR director, with whom I had met separately a week after my boss. I wouldn't get a response for another six months. My personal undertaking didn't seem to be considered worthy of encouragement or collaboration, or indeed, any reaction from my employer. I was a cog, a lowly subordinate. It was at once deflating and illuminating. My personal ambitions and this so-called "noble pursuit" mattered not at all. I could understand that. Many employers would respond the same, but perhaps not enlightened ones that had compassion for employees as individuals and cared about engendering loyalty. In any case, I couldn't wait for that train to leave the tracks; I had to hop aboard another train and accept that the destination, at least as far as my employment was concerned, would remain unclear.

## SEPTEMBER 21, 2013 – GET ME
## TO THE CHURCH ON TIME

After Rock God's annual fundraiser, the other event I attended as a political indoctrination and to convince myself to jump into the pool like Man of the People at my neighborhood pool party was rising star Christina Wilkinson's "surprise" announcement that she would be the Democratic candidate for Howard County executive, the top county government position.

Though the event was not billed as Wilkinson's launch for county executive, it was no surprise at all. Wilkinson for County Executive signs were posted all around the event location and supporters were decked out in Wilkinson for Executive t-shirts, stickers and buttons.

These events are like Grateful Dead concerts: Hardcore groupies appear without fail to form the inner circle; more casual followers, the satellite groupies, fill the outer circle.

In line to check in, I stood next to Fireman, the delegate whose seat I was considering running for and whom my wife had roomed with. He didn't recognize me. But when I introduced myself as Amy's husband, he became gregarious and patted me on the back like a good friend.

As a virtual fly on the wall, I observed the political insiders. Like young children who learn and imitate through modeling from their parents, the political caste modeled learned behavior. Never alone, they talked to a companion for a bit, tilted their heads back and laughed. Talk, tilt, laugh, and repeat, all around the room.

Like any good political event, Wilkinson's affair featured theatrics. A politician is a marketer, promoter, party planner, socialite and performer as much as a policy maker. Box-office appeal and style points count.

A band made up of a tuba, a trombone, and a trumpet established the atmosphere, like musicians at a wedding before the bride and groom appear. They played a Sousa March as a build-up to the introduction of the candidate. The event's dignitaries appeared one at a time from a backroom to the rhythm of different songs over the stereo system, soaking in applause as they traversed a center aisle dividing the crowd. First was lean and handsome Congressman John Sarbanes, scion of longtime U.S. Senator Paul Sarbanes of Maryland; next came the youthful Howard County Executive Ken Ulman, the Maryland lieutenant governor candidate; then, like the bridesmaid, Wilkinson's friend from college shuttled through and took the stage to introduce the candidate, telling stories of the 30 years of evolution she had observed her friend make through college and business school, career, marriage, family, activism in the schools, and immersion in local politics, coming to a pinnacle in the journey as the uncontested Democratic candidate for the top political job in one of the wealthiest counties with one of the highest-achieving student bodies in the nation.

Finally, Wilkinson was introduced, and burst through the "green room" backstage and acknowledged the crowd on her way to the stage to the tune of The Jackson 5's *ABC*. By God, it *was* like a wedding procession. I was looking for a groom.

This is how it's done when you have money, volunteers, and institutional and popular support built through the accumulation of good will and recognition over years of service and dedication. You put on a show, a little bit of Hollywood, to create the image, or maybe the illusion, of the larger-than-life candidate, the charismatic leader who can inspire legions of followers. While politicians like Wilkinson and Rock God were the stars in this ostentatious realm, I was more like the extra, someone who might show up to a cattle call audition for a Chicago parade-goer in *Ferris Bueller's Twist and Shout* scene.

# September 26, 2013 – Aiming for a Win-Win

I showed up on time to meet my HR director to discuss options for a flexible working arrangement should I be successful in my General Assembly run. The director wasn't there. That was a bad sign, reinforcing my status as an expendable cog. I waited outside her office for 20 minutes, when she came in holding lunch, looking at me surprised, like she was about to bonk her head and announce, *I could have had a V-8!* She invited me into her office, saying she could eat and talk at same time. I already felt the negative vibes.

The HR director did not embrace my noble pursuit, but didn't dismiss it out of hand either. She said she would have to consult with association leaders, up to and including the CEO. She conceded there was no precedent. She checked for an HR policy on running for political office, but found none. She wanted me to outline the details and project how the endeavor would affect my job, then see if we could work out a "win-win." The possibility of a workable arrangement remained open.

# October 3, 2013 – Courage

*"I wanted you to see what real courage is, instead of getting the idea that courage is a man with a gun in his hand. It's when you know you're licked before you begin, but you begin anyway and see it through no matter what."*

Atticus Finch, in author Harper Lee's *To Kill a Mockingbird*

Just 17 months previously, I found it difficult to get through the day in a suddenly and unexpectedly redesigned life with limited mobility, rehabilitating from surgery for a broken leg, unable to drive and working from home, as my concentration diminished, depression set in, and motivation plummeted. I reflected this day in amazement that one can bridge a gap between suffering during a low point in life and embracing a daunting task like a political campaign with enthusiasm, energy, daring and even a little courage.

Some people told me about the courage it takes to run for public office. It might take a certain kind of courage to expose oneself to public scrutiny and judgement, step into the spotlight and put reputation and ego on the line. But I never thought of running for public office as something that requires *real* courage. To me, *real* courage defines people who put their lives on the line, military members who defend our country and liberate other people, or police officers, firefighters and other rescuers. Or teachers who face the toughest challenges in the roughest school districts. Or people who take a stand despite risks and public condemnation, whistleblowers and civil rights activists such as Martin Luther King, Jr., Nelson Mandela and Harvey Milk. Or people who are unflappable and unstoppable in the face of abuse, tragedy, disease or disability.

For me, entering a political race was more like throwing a hat over the wall. "Throwing a hat over the wall" was the metaphor used by President John Kennedy, referring to America's determination to explore space and land a man on the moon. Kennedy appropriated the expression from Irish author Frank O'Connor, who wrote a parable about two adventurous boys who were halted in their journey by an imposing stone wall—until one threw his hat over the top, inspiring them both to scale the barrier to retrieve it. For me, it was crossing the line from consideration to commitment—throwing my hat over the wall.

•  •  •

Few people think about running for office, and of those who contemplate it, nearly none do. In *Becoming a Candidate,* Lawless cited a survey by a government research firm of more than 2,000 respondents that revealed 95 percent had never considered a candidacy, and less than 1 percent had run for any elective position. In Lawless's own surveys of more than 3,500 individuals considered "eligible candidates" in the four professions (law, business, education, political activism) that most often precede a career in politics, about 1 of 7 had given "serious thought" to running and 1 in 10 ran.

Lawless found that for many "eligible candidates," running for office requires "too much risk for too little reward...the courageous step of going before an electorate and opening oneself up to potential examination, scrutiny, loss of privacy and family time, possible rejection, and disruption from regular routines and pursuits…In many cases, the end does not justify the means."

Lawless' interview subjects had strong views for declining to run. "No degree of civic duty or sense of obligation would lead a sane person to enter the trenches," said one. "Mudslinging. Money-grubbing. Mayhem. That's all it is. Why would anyone ever decide to get involved in that?" offered another.

Novice candidates "are moving into unfamiliar territory and cannot fully envision what a candidacy would entail and whether they could endure it," Lawless found. "Most eligible candidates express distaste for the nuts and bolts associated with a political campaign."

Many of Lawless' survey respondents would have been more interested in political office if they did not have to campaign at all—like being a farmer who doesn't want to mess with planting or cutting the harvest—and harbored disdain for the political process. Her interview subjects described the prospects of fund-raising as "daunting," "petrifying," "disgusting," "off-putting," and "more painful than a root canal without anesthesia."

Many stood on the high dive, peered over the edge into the blue pool bottom, and turned around to descend the ladder, too scared to jump.

"I have thought about running for office for the last 25 years," said a civil rights activist. "But anytime I try to talk to anyone else about it, I get frazzled and worried. What if people don't like me? What if they won't vote for me? What if I can't raise the money?"

Another political activist confessed, "I thought about running many different times…I always made excuses, but I guess…I just never had the nerve."

•   •   •

I shared many of the survey respondents' sentiments. Nevertheless, I drove to a nondescript, red-brick State Board of Elections office in Annapolis, threw my hat through the third-floor window and, for a $50 fee, filed my official registration papers as a candidate—the ethics and financial disclosure statements and my Statement of Organization for Campaign Finance Entities. I named my campaign "Adam Sachs for Delegate-HEAL" to emphasize the health care theme, and appointed myself as campaign chairman because I had no other. I could serve as both candidate and chairman, but I couldn't register a campaign entity without a separate treasurer. Fortunately, I was able to sweet-talk, or guilt, wife Amy into taking the job the night before to clear the way for registration.

I had told my 17-year-old daughter Rebecca, who had just started college, about my plans the day before registering. She was supportive. The same day I talked to my 15-year-old son and budding computer scientist Daniel about being my "Chief Technology Officer" —a cool title that wasn't to be found on the state registration forms. Daniel already knew about my potential candidacy; he had helped me shoot a video promoting a single-payer health care system.

I knew I couldn't rely on either of my teen-agers to be big-time volunteers, with one in college and each with big academic loads and teen social lives. More importantly, I hoped I could serve as a model for striving for something meaningful, accepting a challenge, and being bold in life—maybe even a little courageous. They had seen me run for county council as 10- and 8-year-olds and had enthusiastically passed out literature to voters on primary election day. Now they had more maturity and wisdom to understand what being a political candidate meant and what it entailed. Still, they were baffled by why I would want to do such a thing, viewing it as another one of dad's quirky "adventures," like when I pulled them on a sled through two feet of snow and over snow banks a mile-and-a-half to Blockbusters, or when I suggested going to a remote, mountainous West Texas national park for Christmas. Regardless their involvement and the outcome, I wanted them to know and remember that I had a dream and wasn't afraid to pursue it, that I strived for a Big Agenda instead of settling for a Small Life even though success was a longshot.

## 'You Play to Win the Game'

Actor and director Ben Stiller authored an article in *Parade Magazine* that captured my feelings about running for office despite long odds in what many would deem an exercise in futility. Writing about pivotal moments and decisions in his life, Stiller referenced a movie he directed, *The Cable Guy*, which he called a "great creative experience" but "a big flop."

"I remember I stopped reading the *New York Times* review after the sentence that said, 'But the true disaster movie of the summer may just be *The Cable Guy*," Stiller wrote. "Dealing with that...taught me that the outcome doesn't always relate to the experience you have doing something—and that doesn't mean it wasn't valid or good, especially if it was what you wanted to do."

There's also the flip side to Stiller's feel-good, new-age, Hollywood-artsy philosophy, expressed concisely by Herman Edwards, ESPN broadcaster and former National Football League head coach. In a press conference famous for the coach's exasperated animation and often replayed on ESPN as a coach's rant for the ages, Edwards admonished reporters after a loss that, "You play to win the game...Hello? You play to win the game! You don't play it to just play it!"

Both Stiller and Edwards had valid points. As I let go of the trapeze swing and made my oath of candidacy, I wanted to win and believed I had a chance, even if slim, to finish in the top three and move on to the general election. But I also wanted to embrace the process and the experience and divorce those from the outcome. While letting go of the outcome can serve as a hedge against disappointment, it's also anathema to the successful political candidate—or NFL coach—whose best assets include confidence, ambition, ruthlessness, tirelessness, comprehensiveness, opportunism, unfailing perseverance, unwavering work ethic and an all-consuming desire to win.

Did I have those assets in bulk? I didn't need to plumb the depths of my soul for the answer. It was clear. I would be running a campaign more apropos of Stiller's philosophy than Edwards' and hoping for the best.

# Staking My Claim: The Liberal Left

> *"I believe in a relatively equal society, supported by institutions that limit extremes of wealth and poverty. I believe in democracy, civil liberties, and the rule of law. That makes me a liberal, and I'm proud of it."*

Paul Krugman, Distinguished Professor of Economics, Graduate Center of the City University of New York, and *New York Times* op-ed columnist.

> *"It is a well- known fact that reality has liberal bias."*

Stephen Colbert, CBS' *The Late Show* host

I purposely staked the position furthest left, risking that I'd be labeled a flaming liberal and out of synch with the moderates or the "center," which is where you should be in an American election if you want to play it safe, according to conventional wisdom, unless you are representing an area known for espousing more polar views, say Democratic House Minority Leader Nancy Pelosi from hippie-dippy, Rainbow Coalition San Francisco or Republican U.S. Senator and presidential candidate Ted Cruz from Bible Belt, ass-kickin' Texas.

The great American electorate is bunched in the middle 80 percent of the spectrum, comfortable with patriotism, ethnocentrism (America is the best at everything), empty platitudes, trite slogans ("Making Maryland Better for More Marylanders" was leading gubernatorial candidate Anthony Brown's), pat lines, simplicity, predictability, cautiousness and steadiness—the status quo, no matter how dysfunctional. Despite occasional rumblings or uprisings to change the status quo, most Americans—a majority of them members of the giant, amorphous darling of all successful politicians, the "middle class"—are reluctant to recalibrate the "quo" in any meaningful way (Whatever did happen to Occupy Wall Street, the 99 percenters protesting the greed, recklessness and fraudulent activities of American financial institutions and obscene inequalities, as well as camping out, smoking doobies and getting pregnant in city squares? Did anything change? If so, I must have missed it. Despite their enduring, in-your-face effort, still only one banker or financier ever went to jail for defrauding millions of Americans into home foreclosure, bankruptcy, unemployment, collapsed retirements and misery.)

Spare-A-Dime and Joker had staked out the conservative "Blue Dog Democrat" position to the right of the party's center, Spare-A-Dime with his anti-tax-and-spend, anti-government intrusion, pro-business rants, and Joker with his socially conservative Catholic roots, lobbying experience and pragmatic approach as a former legislator.

The seven other candidates all were vying to be the standouts somewhere along the continuum of the center. I knew I had no chance there, so zagged left to occupy my own territory by promoting adoption of a publicly financed health care system that would cover everyone, a ban on political action committee (PAC), corporate and union campaign contributions in favor of a public campaign financing option, and an income tax cut for working- and middle-class earners based on closing a corporate tax break loophole.

I rejected the often regurgitated claim that a universal coverage health care system would be a "government takeover" of health care, arguing that we currently were pawns under a "corporate takeover" and needed a "people's takeover." I coined my own pseudo-PAC, the P-PAC

(Placing People Above Corporations), as a slogan for my campaign and used it for campaign literature and speeches. I walked on the edge, calling the redistricting process out-and-out "corrupt" at a forum and railing against naysayers who claimed "it's not possible" to enact single payer health care or change the redistricting process, saying the only reason "it's not possible" was because of voters' unwillingness to elect people willing to stand for it.

I was the Bernie Sanders of District 12, minus the unkempt white hair and glasses, the Brooklyn accent, the Pied Piper charisma, the added dash of fire and brimstone, and a catchy play-on-name campaign slogan like "Feel the Bern." ("It's in the Bag with Sachs?" Nah, too corny.)

I embraced consideration of progressive ideas that represented a departure from the status quo with debatable pros and cons, such as legalization and taxation of marijuana. But I did not consider myself a flaming liberal. It's an easy but inaccurate label. I favor some libertarian or conservative principles such as individual responsibility and free choice, and am not a proponent of excessive "government handouts," as conservatives label the assistance programs, as a solution to problems. For example, I support experimenting with different types of public schools, such as single-sex schools and leadership/character academies, especially in areas where public schools are failing students. I believe strong families with involved fathers are the cornerstone of strong communities, and that government welfare can breed generational dependence. I object to wasteful spending on government programs with no proven results, and believe such waste should be eliminated, or at least redesigned, through more frequent audits and follow-up actions on findings of ineffectiveness or poor return on investment.

But none of that mattered much in this campaign to carve out ground in the crowded field. Positions such as favoring public charter or experimental schools did not go over well with the Democratic base, not to mention the powerful education union. I field-tested my idea for public all-boys' schools, based on a model showing success in Newark, New Jersey, during a dinner with African-American friends. They frowned upon it, saying boys and girls have to learn how to deal with each other in the real world so shouldn't be segregated in schools. Views may have been different in Baltimore, but these were parents from affluent Howard County, which was my base.

Rooting out government waste sounded good as a platitude and could win converts. But to have more than a superficial knowledge of the problem would have required a substantial investment in research that would be much easier for insiders, such as current delegates who benefitted from easy access to legislative reports and audits, connections in state agencies, annual testimony in legislative committees and staffs to pursue research. I didn't have time—or, declined to make time—to do the painstaking research. If I had, it would have consumed much of my time set aside for campaigning.

In hindsight, a platform focused on reducing government waste, and therefore taxes, with sound and specific evidence and proposed remedies, may have been the best avenue to pursue—voters latch onto government corruption, waste and inefficiency like UFO trackers pointing to photos of fuzzy lights illuminating darkened skies. In the end, I didn't have the inside knowledge, and didn't believe I had the time or resources to pursue this angle in depth, so only gave it cursory mentions on the campaign trail. I knew more about health care. I was committed to the left flank, for better or worse.

Apparently, some outspoken observers thought it was worse. The Baltimore County Blue blog charged that my "laser-like focus on single-payer healthcare…gives off negative energy." (Well, at least Blue thought my position had *some energy!*)

# OCTOBER 8, 2013 -- TRAGEDY

The Adam Sachs for Delegate-HEAL official campaign got off to a tragic start. Just five days after registering, I went to my mother's apartment after not being able to reach her on the phone for two days and found her dead on the floor. I had never told her I was considering running—our relationship had become strained as her mental and physical health had declined. I didn't want to mention a political run until I was fully committed and felt she was on firmer ground. I had planned to let her know I was in the race the next time I saw her. I never got that opportunity. I felt terrible I had never shared the news.

On the same day that Amy and I found my mother dead in her apartment, a profile story on my candidacy appeared in the *Baltimore Sun*.

## October 8, 2013 -- Foxes
## Guarding the Hen House

*The Sun* reported my campaign was focused on bringing health care to every Maryland resident, streamlining health care to eliminate costly administrative fees, and creating a system "where health care is treated as a human right instead of a privilege, and health care is a public good, instead of a private benefit."

It noted my background working in communications for the health insurer CareFirst BlueCross BlueShield and a health care professional association, lending credibility to my campaign theme. "It's a very costly system that we have in America," I was quoted, "and a lot of the costs don't really go to actual health care."

I came up with a catchy quote to explain why I believed Maryland should go further than Obamacare. I noted that Obamacare did some positive things, but overall it represented a patchwork approach to addressing a complex system.

Comparing for-profit health insurers to hungry predators searching for new prey, I said, "The problem with Obamacare is that it leaves the foxes guarding the hen house, offers them a new luxury coop and delivers them a million more hens."

"I decided to run because I believe I can be bold enough to be a voice to raise the issue," I said, "where I didn't really see it happening with the other candidates."

The next day, I was pleased to see a reader write in the online comments, "I thank this candidate for shouting loudly and strongly for Universal Care." It confirmed there were "true believers" in the electorate.

·  ·  ·

*T he Sun* article provided me a nice opening salvo. Now I just had to back it up with real action. That is, as soon as I could plan a memorial service for my mother, meet and make plans with funeral directors, coordinate with out-of-town family, untangle her financial affairs, launch the bureaucratic estate settlement process with the Register of Wills, negotiate with her landlord, make repairs to her apartment, sell her furniture on Craigslist, and move all her other belongings out of her apartment within three weeks. Not the ideal way or frame of mind to launch a campaign.

So the first month of my campaign was put virtually on hold while I dealt with my mother's affairs and coped with the sudden loss emotionally. In a spiritual way, I felt Sandra Sachs with me during the campaign, watching over me as I traveled door-to-door and marched with people who were struggling day-to-day. It occurred to me that maybe it was fate that I was running at all. It was my mother who loved politics and took pride in identifying herself as a Democrat, the party of inclusion and champion of the vulnerable, with her roots as the daughter of Eastern European immigrants who settled in the gritty outskirts of Boston and who lived a hardscrabble, working-class life. She would have been proud, I thought, looking down. No one from my family had ever run for political office before. The Kennedys we were not.

Reeher determined in *First Person Political* that about two-thirds of state legislators "to a large extent inherited political commitment and interest from relatives…These relatives' civic engagement, on the whole, far exceeded the involvement level of the average citizen." That was true in my case; if not for Sandra Sachs' passion, the thought of running may have never crossed my mind.

Lawless echoed Reeher's survey findings in *Becoming a Candidate*, saying a "politicized upbringing lays the foundation for political ambition" and that an "early political socialization process can clearly instill in many individuals the belief that they have the power to take part in the democratic process."

Those characteristics were evident of others in my race, including most prominently Anointed One, Ballerina and Gadfly. For them as well as me, the apple did not fall far from the politically-rooted tree.

# OCTOBER 23, 2013 – ROCK GOD IN CONCERT

Four months after Rock God announced his Senate bid at his pizza fundraiser, I attended Rock God's "kickoff" event for his Senate run at The Great Room at Savage Mill, an elegant hall with high ceilings and magnificent windows converted from a former 19$^{th}$ century mill building and rented out for weddings and galas. Like a wedding reception, two stations were set up with catering staff carving roast beef and turkey, with mashed potatoes and gravy. Bartenders served drinks. Five varieties of dessert cups lined tables. All that was missing was the lineup of single ladies to catch the garter. Raising big money as a politician does have its perks.

The Lion of the Senate Mike Miller attended to introduce Rock God, telling the crowd how lucky they were to have Rock God working on their behalf in Annapolis.

Rock God took center stage, a huge banner behind him screaming "Big Team 13." He announced there were 100 sponsors of the kickoff event, all bidding on a little piece of Rock God's political pie.

He talked about his legislative work and its unpredictability. He welcomed the newbie to Team 13, the candidate all but anointed to take his place as delegate, Howard County school board member Regina Hassan. "Working as a team is important," he said. He lamented the antagonism and dysfunction in Washington and said his philosophy is to strive to work with people who don't agree with him.

"The team will be back together to do good stuff in Annapolis," he declared, adding more lines about "working together" and "working hard" and being "proud."

It sounded earnest, but struck me as rather dispassionate and lack-luster for the momentousness of the occasion, failing to spark emotion. People were standing silently, motionless, holding their drinks and nibbling their food, chatting in hushed tones. Where was the raucous cheering and fist-pumping? Wasn't politics all about emotional, visceral connection?

Rock God said he was "excited and energized" to launch his Senate bid. He may indeed have felt that, but the speech did not convey it. "..And with that, I will kick off this campaign," he concluded to modest applause. Then, everyone returned to talking to their neighbor.

・ ・ ・

H e didn't say much of substance, and certainly didn't climb out on a limb on any specific issue. But then, I thought, he probably couldn't, even if he wanted to. How much of a risk-taker can you be when you are an insider and feel compelled to act in that role and are trapped in a box? The Senate president was there. Is he going to sup-port someone throwing grenades for universal health care coverage or legalization of drugs or overhaul of the redistricting process or revision of the income tax structure if that is not on his agenda? Is a grenade-thrower going to reap the career-ladder rewards that come with being a good foot soldier? How passionate can you be when most of what your typical legislator will do is preserve the status quo while maybe nibbling at small changes around the edges, knowing political bosses will tolerate nothing more, and try to appease the desires of powerful special inter-ests and others with the most access, except in rare instances of true, meaningful breakthroughs after years or even decades of percolation, like gay marriage?

For God's sake, the Democratic-controlled Maryland Assembly failed to pass a bill in 2016 that would have required employers with at least 15 employees to offer workers a minimum of seven paid sick leave days per year, the fourth year in a row such a bill had died. Senate Lion Miller said the bill came to the Senate from the House too late, and there would be a strong push "next year." Convenient excuse. Translation: Politicians killed it deliberately through legislative maneuvering and delay tactics, sparing all of them who collect wads of cash from businesses an up-or-down vote. Always "next year." Kick the can. Next year, maybe no one will remember the shirking of responsibility *this year.* How will starting from scratch *next year* help workers with illnesses or sick kids to care for *this year?* Where's the courage to offer struggling, working families a small measure of decency and humaneness? Would one allowable sick day every two months really kill an employer's productivity or break its bank? Just who do these politicians really represent, and whose status quo are they protecting?

And in 2016, for the second year in a row, a 44-year-old Maryland delegate who suffered sexual abuse as a child could not get his bill providing more rights to the victims of sexual abuse out of legislative committee. The bill would have extended the statute of limitations for a victim to file a civil suit against the abuser beyond seven years from the time the victim is considered an "adult" at age 18, recognizing that victims often repress the memories for many years. The House Judiciary Committee Chairman declined to allow a committee vote. Which organization was a powerful opponent, sending lobbyists and submitting testimony to defeat the measure? The Catholic Church (Maryland Catholic Conference), an institution tainted worldwide by scandals and cover-ups of priests sexually abusing children. Just who are the politicians protecting?

• • •

R ock God never blew me away with his soaring oratory or fire for a cause, or made me want to follow him to the ends of the earth because of his infectious charm or charisma, a la Bill Clinton. No, Rock God was a grinder—a balcony-sitter, not a ledge-walker—steady, reliable, ever-present and dogged, playing the percentages, like the tennis player who has the patience, point after point, to tough it out for one more conservative mid-court shot than his opponent is willing, the son of a steelworker who grinded out a living with a lunch bucket, a helmet and a blow torch.

## October 26, 2013 – A Hard Sell on the Streets

After attending to the depressing and energy-sapping details of my mother's funeral and estate, I was ready to make my first public foray as an official candidate at the Health Care is a Human Right Rally in Baltimore. I viewed the event as a good opportunity to make connections with like-minded activists.

I made an impromptu flier to announce myself as a candidate who was promoting universal health care and to soft-pedal a plea for financial support. I met up with four HCHR activists from Howard County, all retirees, and traveled to the city.

It felt odd to contemplate approaching strangers and introducing myself as a candidate for delegate. It had been seven years since my first run for public office, which I believed would be my *last,* and it had been daunting then. The one thing that helped me most then was my experience as a newspaper reporter, where I constantly was faced with approaching strangers, introducing myself and asking questions. But I was out of practice.

The marchers convened at a converted movie house. I stoked my courage and lit my extrovert fuse, introducing myself to attendees and telling them I was running for delegate on a "single-payer" platform. I handed them my homespun campaign card to encourage donations.

To my chagrin, I found that people had difficulty making the connection between the fact that I advocated for their cause and the necessity to raise money to generate support and deliver the message.

Most marchers were more concerned about what district I lived in and whether they could vote for me. That interest was nice, but truth be told, it wasn't what I needed from this event. I needed money. If I couldn't get financial support from this crowd, as one of the few, if not the only candidate statewide championing single-payer health care, who could I realistically expect to get it from?

What I quickly recognized was that a good portion of the universal health care crowd was poor and had no money to spare for political donations. Many of the activists I met and heard tell stories of health care woes and going without health insurance were students, the laid-off and unemployed, the once- and nearly-homeless, the struggling self-employed, low-wage workers and quirky outsiders, such as Green Party candidates.

But there were also professionals and comfortable retirees, including those from my home county, who could contribute. I passed out about 60 fundraising cards before the march and along the route, yet didn't even break even on my $7.50 investment to produce the cards. Fundraising was not going to be an easy task.

A drum line corps, dancers and cheerleading squads in full regalia joined the march, which snaked for two hours through old Baltimore neighborhoods to the waterfront's gleaming, high-rise headquarters of CareFirst BlueCross BlueShield, the giant health insurance company for which I once worked. Leaders chanted: "What do we want?" "Health care!" "When do we want it?" "Now!"

In a city park, "street theatre" performers acted out a portrayal of the U.S. health care system in which Big Insurance showed indifference to Sick People, with Uncle Sam's complicity. The march brought residents to their windows, balconies and front stoops to check out the commotion, as marchers ran to deliver fliers to the onlookers.

The march had not only a festive feel, like a parade, but also the aura of something significant. I felt proud to be part of it, since I knew I could have an influence in raising awareness of the cause through my campaign.

After reaching the CareFirst building, marchers gathered at an adjacent riverside park, formed a large circle, held hands, listened to leaders speak about pressing forward with the movement, congratulated ourselves—though omitted a rendition of *Kumbaya*—then quickly dispersed to take cover from the wind and pending darkness. It was at once inspiring and anti-climactic. It was a Saturday. No CareFirst executives or influential politicians were present to witness the demonstration or, heaven forbid, engage with any of the advocates—just a cold, steely, indifferent corporate monolith casting its long shadow over a plucky, brave but largely powerless citizenry.

# OCTOBER 28, 2013 – MY DISTRICT 12 DEBUT

*"It is hard to talk about a middle ground for
something that is a fundamental right."*

TERI REYNOLDS, CONTRIBUTOR TO TARIQ ALI'S *THE
OBAMA SYNDROME: SURRENDER AT HOME, WAR ABROAD*

The Southwest Baltimore County Democratic Club Forum was the first event where all the District 12 candidates appeared together, except Spare-A-Dime, who had not yet entered the race. The club gave each candidate five minutes to pimp themselves.

With the recent *Baltimore Sun* story announcing my entry and emphasizing health care, and with my experience working for a health care insurer and a health care professional association, I decided to go all-in on promoting universal health care coverage to distinguish myself from the pack. I knew my emphasis on this issue could break either of two ways: position myself as a bold candidate unafraid to speak the truth, break with political faint-heartedness and challenge powerful Establishment interests; or peg me as a single-issue radical candidate occupying an unwinnable fringe.

In a dark parking lot outside an unremarkable, modular former elementary school, I sat under a light for a few silent minutes, contemplating my readiness to compete, to project confidence, to fit the part, to face candidates I knew were better resourced and better known, to engage with constituents in a way to convey that I really cared about them and their concerns upon first introduction—whether I truly did or not—and talking myself into believing that my ego would survive no matter what unfolded.

By luck of the draw, I was the first candidate selected to address the 50 club members seated like students in the former classroom. I took a deep breath, stood up, walked to the front of the long table where the candidates were seated and crossed the threshold into the limelight of the real public campaign.

I told the members that all nine candidates would take similar positions on many of the top issues, such as education, environmental protection and the economy. Then I asked them point blank: Do you want to elect someone who is not beholden to The Establishment, who will buck the status quo, who will stand up for something bold that will truly make a significant difference in the lives of every Maryland resident?

I would do that, I told them. Then I unveiled my campaign's health care platform, Healthcare for Everyone All Lifelong, or HEAL:

- Publicly-financed, universal health care coverage—everybody in the system, nobody outside
- Health care as a human right, a public good
- A single administrative, nonprofit entity to set rates and pay bills
- No haggling with for-profit private insurers, because they'll no longer be running the show
- Full choice of health care providers and hospitals, eliminating high "out of network" rates, because they're all in the same system
- No monthly premiums, deductibles and copays
- No medical bankruptcies
- Health care coverage that travels with you, not tied to a Big Brother employer
- Equitable health care that is not based on personal wealth

It was nothing short of a tragedy and a disgrace for the wealthiest nation to leave so many of its people without any or adequate health care, living in fear of going broke because of a medical condition and putting off needed care because they couldn't afford it, thereby creating even more serious and costly medical problems instead of preventing them, I told the audience.

For those inclined to label anyone challenging the current system a "socialist" or part of the "far-left liberal fringe," I said that's exactly the propaganda the corporate and political Powers That Be wanted citizens to believe so they could preserve the status quo.

I cited research that showed the costs of continuing to travel the current path: The average annual health care costs for a U.S. family of four in 2013 was $22,000, with more than $9,000 coming out of pocket; annual U.S. spending per person on health care was $7,300, while spending in other industrialized nations, including Canada, Germany, the United Kingdom and Australia, was half the U.S. total or less. To boot, the U.S. had worse health outcomes on almost every common health measure than other comparable nations.

I referenced the obscene costs of health insurer executives' compensation. In one recent year, a small group of top executives from the top seven publicly traded health insurance companies were compensated $225 million. One former CEO accumulated $1.6 billion in stock options before he was busted by the Securities and Exchange Commission for illegalities. The top insurer in Maryland, CareFirst BlueCross BlueShield, had recently given its former CEO an $18 million severance parachute.

"How did you all like paying that CEO $18 million to get fired as part of your health care plan," I asked the club members. "Did that improve your health?"

I noticed some heads nodding and sensed that the crowd was paying attention.

I talked about Obamacare making some positive changes, but having the fatal flaws of empowering and enriching private health insurers, making a complicated, patchwork system even more convoluted and still leaving millions uninsured. Maryland's projections were that 400,000 residents would still be uninsured, even after Obamacare implementation.

I highlighted that Vermont recently had become the first state to enact laws to create a universal health care system, and that Maryland had considered a bill several times previously to do the same. I asserted that, according to one independent economic analysis, Maryland's proposed legislation would save $6.4 billion annually in health costs, or $1,000 per Maryland resident.

I closed by quoting Wendell Potter, a health insurance public relations executive turned industry critic who authored the insider tell-all book *Deadly Spin.* "The health insurance industry is dominated by a cartel of large, for-profit corporations…[T]he top priority…is to 'enhance shareholder value,'" I quoted Potter. "When that's your top priority, you are motivated more by the obligation to meet Wall Street's relentless profit expectations than by the obligation to meet the medical needs of your policyholders."

The feeling sunk in that I was part of something big and meaningful, that I would be taking an unpredictable and exciting journey with these eight other valiant souls—with Spare-A-Dime to join the gang later—with our paths crossing frequently. We would come to respect or distrust each other; we would offer each other support and collegiality in the heat of battle or treat each other strictly as adversaries with disdain; we might become friends or enemies; we might attack and tear each other down or focus on ourselves and our own attributes and ideas. It would play out over the next eight months at public forums, in newspapers, on social media, at community events, in endorsement meetings and on neighborhood streets. I felt proud and honored to be part of the whirlwind.

As I circled back to take my seat along Candidates Row, the candidate next to me in alphabetical order, Next Big Thing, who had received strong advance publicity and buzz, whispered, "Nice job."

"Thanks," I replied, surprised by the compliment. It was the first time we had met. A more cutthroat candidate would have said nothing at all, wouldn't even have acknowledged me. *This guy is alright,* I thought, *I can see why he's got the buzz.*

# The Next Big Thing

Next Big Thing had the look: youthful, tall, dark and handsome. Rotating images on Next Big Thing's website, which promoted the up-and-comer as a "Solutions Guy," depicted Next Big Thing smiling with Maryland Gov. O'Malley and hobnobbing with Fireman, who he was seeking to succeed as delegate.

"The Greatest Candidate…Who Has Never Run for Anything," Bill Woodcock, the self-anointed Marshmallow Man, author of the political and community blog 53 Beers on Tap, crowed of Next Big Thing.

Next Big Thing always emphasized that he served as a speechwriter for O'Malley, soon-to-be Democratic presidential candidate, at forums and on his website and campaign literature, giving him political cache'. That connection also paid off monetarily. O'Malley's O' Say Can You See PAC contributed $4,000 to Next Big Thing.

Next Big Thing didn't only have the governor as an influential connection; his employment at the law firm Saul Ewing, LLP linked him to more political high places. The chairman of Next Big Thing's campaign was John Joseph "Max" Curran, who was a partner at Saul Ewing. Max Curran was the son of J. Joseph Curran Jr., the longest-serving attorney general in Maryland history. And Max Curran's sister was Katie O'Malley, Gov. O'Malley's wife and a Baltimore City District Court judge.

## My Good Friend

Next Big Thing's association with Fireman also was more than just a chance photo op. There was no doubt Next Big Thing and Fireman had formed a budding "bromance" in amazingly short order. Next Big Thing even referred to Fireman as a "father figure" in a glowing tribute to the outgoing delegate.

In October 2013, Fireman spearheaded Next Big Thing's campaign kickoff, just several months after Next Big Thing moved into the district. Fireman introduced the fledgling Arbutus candidate to the new Next Big Thing supporters, many of whom were old Fireman supporters. As the Next Big Thing campaign was gaining momentum closer to the primary, Fireman emceed another Next Big Thing event with ever more passionate bromantic vibes to sing Next Big Thing's praises and offer the upstart candidate his official endorsement.

Fireman's introduction was an ode to his hoped-for heir apparent, putting the weight of the lifelong Arbutus resident's and local firefighter's 20 years of legislative experience, responsive constituent service, accumulated good will, deep roots and connections and intimate community knowledge squarely behind The Fireman Protégé.

"Next Big Thing is one of these guys who as soon as you meet him, you'll like him. And he's genuine. There's a lot of people in politics these days…they're not genuine. And that's not something you can fake. That's something that's built inside of you… When you sit down and ask for his help, he listens. He's not one of these people who asks you, and then doesn't listen for the answer.

"…[H]e also works for the little guy…To me, the most important thing is constituent service. I tell people all the time: It's what you do the other 275 days [outside of legislative session] that makes you a good elected official.

"The big announcement is…if you look on his lapel, you'll see a little state firefighters' helmet. Tonight I officially endorse Next Big Thing… I'm going to do everything in my power. Everybody in all of District 12 will know that Delegate Fireman is endorsing Next Big Thing when they get their mail in the next couple days."

And then, a classic Fireman finale of endearing—or cloying—references: "So with that, my good friend, my buddy, he's a great husband, my good friend, Next Big Thing."

True to his word, Fireman gave the Next Big Thing campaign an in-kind donation of more than $5,300 to send a mailing to District 12 voters announcing Fireman's endorsement of Next Big Thing. On the homepage of his campaign website, Next Big Thing featured an official-looking seal saying "Endorsed by Del. Fireman" and the video of Fireman introducing him to the cheering crowd as "my good friend."

Wow. What an amazing advantage it would be to have a popular politician like Fireman, whose constituents had been voting for a Fireman on the ballot stretching back five decades, channeling his backers to your camp. From the 1960s through the 1980s, they voted for Fireman's father, who served three terms as state delegate and two terms as Baltimore County sheriff. Beginning in 1994, those same voters had five opportunities to elect the younger Fireman as state delegate.

And it wasn't just Fireman who attended Next Big Thing's passing of the torch celebration. Before Next Big Thing was done, he acknowledged that Rock God, the impending shoo-in for state senator, was in the crowd. To have Rock God in your corner could send your political stock through the roof.

I looked at Next Big Thing, palling around with Fireman, his father figure and mentor, attracting a revered statesman like Rock God, and I couldn't help but be a little jealous about the payoffs. The political gatekeepers had opened the Political Pearly Gates to Next Big Thing with a "Welcome Honorary Club Member" sign. I didn't have any heavy-hitters stoking my fire along the campaign trail. What it would be like, I wondered, to have someone of Fireman's status and caliber to announce to his devotees, "I believe in you, Adam Sachs, and I want you to replace me as delegate."

· · ·

I actually made a stride toward seeking such a coup, but in the end, I didn't have the nerve to follow through. I asked retiring Delegate

Drummer at an event if she would meet with me, planning to gauge if she would offer another endorsement in addition to Anointed One. She responded she would, but requested that I wait until after the General Assembly session ended, and to allow time to grieve her grandson's recent death from brain cancer.

I never did get back to Drummer. I could say that I just got busier as April came, the weather improved and daylight expanded, allowing more opportunity for door-to-door campaigning, and candidate forums ramped up. I could claim it was too late in the campaign to seek an endorsement anyway. But those would be lies, excuses. Truth is, I punked out. I was afraid I would be rejected as an unworthy, inadequate candidate, a longshot without the political chops or campaign operation, certainly not one upon which a local political legend would stake her reputation. That was my loss. In a political race, you have to try everything. And ask, ask, ask until you're blue in the face. Every candidate has to get in touch with his inner salesman, his Dale Carnegie persona, or the fortitude to develop one quick. If you fear rejection or are hesitant about asking, you might as well stay home.

## You Are Never Alone

Next Big Thing alternately flattered, extolled and teased Fireman as if he was toasting him at a wedding, telling the story about when he introduced himself at constituents' doors:

"They'll say, 'Well, is Fireman running again? And of course they're on a first name basis with [Fireman]. I think they're trying to figure out if I have what it takes, if I'm fit for office…And then they say, 'Are you trying to fill his shoes?' No, you can't, you absolutely can't. I mean that. It's not just because I don't have enough cologne." The audience erupts in laughter at the inside joke that's so well-known it's public knowledge—Fireman wears too much cologne. And Next Big Thing is close enough to Fireman to rag him about it and get away with it.

"I think there's this understanding…that you can count on Fireman when you need something…Dare I say it, 'You Are Never Alone…'" He didn't need to finish his sentence; more guffaws filled in the unspoken, universally recognized punch line: "'with Fireman Petrone.'"

"I've learned a lot from you…I've learned how to greet people on the street: 'Hey, buddy. Hey beautiful.'" Next Big Thing cracked himself up at the thought of himself delivering such Firemanisms on street corners. Then he regained seriousness about his mentor and his campaign's philosophy, which apparently was to emulate Fireman and snare his votes:

"What people want most is someone to count on, and there's two words, Fireman mentioned them: constituent service. That's what it comes down to, and that's what he's really stressed to me. So I will be that guy."

## Constituent Service: A Legislator's Responsibility?

Good for Next Big Thing for buying into the politicians' gospel. I have to admit, I rarely mentioned a job requirement called "constituent service" during my campaign.

Constituent service is to politics as entertainment is to Disney: without it, you might as well fold up shop. But constituent service wasn't why I was running. Constituent service, what is that? (Here's where I get pilloried by the purists and career politicians). It's doling out scholarship money; granting honors to Eagle Scouts; signing hollow proclamations; giving out flags; gripping and grinning for photo ops; appearing as window dressing to increase the significance of events; mollifying squeaky wheels; making others feel important; and most practically, using the power of your office and your connections to run interference, break red tape and attempt to solve problems for people who need government attention. And that's why you have staff. You pay *them* to do that grunt work that has little to do with setting policy and governing a state.

I wanted to work on big issues that could affect everyone statewide, stand for people who didn't have a voice and advocate on policies that would challenge the status quo. If I held office and didn't stand for anything significant or make a trace of difference legislatively for eight years, I'd fire my ass into self-imposed retirement out of frustration with a recalcitrant system and save voters the trouble. Maryland wouldn't have needed my unique abilities for constituent service, because they wouldn't have been unique. Any monkey could do it.

Constituent service? It sounds so benevolent. So altruistic. So…obvious! Who wouldn't embrace being the Political Wizard of Oz? What good politician *wouldn't* say he was a true believer in the most utilitarian tool in the politician's toolbox? Certainly not Next Big Thing, the Fireman disciple.

The nonprofit organization City Ethics questioned whether "constituent services" should be handled by legislators at all, highlighting their political rather than legislative nature and the potential for preferential treatment and corruption. Politicians often can get around ethics provisions and justify preferential treatment by claiming they were merely providing constituent services. But under scrutiny, constituent services often are proved to be offered to constituents or groups with a special relationship to the politician and involve special favors or repayment of a political debt, said City Ethics.

"Local legislators are elected to determine policy, not to deal with nitty-gritty matters. This is what administrators are supposed to do," said City Ethics. "Considering how important constituent services are to re-election, this area of government blurs the line between governance and election campaigns."

## Carpetbagger

At the Fireman endorsement event, Next Big Thing indirectly addressed the elephant in the room, the fact he couldn't escape: He was a carpetbagger, a "parachute candidate."

"There is plenty of homegrown local talent to give residents the options they need. We didn't need folks…moving into our district to run for office," Man of the People derided, referring to Next Big Thing and Joker.

Next Big Thing lived outside District 12 before buying a new house in Fireman's Arbutus hometown 11 months before the primary. Within several weeks of the purchase, Next Big Thing officially filed his candidacy for District 12 delegate. And about two months later, Fireman introduced Next Big Thing as his Chosen One at a campaign kickoff.

For all his attributes as a candidate, Next Big Thing encountered suspicion, vitriol and disdain because of his abbreviated residency in the district, lack of dues-paying and his insider bonds with Fireman and Gov. O'Malley.

Baltimore County Blue blog questioned whether "the O'Malley Machine" prodded Fireman to endorse Next Big Thing. "The O'Malley Machine may have its hand in the cookie jar," the blog said, drawing the lineage from Next Big Thing through the prominent Curran clan to Gov. O'Malley. "If the O'Malley Machine is so interested in having influence on district elections, why didn't they seek a candidate who already lived in the district?"

A commenter on the blog certainly saw treachery and conspiracy, charging that Next Big Thing's sudden enthusiasm for attending local business group and community association meetings, marching in the Arbutus 4th of July parade and volunteering at the fire department's carnival while his house was under construction was mere political expediency to become a "quick study" in District 12.

"Almost all of the other candidates…have more connections to the district and experience than Next Big Thing…Let's help voters educate themselves on this carpetbagger…Clearly with Next Big Thing it isn't about what you know or have done but who you know."

## The Real Deal

Next Big Thing inspired strong emotions on each side among the Baltimore County faithful and deep-rooted. But as for me—though Next

Big Thing had plenty of traits and connections of which to be envious, and in a political race, downright spiteful of—I liked him from our first introduction. I couldn't fault Fireman for backing Next Big Thing; I came to believe Next Big Thing would make an excellent representative as both a smart and diligent policymaker and a likable, personable, sincere, well-intentioned and honest man.

At several forums, where candidates lined up like cattle, I sat next to Next Big Thing, and he was always friendly, even helpful. When I arrived late to one forum because of horrendous traffic, Next Big Thing graciously filled me in on the proceedings, when he could have left my tardy ass hanging out to dry.

Next Big Thing was the type of guy I'd like to call my friend, even, as Fireman would say, "My good buddy." One weekend day while campaigning door-to-door, I saw Next Big Thing and a volunteer in the distance coming toward me.

"I heard you had appendicitis. How are you feeling? Are you recovering?" I asked him, knowing he had had surgery and had missed a recent forum.

"I'm feeling good, much better," he responded.

"Lucky weather for February, it's a good chance to cover some ground without slipping on ice."

"That's what we're trying to do," Next Big Thing said. "We're getting a good number of people at home today."

"Good to see you out," I said.

We chatted for a few minutes about the campaign, two rival candidates in the middle of a residential street, then continued in opposite directions, banging on doors. I appreciated that Next Big Thing was running a hard race, but could still be personable and gracious with his opponents. At that moment, I thought I wouldn't mind seeing Next Big Thing finish in the top three.

At 29, he was about the same age as Man of the People, but Next Big Thing had something that Man of the People did not—The Look, and therefore The Aura that he was meant for this line of work. Next

Big Thing was about 6-foot-3, good looking with thick, dark hair, solidly built, affable, and likably humble. And for such a young man, he had an incredibly strong resume.

Next Big Thing was named one of the "20 in Their 20s" honorees described as "the future leaders of Maryland" by the *Daily Record,* a venerable Baltimore-based legal and business publication.

Next Big Thing first latched onto O'Malley as a "mayoral fellow" in the communications office of the then-Baltimore City mayor after college in 2006. That was a savvy and timely move, as O'Malley was in the throes of running for governor. Next Big Thing followed O'Malley to the Governor's Mansion, working in his communications office.

From O'Malley's staff, he graduated from George Washington University law school and worked as a judicial clerk for the Maryland Court of Appeals before moving to the law firm Saul Ewing.

In the *Baltimore Sun,* Next Big Thing declared that he decided to run for office after hearing that the three District 12 incumbents had decided not to seek re-election, calling it "a terrific opportunity." In other words, he said his move to the district preceded his knowledge of the political opportunity. Next Big Thing's version of the order is debatable. What isn't debatable is that, with his Fireman, Gov. O'Malley and law firm connections, Next Big Thing entered the race running on all cylinders, regardless of his "carpetbagger" label.

Why Fireman supported a newcomer when three District 12 lifers (Man of the People, Energy and Ballerina) and another 20-year resident (Gadfly) were in the race may have been as simple as Fireman believed Next Big Thing was the best candidate with the brightest future. Or, the link may have been made through a series of insider connections. Regardless, it was highly unusual for a sitting politician to throw his support behind a new contender with less than a year's residency and no track record, demonstrated service to the home community or personal connections to its local leaders. And Fireman's support undoubtedly gave Next Big Thing a big boost, including financially. He racked up campaign endorsements and contributions from police and firefighter unions that normally supported Fireman, and working class labor unions such as the United Food and Commercial Workers (UFCW), an organization which gave Next Big Thing $3,500 and was a frequent contributor to Fireman, right up Fireman's alley as a blue-collar union man himself.

I can't say for sure whether those contributions were the residual of Fireman's perennial largesse from the unions, or actually earned by Next Big Thing. That's part of the unseemly gray underbelly of politics. But it begs this question: Why would workers in food processing and meat packing plants, and grocery and retail stores throw their support to a corporate attorney representing white-collar firms for a big Baltimore law firm who apparently had never been a union member, and whose law specialty was corporate governance, securities and white collar enforcement, not exactly the resume of a defender of the rights of food workers getting trampled by their corporate bosses?

The answer: It doesn't matter. Those paycheck-to-paycheck grinders, through their union honchos, can invest in a share of future loyalty from a budding politician like Next Big Thing the same way attorneys comprising the Maryland Association for Justice, which also contributed to Next Big Thing, can. That was the crossover appeal, and political pull, of Next Big Thing.

## October 29, 2013 – I'm Not
## Wearing a Wire, I Swear!

Building on the momentum from the Health Care is a Human Right rally in Baltimore, one of the rally's attendees from the HCHR Howard County chapter said several members wanted to meet with me. I took that as a positive sign. I could have used any support the organization could have offered, though I was unsure whether the nonprofit could endorse, assist, or make donations to political candidates. But certainly individual group members could do those things on their own, and that's what I was seeking.

The chapter's leader, Dr. Glickstein, couldn't attend. So I met with another advocate and a man who seemed to be a covert, KGB-like operative of the group, a primary care physician who apparently didn't want to be publicly recognized as a supporter of universal health care.

Over butternut squash soup and a turkey sandwich at Panera Bread, our meeting started auspiciously. It felt like an interrogation, as if I was an impostor or an undercover spy infiltrating an underground movement.

"Why are you interested in universal health care?" the covert doctor opened. "What have you done for single-payer before?"

Not "glad to have you on board" or "what can you do to help us?" The doctor wanted to know my bona fides—what was my allegiance to the movement—essentially to prove that I was a "true believer" and not a fraud, a fly-by-night pretender, or even worse, a "mole" in espionage parlance. I had visions of myself gagged and bound, strapped to a chair in a dank warehouse, water dripping, a bright light in my eyes (once the duct tape was removed), about to be interrogated by masters of torture. I'm surprised they didn't take me out back beyond Panera's kitchen and strip search me for a wire and rough me up as a warning.

"I advocated for passage for the Affordable Care Act in my job. I came to believe that a single-payer system was a much better solution," I told the operatives. "What better way to promote it than running for office?"

"We haven't seen you before," said the doctor, implying I did not have the proper credentials to be representing the cause. I hadn't served in the trenches, been beaten down at every turn by Corporate America, Big Insurance and Status Quo Politician. I was Johnny-come-lately, looking to ride the old troupers' coattails. I got the sense these guys had been battling for this change for a long time with little progress, much frustration, waning faith and growing suspicion.

I had already been to several HCHR-Howard chapter meetings, announced that universal health care would be a cornerstone of my campaign for delegate, and participated in the Baltimore health care rally. I professed belief in the group's principles. Maybe they wanted an oath signed in blood?

*What's with these guys,* I thought. It's not like they have a bunch of candidates banging down Dr. Glickstein's door to represent their cause. Incumbent legislators and candidates were accepting thousands of dollars for their campaign accounts from entities with huge stakes in *preserving the system,* not radically *changing the system.*

The doctor was skittish about going public with his affiliation with the cause. As much as some physicians may not like the current structure of the health care system from a moral standpoint and abhor dealing with health insurers, they may enjoy the capitalistic perks and feel business pressures not to rock the boat or bite the hand that feeds them.

Eventually we discussed how to educate the public in simplified terms about the principles of universal health care coverage and counteract propaganda like "a government takeover of health care."

While I stayed true to my beginnings and promoted the concepts behind universal health care throughout my campaign, I felt let down by Health Care is a Human Right, even resentful. Perhaps I was naïve in thinking that my public advocacy for a cause that no one else in the district, let alone State House races statewide, was championing would earn me some volunteer assistance or financial support. I made a pitch for support at several meetings at Dr. Glickstein's house, and followed up with members several times by e-mail. But I couldn't generate contributions—only a few volunteers for video interviews—and I didn't feel like being a beggar. Eventually I stopped asking.

Leaders of the group seemed to cling to the hope that a current Howard County legislator would carry their banner in the General Assembly, specifically Rock God, or possibly Delegate Pendleton. Why hand the ball to a Single A Minor League pitcher for the big game when you have a Major League Cy Young Award winner on your roster? But these were false hopes.

Rock God had been one of about 30 delegates to co-sponsor a bill in a prior year that would have established a universal access, single-payer system. But when Rock God had speaking platforms before large political audiences to make such a bold proclamation of support—his announcement of his Senate run and his Senate kickoff event—he never mentioned single-payer health care. It would have been politically risky to step onto that ledge and take a fringe position, what with his soon-to-be upgraded status as a new senator, the state's leaders emphasizing focus on the botched implementation of Obamacare and the overt expectation to stay in line with the Democratic Party Machine. And Pendleton, vice chair of the House health care committee, received more than half of her campaign contributions from health care and health insurance-related entities in 2012, including Maryland's largest health insurer, CareFirst BlueCross BlueShield, Medical Mutual health insurance, prescription benefit management company Caremark Rx, the Maryland Hospital Association and others. With that kind of support from protectors of the status quo, she wasn't likely to upset the applecart.

Of course, I have to look at myself for the reason I didn't generate the support from HCHR I had hoped for, however small and resource-poor the organization was. Either I wasn't compelling enough, authentic enough, or viable enough, or all. It may have been that I was not proficient at asking for help and building a team of loyalists. I tended toward the characteristics of the lone wolf, which is sacrilege for a politician. It also may have been that the small cadre of HCHR regulars, maybe a dozen, recognized that I was a longshot and not a natural politician and wanted to hedge their bets and not be seen as affiliating too closely with a losing proposition.

Still, I was deeply disappointed by HCHR. I expected more from this group which mostly remained in the shadows, when I was strongly advocating for the principles in which it believed and bringing its issue into the sunlight. The feeling of being interrogated and doubted at the outset of my meeting at Panera, treated like an outsider instead of embraced, was a turnoff. I never talked to Deep Throat the Doctor again. If I had to twist and turn to galvanize support from these people, Lordy Be, what would it take to attract others to my effort?

# OBAMACARE: OBAMA'S RUBIK'S CUBE

*"Healthy citizens are the greatest asset any country can have."*

WINSTON CHURCHILL, BRITISH PRIME MINISTER

*"The lily-livered method that Obama chose to push health care into being is a crystal-clear example of how the Democratic Party likes to act—showering a real problem with a blizzard of ineffectual decisions and verbose nonsense, then stepping aside at the last minute to reveal the true plan that all along was being forged off-camera in the furnace of moneyed interests and insider inertia. While the White House publicly eschewed any concrete 'guiding principles,' the People Who Mattered, it appeared, had already long ago settled on theirs... no single-payer system, no meaningful public option, no meaningful employer mandates and a very meaningful mandate for individual consumers... All that's left of health care reform is a collection of piece-of-shit, weakling proposals that are preposterously expensive and contain almost nothing meaningful. And it's virtually guaranteed to sour the public on reform efforts for years to come."*

JOURNALIST AND AUTHOR MATT TAIBBI,
IN *ROLLING STONE* MAGAZINE

The Affordable Care Act (Obamacare) is a Rubik's Cube—lots of turning, spinning, head-scratching, reverses, glitches, bad moves and confusion. Historic and groundbreaking yet torturously over-wrought, the law certainly does some good, but adds yet another layer of preposterous bureaucracy and complexity and supposed "consumer choice," which really is massive consumer overload and confusion, onto a preexisting byzantine miscreation, and will become another cement-hardened convention impossible to undo.

Even after the law had been implemented for a year, 33 million Americans, or 10.4 percent of the population, had no health insurance throughout 2014, according to the federal Current Population Survey.

Among the uninsured was the illogical category of individuals who fell into the "Medicaid gap." How's this for absurd: These were people who had incomes that were too high to qualify for Medicaid, the federal health insurance program for the low-income, *but too low* to qualify for Obamacare health insurance premium subsidies. Because governors in 20 states declined to accept federal money to expand Medicaid, these people were left in the lurch.

After Obamacare's first open enrollment period concluded on March 31, 2014, President Obama acknowledged that "despite this law, millions of Americans remain uncovered in part because governors in some states for political reasons have deliberately refused to expand cov-erage under this law... So, no, the Affordable Care Act hasn't completely fixed our long-broken health care system...As messy as it's been some-times...[the law] is making sure that we are not the only advanced coun-try on Earth that doesn't make sure everybody has basic health care."

Uh, no, it's not; it's going to fall well short. The Congressional Budget Office projected in 2015 that there will be between 25 million and 30 million uninsured people in the United States every year between 2016 and 2025 because of holes in the system, sometimes due to the whims of state governments and the unpredictable choices and behaviors of individuals.

Aside from immigrants, young adults and those plunging into the "Medicaid gap," more than 14 million other Americans didn't have health insurance in 2014. Most were working-age adults. About three-quarters of the adults had jobs at least part of the year, and nearly half worked full-time all year. They generally earned less than $50,000 annually, and likely decided that health plan options labeled "affordable" by Obamacare's architects were, in reality, anything but.

Another problem with Obamacare that the designers did not anticipate in their rush to claim affordability turned out to be that private insurers severely limited the physicians, hospitals and other health care providers in their plans' networks to keep costs down, thus restricting consumers' choices. These "narrow networks" typically meant prohibitively high costs for plan members going to out-of-network providers.

The American public generally was so ambivalent about, or vehemently opposed to, the Affordable Care Act—the result of widespread miscomprehension, inflammatory propaganda against it, and the law's own discombobulating constitution—that the White House felt compelled to trot out celebrities to encourage people to sign up for health insurance.

## Obama, Congress & Kumar Go to White Castle

In advance of the first open enrollment period, the White House brought comedian Amy Poehler, actor Kal Penn, American Idol singer and Oscar winner Jennifer Hudson, and representatives for talk show host Oprah Winfrey and pop stars Bon Jovi and Alicia Keys to a meeting to enlist their help in enrolling young adults, deemed the target group most likely to shun the sign-up effort.

Only in America would the Leader of the Free World rely on the dude best known as the pot-smoking stoner who fools his trusting Indian father into thinking he is grinding through med school and who has an unquenchable hankering for the little burgers at White Castle and goes on a quixotic nighttime quest through the off-ramps of New Jersey to satisfy the munchies (Penn, the Kumar of *Harold & Kumar Go to White Castle*) to convince young adults that they should shell out a large chunk of their modest income for health insurance. Why would they want to do that? They want to enjoy life, not be broke every month even when they might rarely see a doctor. There may be no better indicator about the pathetic state of a nation's health care system than the apparent necessity to have Kumar shill to protect uninsured individuals from the likelihood of medical bankruptcy in the case of even a moderate accident or unforeseen health condition.

Another indicator is the money invested and the great lengths the government went to just to make citizens aware of the new health insurance options and educate them about the complexities—an effort that would be wholly unnecessary under a single-payer health care system in which all individuals would have access to essential health care needs as a right of citizenship. Prior to the enrollment period starting in late 2013, the Obama Administration awarded $67 million to organizations nationwide serving as "navigators" to help the uninsured understand their coverage options and enroll.

There was good reason to fear that Americans had little concept about how the new complex layer of health insurance provisions grafted onto the existing health care contraption would work. Just two weeks before the enrollment period, *USA Today* reported a poll showing widespread confusion and misinformation about the law, especially among the law's main targets. Among those who were uninsured, nearly 40 percent didn't realize the law required them to get health insurance; among young adults, only 56 percent realized they were mandated to be insured or they'd face a fine. Overall, one-third said they had little or no understanding about how the law would work.

One of the most ridiculous—yet popular and widely trumpeted—provisions of the law was Daddy's Got You Covered, which required that health insurance companies allow individuals under age 26 to be eligible for coverage through their parents' plans, applicable regardless of whether the "dependents" were married, employed or living separately from their parents. Here we have people under age 26 dying while fighting wars in Iraq and Afghanistan, and others working two jobs to get through school or make ends meet as responsible and independent adults, and yet we are codifying that it is acceptable, or worse, something to encourage or brag about, that a 25-year-old should rely on mommy and daddy for basic health care.

## America: We're Number 37!

*"America's health care system is neither healthy, caring, nor a system."*

WALTER CRONKITE, LEGENDARY *CBS NEWS* ANCHOR

Obamacare created even more demographic subsets of the population to insure—immigrants; young adults who were not independent; young adults who just didn't care or who didn't want to pay the high costs; people who made too much money to qualify for Medicaid but too little to afford private health insurance; low-income adults with no children; employers with less than 50 employees; employers with more than 200 employees; and on and on. This obsession with breaking the citizenry into distinct categories defines what is oddest about the U.S. health care system compared to all other similar, developed nations. People get health care coverage not based upon their inclusion in society, but upon their category: elderly, low-income, disabled, military member/veteran, employee, union member, job-loser/unemployed, retiree, children whose families earn too much to qualify for Medicaid, and so on.

Book author and journalist Matt Taibbi wrote a scathing article about the Affordable Care Act and the process by which it was created for *Rolling Stone* just after the legislation was enacted in 2010.

*"America has not only the worst but the dumbest health care system in the developed world...a bureaucracy so insipid and mean and illogical that even our darkest criminal minds wouldn't be equal to dreaming it up on purpose. The system doesn't work for anyone. The cost of all of this to society, in illness and death and lost productivity and a soaring federal deficit and plain old anxiety and anger, is incalculable. The bad news is our failed health care system won't get fixed, because it exists entirely within the confines of yet another failed system: the political entity known as the United States of America... [W]e have a government that is not equipped to fix actual crises. What our government is good at is something else entirely: effecting the appearance of action, while leaving the actual reform behind in a diabolical labyrinth of ingenious legislative maneuvers."*

Taibbi submitted that the only consequential reform with any teeth to come out of Obamacare was the provision "forcing everyone to buy some form of private insurance, no matter how crappy, or suffer a tax penalty," a capitulation to the private health insurance industry.

"Health care reform will simply force great numbers of new people to buy or keep insurance of a type that has already been proved not to work," Taibbi wrote.

Despite America's strong tendency toward ethnocentricity—the prevailing sentiment that the United States is inherently superior in everything we do—there is plenty of empirical evidence to show that health care is not one of those areas.

The U.S. received a wake-up call in *The World Health Report 2000, Health Systems: Improving Performance,* an evaluation of the overall health care efficiency of the 191 member nations of the World Health Organization (WHO) conducted by WHO, in which the U.S. ranked 37th, one spot behind Costa Rica, eight places behind Morocco, and 13 slots below Cyprus. Every four years, the Americans far outpace the Costa Ricans, Moroccans, and Cypriots in Olympic medals, but apparently not in health care efficiency.

In a study updated every few years by The Commonwealth Fund, a private nonpartisan foundation that supports independent research on health and social issues, the United States health care system ranked as the most expensive in the world, but consistently underperformed compared to 10 other nations on measures such as quality, access, efficiency and equity. Yet per person spending on health care in the U.S. in 2011, $8,508, was nearly double the average per capita cost of the 10 other countries in the study.

Health care costs are punching ever bigger holes in the budgets of working Americans. In 2015, health care costs for a typical American family of four covered by an average employer-sponsored preferred provider organization (PPO) plan was $24,671, more than 40 percent of which, or about $10,500, was paid by the family, according to a leading actuarial analysis, the Milliman Medical Index. The Commonwealth Fund found that employee premium contributions for employer-sponsored family health plans nearly doubled from 2003 to 2012, from $2,283 to $4,236. And the U.S. Centers for Disease Control and Prevention found that more than one in four U.S. families had recently experienced a financial burden due to medical costs.

For many families, the consequences of unaffordable medical bills are dire. A 2009 Harvard Medical School study on medical bankruptcy found that 62 percent of all bankruptcies in 2007 were medical-related. Contrary to popular belief, these bankruptcy filers weren't deadbeats. Most were well educated homeowners with "middle-class occupations," and 75 percent had health insurance.

Consequences could go far beyond financial ruin for the uninsured. Nearly 45,000 annual deaths were associated with lack of health insurance, according to a 2009 study conducted at Harvard Medical School and Cambridge Health Alliance. The study found that working-age Americans without health insurance had a 40 percent higher risk of death than their privately insured counterparts.

# Medicare for All

*"Everyone should have health insurance? I say everyone should have health care. I'm not selling insurance."*

Dennis Kucinich, former Ohio Democratic
congressman, two-time presidential candidate

For many health care advocates, a transformation to a nonprofit system in which all individuals are covered (universal access) for essential health care services, streamlined so that one administrative entity enforces standards, sets rates and pays bills (a single-payer)—the basic concept used by nations in The Commonwealth Fund study that outperformed and underspent the U.S. —is the obvious solution to America's health care miseries. But the political, economic and institutional barriers to arriving at that solution have been impenetrable.

Amid the hubbub of Obamacare's debut enrollment period, political commentator David Sirota wrote in *Salon* that politicians missed an opportunity to provide better health care through a simpler, single-payer system, coined "Medicare for all."

Sirota highlighted Obama's meeting with "Obamacare's middlemen"—private health insurance executives—during the rollout as indicating who was in charge.

"The spectacle of a president begging these middlemen for help was a reminder that Obamacare did not limit the power of the insurance companies as a single-payer system would," Sirota wrote. "The new law instead cemented the industry's profit-extracting role in the larger health system—and it still leaves millions without insurance."

A second signal of the missed opportunity, Sirota said, was the misplaced emphasis on developing a health insurance enrollment website, rather than on improving health care. "That's because the insurance industry wrote the Affordable Care Act, meaning the... top priority isn't delivering health services. Obamacare is primarily about getting the insurance industry more customers and government contracts."

Medicare is popular because it "guarantees access to decent, cost-effective health care rather than just meager health insurance," Sirota argued. Obamacare "doesn't guarantee better health care or a more simple health system. Those Democrats who pretend it does are just as dishonest as the Republicans who ignore Medicare and pretend government cannot effectively manage healthcare. All of them are making noise to drown out the single-payer signal."

Taibbi, the *Rolling Stone* writer, drew similar conclusions. "There was only ever one genuinely dangerous idea out there," Taibbi wrote, "and that was a single-payer system...[N]othing except a single-payer system makes any sense."

Taibbi noted that health care providers and facilities must hire whole staffs to deal with more than 1,000 private insurers' unique policies, jacking up costs astronomically. Administrative savings under a single-payer system could "pay for the whole goddamned thing, if anyone had the balls to stand up and say so," he argued. Indeed, a 2013 Commonwealth Fund survey found the U.S. spent $606 per person on health insurance administration, more than four times the average of 10 comparable nations.

In one door-to-door conversation, I discovered a constituent with a health insurance nightmare. I later met her at Starbucks to learn more about her personal story, which encapsulated the convoluted nature of U.S. health care:

*"I'm working two part-time jobs, but neither offers health care," said the woman in her 50s, married to a husband on Medicare and with a 21-year-old dependent son at home. "I had coverage through an actors' union, but I didn't work enough hours to keep it. So I went on COBRA (continuation of a former employer's plan), but it cost $740 per month, which was half of my take-home pay. It was a hardship on my family. If I missed a COBRA payment by a day, I'd be in fear. I'd get calls from my doctor's office saying I wasn't insured. Then I'd have to call and haggle with the insurance company. It was a constant battle.*

*"When my husband left his job, my son didn't have coverage, so we got a high-deductible catastrophic policy for him before Obamacare. But when he had to be hospitalized for 10 days, we paid $5,000 out-of-pocket.*

*"It's tough when you're solidly middle class, and all your money is going out because you're not getting health care coverage from the workplace. It's crushing and confusing to be paying all this money, then have to be on the phone and expecting service, but that's not what you're getting."*

Hearing her story reaffirmed for me that there had to be a better way that would reduce costs, fear and anxiety for so many families and individuals. In taking up the single-payer health care mantle, I aimed to stand for something that would make a meaningful difference in my campaign, something that would advance justice, equality, decency and common sense.

But some were not impressed with my explicit aspiration, apparently preferring candidates with a broader, conventional, more ambiguous or less contentious focus.

The Marshmallow Man blogger, in introducing me as a candidate, identified single-payer health care as my "centerpiece." "Wow, that won't be controversial," Marshmallow wrote. "That's a big ambition. I'd be curious to hear how a freshman delegate from a district with three freshman delegates is going to accomplish getting that passed."

The Baltimore County Blue blogger was similarly skeptical and dismissive, arguing that I was a "good man with progressive views," but that my "single-issue focus" on health care was too limited. Citing no evidence, Blue asserted Maryland "serves the health care needs of its citizens far better" than many states. "We don't disagree with Mr. Sachs, we even like him, but it is not enough."

One commenter on the Baltimore County Blue blog was more blunt in her assessment of me: "One dimensional. In the few times I have heard you speak, you focused solely on single-payer health care. It is a great concept. But please address other issues facing the residents of District 12."

To a certain degree, the commenter was right. I didn't care much that some schools in Baltimore County were lagging and certain commercial areas were dying, nor did I think I could affect those issues on the state level; they were more local concerns to be addressed by elected officials with more direct jurisdiction. No, if I was going to be a politician, I was going to have bigger fish to fry.

# The (Corrupt) Art of District-Making: Can You Draw a Broken-Winged Pterodactyl?

*"Politics is the art of controlling your environment."*

Hunter S. Thompson, author and Gonzo journalist

Maryland's District 12 made no sense. But then again, why should it? Maryland is known for having one of the most corrupt, politically-influenced redistricting processes in the nation. In 2015, the watchdog group Judicial Watch filed a voter lawsuit challenging the constitutionality of Maryland's gerrymandered congressional district maps, charging that the districts are the most distorted and confused in the country. One particular district was so distorted that, when challenged in federal court, a judge described it as a "broken-winged pterodactyl, lying prostrate across the center of the state." Political publications labeled it a "monstrosity of a district" and "The Pinwheel of Death," with one including it among its list of the nation's five "most oddly shaped districts."

There's nothing stopping the Maryland legislature from creating the same type of amorphous creatures out of the 47 state legislative districts for the barely concealed purpose of protecting incumbents, diluting Republicans' strength and preserving Democratic enclaves to ensure a perpetual majority. That is, if the legislators don't mind violating the spirit, if not the letter, of the Maryland Constitution and the laws they are sworn to uphold.

The Maryland Constitution requires that legislative districts "be compact in form" and that "due regard shall be given to natural boundaries and the boundaries of political subdivisions."

## Copout

Maryland Democrats were given the opportunity to end the camouflaged corruption and institute equity in the boundary-drawing process in 2016, after Maryland's new Republican governor appointed a bipartisan panel to develop a new system. The governor's commission presented a proposal for a nonpartisan Redistricting Reform Commission that would be independent of politicians. In a shameful display of cowardice, manipulation, deceit and willful ignorance of the people's will, none of the 20 Democratic House and Senate committee chairs and co-chairs co-sponsored the bill, which never got out of committee.

Instead, Democrats punted, introducing a resolution to make it appear they were doing something without doing anything at all. The art of making noise, creating distraction or diversion, earning style points without substance, employing bait-and-switch tactics to obscure real agendas, generating much "ado" that adds up to nothing—these are the tricks of the politicians' trade, and when it comes to literally protecting their own turf, the lines that delineate their kingdoms, they'll use them all.

Forty-seven delegates supported a disingenuous resolution that called on Congress and President Obama to pass and sign legislation establishing "uniform standards and procedures applicable to each state" for the creation of congressional election districts. REALLY? They've observed Congress during the Obama era. Have they seen any compromise? Seen anything pass? And they want Congress members to agree on legislation that would affect all members' re-elections? And they expect a Republican-controlled Congress that abhors federal rule and champions states' rights and flexibility to impose an edict from Washington on all states? What a copout!

. . .

District 12 was one of those unruly pterodactyl- or pinwheel-shaped districts that blatantly violated Maryland's constitutional requirements by, for one thing, unnecessarily blending political subdivisions.

In my published letter to the editor, I advocated removing politicians from the once-per-decade boundary-redrawing process, like the new governor later proposed. I argued the boundaries should be based on compactness and natural borders, not created by current office holders "to protect cronies."

I compared District 12 to a barbell, with 50-pound weights in the west and east and a thin bar running a long expanse of central terrain to connect the ends. District 12 spanned about 25 miles, a 45-minute drive end to end. I could see no logical reason for it. It had to be an opaque, backroom arrangement to carve out territory to protect Democratic turf. Residents of Columbia, the western part of the district where I resided, lived life removed from Baltimore, 20 miles away—out of sight, out of mind. Yet the eastern part of the district abutted the Baltimore City border, where a constituent could stand at the peak of Baltimore Highlands and have a clear view of downtown Baltimore. "This range may be appropriate in a rural area," I wrote in the letter, "but is hardly necessary to achieve the target population count for a district in the densely populated Baltimore-Washington megalopolis."

The "tortured drawing" set up "a district of dichotomies," making it more complicated and challenging for anyone to represent because of its oil-and-water composition, I wrote. By ignoring natural borders, such as county lines, legislators created a district with "big swaths of two counties (Howard and Baltimore) with different sets of elected officials and widely varying cultures, histories, traditions, demographics, socio-economics, problems and issues. Diversity is great ... but so is common sense."

At forums and in media interviews, the candidates consistently were asked how they would reconcile their representation, priorities and positions for the two distinct and largely dissimilar areas of District 12. Invariably, candidates offered the politically correct, expedient, inclusive and non-provocative Pablum—that the two jurisdictions had far more similarities than differences, and that they could get to know and represent each area equally well and fairly. There were kernels of truth in this non-answer, but it ignored stark realities, and it was a calculated, pandering response, if not outright disingenuous. I wasn't immune. I said something to that effect, too. But that's politics, and I was bending to its will.

# A TALE OF TWO ZIP CODES

*"First of all Rat, you never let on how much you like a
girl. 'Oh, Debbie. Hi.' Two, you always call the shots.
'Kiss me. You won't regret it.' Now three, act like wherever
you are, that's the place to be. 'Isn't this great?'"*

MIKE DAMONE, *FAST TIMES AT RIDGEMONT HIGH*

The glaring differences between the Howard County and Baltimore
County portions of my District 12 are evident in the U.S. Bureau of
the Census' 2013 American Community Survey demographic data for
two primary ZIP codes in the district: 21044 (Columbia, Howard County)
and 21227 (Arbutus, Halethorpe and Lansdowne, Baltimore County).

|  | Columbia Howard County (21044) | Arbutus, Halethorpe, Lansdowne Baltimore County (21227) |
|---|---|---|
| **Population** | 41,704 | 33,534 |
| **Demographics** | | |
| White | 57.2% | 75.2% |
| African-American | 25.4% | 15.2% |

| Median Income | $98,428 | $55,168 |
|---|---|---|
| Household Income $100,000+ | 49.4% | 19.7% |
| Unemployment | 6.6% | 10% |
| **Education** | | |
| High School Graduates | 96.1% | 79% |
| 25+-Year-Olds w/ Bachelor's Degree | 69.7% | 18.2% |
| 25+-Year-Olds w/ Grad/ Prof'l Degree | 36% | 5.9% |
| **Occupations** | | |
| Management, Business, Science, Arts | 67% | 30.8% |
| **Poverty** | | |
| Poverty Rate (Individual) | 7.4% | 13.7% |
| Food Stamps Recipients | 4.5% | 11.8% |
| **Housing** | | |
| Housing Value – $300,000+ | 69.2% | 12.6% |
| Houses Built, pre-1970 | 13.9% | 73.4% |

Compared to the Howard County 21044 ZIP, the Baltimore County 21227 ZIP was significantly whiter, less educated and affluent and more blue-collar and jobless. Baltimore County had nearly double the poverty rate, and two to three times the number of government assistance program recipients.

The Howard County region, dominated by the New Town of Columbia, was much newer and more transient than timeworn, deeply-rooted Baltimore County. Howard County had more modern schools, roads, housing, public utilities and other infrastructure, while some of Baltimore County's infrastructure was crumbling, business districts slumping and housing falling into disrepair.

Columbia, Howard County was *The Jetsons,* a vision of Utopia, an aspiring haven for upwardly mobile futurists, pioneers and seekers; Lansdowne, Baltimore County was *The Honeymooners,* a nod to yesteryear, an unadorned roost for lunch-pail bus drivers and sewer workers like Ralph Kramden and Ed Norton.

## Intergenerational Dysfunction

Those were the cold, hard statistics stratifying the polar ends of District 12. A teacher I met from working-class Lansdowne Middle School in Baltimore County described the differences in more personal, first-hand observational terms.

"A lot of students just don't care," he said. "Some of my students just refuse to take a test. A lot of them don't like to read and write. Some will accept detention instead of doing their work. Then they'll skip detention, and then when I talk to their parents, I find out they just don't care."

The teacher described an intergenerational dynamic that had taken hold in the area that manifested in dysfunction and malaise. He had encountered many parents who didn't do well in school, had developed a "negative attitude" toward education and passed it along to their kids. Numerous families, many of them single-parent, were "living off the government dole" —welfare, food stamps, disability. Kids had become reliant upon their families as safety nets into adulthood. As a result, many kids grew up and never left the area, continuing to live with parents and grandparents under the same roof.

"Even the kids that try working at Burger King or McDonald's quit after a few weeks because it's too hard," the teacher told me. "A lot of them think they will get a menial job after high school and live at home. Some try community college but bomb out because they have to work." A gradual transition is taking place, the teacher observed, as Hispanic,

Middle Eastern and other immigrant families who are "still striving" are moving in because of the affordable housing.

My Baltimore City firefighter friend who worked at a city firehouse across the city line from Lansdowne and Baltimore Highlands described that area of District 12 to me as "rough." He rethought his description and came up with a more precise word: "raw."

## Princess and Her Step-Sisters

Baltimore County's District 12 was divided into the Princess, Catonsville, the larger, wealthier, higher-educated town that many believed received preferential treatment from county government, and a bunch of red-headed step-sisters: Arbutus, Halethorpe, Lansdowne, Relay and Baltimore Highlands. Catonsville's large Victorian and Colonial homes were built by wealthy Baltimoreans as summer residences in the 1800s before automobiles and the electric trolley brought more families to the Baltimore outpost as year-round residents and transformed it into a bedroom community. Downtown Catonsville, with its outdoor theatre, weekend farmer's market, summer concert Fridays, and main street cafes, flower shops, art galleries and music stores—the Maryland legislature issued a proclamation declaring Catonsville "Music City, Maryland"—surrounded by neighborhoods of Victorian mansions give it a quintessential American small-town ambiance.

Lansdowne, on the other hand, became known as a blue-collar Baltimore and Ohio Railroad town, with many of its residents working for the B & O founded in Baltimore in 1828. By the 21$^{st}$ century, Lansdowne, along with neighboring Arbutus, Halethorpe, Relay and Baltimore Highlands, had largely stagnated.

## The Next America

Columbia was originally billed as "The Next America" by its ambitious founder/developer James Rouse when he covertly bought up contiguous farmland in rural, Howard County, Maryland in the 1960s to create an idealistic new community on a grand scale. It's the type of meticulously engineered place outsiders and non-believers mock for its saccharine sensibilities, high-mindedness and idyllic blueprint. Streets and communities are named after poets and great literature. Aesthetics were paramount, with planning that avoided the visual eyesores characterizing many suburbs: telephone and power utility lines were buried underground; architectural "covenants" governed and standardized the look of neighborhoods and homes; and signage was strictly controlled. Visitors couldn't find commercial destinations because they blended into the environment. Drivers were more likely to cruise a "garth," "downs," "way," "row" or esoteric "The Bowl" than a more bourgeois "road," "street," "lane," or "drive." The community was built around forests, instead of destroying them, and included nearly 100 miles of pathways traversing lakes, streams and rivers.

I live within walking distance of two manmade lakes ringed by walking paths, streams and woods, including Lake Kittamaqundi, a tribal Indian word that translates to "meeting place;" the symbolic People Tree, exemplifying the highfalutin concept of interrelatedness through a 14-foot-high metallic statue with a cluster of 66 connected human figures emanating from a central pole; and the community recreation association's high-brow Haven on the Lake, a spa and exercise facility offering such services as crystal salt therapy room, tropical rain shower and Barre and Pilates classes. You won't find anything so fancy-schmancy in Arbutus or Lansdowne.

Howard County was the third wealthiest county in the U.S., with a median household income around $110,000. And Columbia, Howard County's centerpiece, ranked in the top 10 of Money Magazine's Best Places to Live in America for five consecutive biennial ranking cycles between 2006 and 2014.

Culture and arts were integrated into Columbia's plan. Merriweather Post Pavilion, an outdoor concert venue, was built as the Baltimore Symphony's summer home. In its formative years, pioneering creative types formed a poetry and literary society and the Columbia Pro Cantare opera chorus.

## A Misfit

I knew I didn't fit in well in much of Baltimore County's District 12. Like a vegetarian at a bull roast or a Mennonite at a nudist camp, I felt out of my element. It's not that I'm an elitist—well, maybe I am, but not in the classic, born-with-a-silver-spoon-in-the-mouth sense. I'm a second-generation American from two families of Eastern European Jewish descent. One grandfather followed several siblings to America, leaving a small family farm and shop in a Lithuanian village to escape the pogrom, the organized massacre of Jews and destruction of their villages, during the World War I era. Knowing no English, he managed to put himself through school, earn a college degree and become a civil engineer for the federal government, working on hydroelectric power projects in the West. My father earned a master's degree from the University of Pennsylvania in urban planning, and spent his career in the city planning, property investment and management, and mortgage fields.

My other grandfather was a Russian immigrant who dropped out of school in the eighth grade to help support his family by selling goods on the Boston streets, ultimately working as a salesman for Prudential. His children, including my mother, were the first generation to attend college. My uncle earned a PhD in history from Harvard University and was a career teacher.

The education ethos wasn't explicitly pounded into me, but early in life I internalized the expectations that I would perform well in school, graduate from college and join some kind of white-collar profession. At the time of my run, I was working on my second master's degree, this one in counseling to add to journalism. My models demonstrated that that's just what my family did.

Data from the Baltimore County 21227 ZIP Code indicated that I would be in the minority there, with only 6 percent of the population holding a graduate degree. Call it elitist, or call it a fact. Either way, I felt like a fish out of water.

# BALLERINA

While endorsements from many obscure or niche organizations may have little influence and may not be worth a candidate's time or effort, others are coveted for their potential impact. Blowing off those endorsement interviews would be a poor choice. Even if you don't get endorsed, at least the leaders of the organization will know you care.

The combined interview of the Howard and Baltimore County teachers associations was one of those mandatory-attendance interviews.

I knew my chances for endorsement were slim. I was competing against two career 30-year educators, Energy, the award-winning high school math teacher, and Ballerina, a former special education teacher and current Maryland Department of Education administrator, in addition to Man of the People, who chaired an educational advisory council. But I filled out the 22-page questionnaire and showed at the interview anyway.

In the waiting room, sitting as if waiting for the dentist's drill, I met Ballerina's campaign manager, who was retired after working as a high-level administrator under two former Maryland governors.

"I've worked in politics a long time, but I never realized how much hard work is involved in campaigning. I have more time now, but I didn't know how much time this would take," the manager said.

"Yeah, there's no way around it," I acknowledged. "When the teachers' union wants to interview you, you can't turn it down no matter how tired you are."

"Politicians must really love their job to do all that work," she said.

"Yeah, I guess they must," I replied. But what I really wanted to say was that they loved the influence, power, status, adulation and ego boost at least as much as the job. However, it did not seem that Ballerina craved those frills.

"Ballerina really hates asking people for money. I have to keep telling her it's just something you have to do. I almost have to make her do it," said Ballerina's manager.

It was my first indication that Ballerina may not have been cut out for this racket.

## Soft Shoes: The Legend

Ballerina had politics in her blood—or at least in her family's. Her father was a Maryland politician for 22 years, earning a reputation as a lawmaker so deft and effective in negotiating complex legislative deals without heavy-handedness, like a ballroom dance, that he was nicknamed "Soft Shoes." Stories about his death described him an "insider's insider," a "living legend," a "legislative magician," "one of Maryland's last old-time Democratic machine leaders" and an "undisputed political lord." Clearly, Ballerina came from good political stock. Unfortunately for her, she did not strike at politics while the iron was hot. If she had jumped into the game earlier, while the trade value of the legendary Soft Shoes name was highest, she likely could have rode her father's coattails to a successful political career. But Ballerina was busy raising kids and working as an educator. Perhaps the political bug had not bitten her, or perhaps motherhood and teaching were higher priorities.

"Women come to the legislature at different times in their lives than men—often at times when the trade-offs are not as severe," Reeher wrote in *First Person Political*. This was the case with Ballerina, and it played to her disadvantage.

In the *Baltimore Sun* article announcing her candidacy, Ballerina said that upon reading about the retirements of Delegates Fireman and Cop,

"I thought maybe I should. And people approached me and said, 'Now's your time.'"

That may have been wishful thinking. At 61, her window of opportunity may have closed.

That may seem cruel, and smack of ageism and sexism, but politics is a cruel game, and there's a reality that can't be escaped. Not only did the window probably close on the potential political windfall of her father's reputation and legacy, but there's no doubt that Ballerina would have shined brighter and appealed more broadly as a younger, more dynamic dancer.

I liked Ballerina; she was a woman one might describe as "lovely" or "dear" or "caring." She was warm and motherly—a grandmother, actually—and always friendly to me. She was sharply dressed and well-coiffed, with bleach-blonde hair. She had one noticeable drawback, a raspy voice, which detracted from her public speaking. We talked casually at political and social events, and I always felt comfortable just chatting with her, not like she was my rival. I could tell her family was concerned about how she would cope with the rough-and-tumble of politics. I got the feeling that Ballerina's family members worried about her sensitivity and wanted to shield her from being offended or attacked. Her father may have excelled in the world of back-slapping and backroom deals, and may have felt comfortable wearing the Teflon armor to deflect affronts, but those attributes may not have transmitted to the daughter's DNA.

Ballerina wasn't cutthroat. If Ballerina and I shared a trait, it may have been that neither of us wanted it bad enough to do whatever it took to win. Despite that, I knew Ballerina had a strong base among women, seniors, education advocates, Catonsville residents and her father's supporters. She could certainly be a contender by energizing those bases.

Ballerina proudly proclaimed that she had lived within a five-mile radius of Catonsville for nearly her whole life. Of the six Baltimore County candidates, three—Ballerina, Energy and Man of the People—could say that they were essentially lifelong residents of their communities.

This deep-rootedness plays well in local politics. Voters love to hear that you love and care about where you live so much—indeed, the same place that *they have chosen to live*, because, of course, it's the greatest place to raise kids—that you would never leave. It's an automatic and visceral commonality and connection, especially in small towns— you're one of them, ergo what they care about, you care about—and why those identified as "carpetbaggers" like Joker and Next Big Thing may get pilloried as uncaring, opportunistic interlopers. But as for life experience, I find this supposed asset of never-changing origins parochial and limiting.

After teaching, Ballerina followed closer in Soft Shoes' footsteps, working for 20 years in government relations for the Maryland Department of Education, frequently meeting with state legislators and establishing a foothold in her father's old stomping grounds.

Education was Ballerina's sweet spot, her go-to issue throughout the campaign. Despite her professional background, political blogger Baltimore County Blue blasted her knowledge of education issues, saying her "20 years of experience in Annapolis is barely noticeable" and noting that teachers' unions bypassed her for their endorsements. The blogger questioned whether her candidacy was merely "a gig for her golden years."

Baltimore County Blue's attack on Ballerina's home turf, her life's passion, may have been unfair. Or it may have illuminated that some candidates, despite having in-depth knowledge on a topic, have difficulty communicating their expertise or passion in a way that stimulates voters.

In a brutal blog post titled, "Ballerina — Go back to school!" Baltimore County Blue asserted that with her political pedigree and education lobbying experience, "you would think that Ballerina would be rolling over her District 12 opponents...But she's not. Ballerina repeatedly fails to do her homework to understand Maryland's challenges."

The Marshmallow Man blogger also was rough on Ballerina, writing after a forum that "her non-answers and rambling answers and wondering why the questions were so hard (they weren't) clearly indicated that she wasn't ready for the part."

I felt bad for Ballerina. The accusations reeked of piling on; Ballerina was not the most natural politician, but I viewed her as having her heart in the right place. But when you put yourself in a public position, you have to expect—and accept—the public's barbs.

• • •

This criticism of lack of adequate comprehension of all the potential issues on which a candidate is expected to be well-versed is vexing. The number of issues is virtually limitless, and each one has nuances and complexities, with multiple pros and cons to weigh and unintended consequences to consider. You can have deep knowledge of a few issues, or broad knowledge of many issues, but it's extremely difficult to go broad and deep across the board.

In his political memoir *The Speechwriter*, Barton Swaim acknowledged the outsized expectations of politicians' erudition: "[N]o normal person can be expected to say something interesting that many times a day, on that many subjects, to that many separate groups."

Ballerina didn't have the steel-trap mind and knowledge-grasp of a Zelig. But she did have ingredients that connected with voters: Mom and Apple Pie.

# November 5, 2013 – Politics 101: Don't Tell Potential Endorsers They're Dinosaurs

I faced a gauntlet of educators on the joint teachers' associations endorsement committee—six teachers, county teacher union presidents and a state education union official. I sat at the head of an intimidatingly long table serving as the firing line, as if preparing to defend a PhD dissertation, girding for the Socratic or dialectical method or any other scholarly mode of inquiry.

The questionnaire that I had filled out and that the educators possessed in front of them included a slew of complicated and arcane legislative background and questions, most of which came down to issues of increased funding—adhering to complex, bureaucratic-sounding financing mechanisms such as the Thornton Funding Formula, Geographic Cost Index and Maintenance of Effort; honoring pension programs and transferring more retirement responsibility from the state to counties; and guaranteeing minimum funding levels for school construction.

## Mo' Money

If I just answered "mo' money, mo' money," for every question, or bellowed Tom Cruise's *Jerry Maguire* line, "Show me the money!" I would have been looked upon favorably. Of course, it also would have been irresponsible and in ignorance of the context of the overall economy, the middle class backslide and government budget struggles. But I was sure the candidates who really coveted the endorsement would go with the "mo' money" responses all day long.

I shouldn't have worried about being honest. It wasn't that the educators were wrong about clamoring for mo' money, but such decisions couldn't be made in a vacuum. Taxpayers had been hit hard—jobs lost, wages stagnated, retirement funds depleted. Other necessary government-funded programs had been cut and were straining to survive.

Could I realistically make promises of supporting increased funding to the educators and not regret it later if I actually was in a position to make such decisions? I decided I couldn't, at least not unequivocally.

Although my chances for an education endorsement were slim to begin with, I certainly put a fork in a shoe-leather steak with responses on teacher pension issues. On my questionnaire, I was blunt—too blunt. I called pensions a "relic of a bygone era" and a retirement-funding mechanism that was "going the way of the dinosaur," not to mention, contributing to cities like Detroit going bankrupt because of underfunded obligations. Obviously, the endorsement committee members picked up on my answers, and they weren't amused by my phrasings. I noted that at my current job, a union position, the pension had been eliminated, a concession to the reality of the 21$^{st}$ century economic climate. My story of my own work experience met unmoved expressions.

The committee asked me to explain my comments on pensions. I reiterated my written comments, saying pensions were dead. The undeniable trend was that individuals would be responsible for their own retirement savings and resultant lifestyles, not the government or any employer, though their benefit programs could help. Committee members didn't bother debating with me, but just glanced at each other, telepathically communicating, *this dude's toast.*

And I dared to raise the heretical notion that mo' money isn't always the answer, noting that four nearby jurisdictions—Montgomery and

Prince George's counties in the Washington suburbs, Baltimore City and Washington, D.C. —each ranked in the top five of the 50 largest school jurisdictions in the U.S. on per pupil spending. Yet Prince George's, Baltimore and Washington performed poorly according to common measures of achievement. Money can certainly help, but it isn't the only solution, I asserted.

I talked passionately about disparities in education, reflecting on my short time as a teacher in Baltimore City, where I observed that many children had long odds to succeed due to many factors outside their control, and offered another notion heretical to the public schools bureaucracy that more innovative school choices are needed where schools are failing students.

The inquisition turned to the usual focus on electoral "viability." Endorsers asked about my campaign plan. What was I going to say to impress them? I planned on riding my Sachs for Delegate BikeMobile around the district and recording a corny rap video on single payer health care for YouTube?

They asked about other endorsements. I'd only been officially in the contest for a month, during which my mother had died. I was nowhere as far as endorsements.

And of course, they asked how much I was going to raise and how much money it would take to win to gauge how serious I was as a candidate and how well I could play the game and work the machinery of politics. No doubt, the education association wouldn't want to back a loser. I made the mistake of being too honest, saying that fundraising was not my top priority and that I would spend my time connecting with people and delivering my messages. Instead, I should have given them some pie-in-the-sky number like $50,000 to connote "viability." Did I need to be brutally honest about my own longshot prospects? Or could I be full of bluster and project the utmost confidence and make exaggerated claims about myself, play the game, something like an experienced politician like Joker would do, to increase the chance of endorsement. I could have left it to the committee to sort out whether an overblown fundraising projection was within my grasp, an overly optimistic estimate or just a bald-faced lie. But I didn't, declining to identify a fabricated fundraising target. I wanted to be evaluated as a candidate of ideas, firmly-held beliefs and integrity, not as an ATM.

# Endorsements: Notches in Your Belt

*"He was the only man I ever knew who could get money from the rich and votes from the poor with the promise to protect them from each other."*

Tommy Douglas, former Saskatchewan premier and leader of Canada's Federal New Democratic Party

*"For many are called, but few are chosen."*

Bible, Matthew 22:14

The groveling and pandering for endorsements from special interest groups is an electoral politics conundrum that few candidates can avoid if they want to increase their chances of winning. Endorsements are the proverbial "feather in your cap," the equivalent of the Boy Scout covering his uniform with merit badges to show accumulating achievements; the high school stud etching notches in his belt to signal conquests; the wealthy socialite wife glittering with bling to proclaim status.

I don't think endorsements show much except a candidate's ability to say everything that the special interest wants to hear, at least for candidates with no official legislative record, which, in my race, included everyone except Joker.

But many candidates would say chasing endorsements is not groveling or pandering. Rather, they'd say it's about demonstrating that your political ideology and positions align with the interest group's agenda, and that you could be relied upon to represent the group's concerns and stances in the legislature.

But here's the problem: Once you receive that endorsement, and especially if it's a group that has endorsed you reliably and loyally multiple times, it is human nature that you are going to be beholden—disinclined, if not outright unwilling, to take a position or cast a vote that runs counter to the group's interest, especially on a high-profile, crucial issue, out of fear that the group will label you a traitor or disloyal, drop you from future endorsements with all the cash and votes that the seal of approval carries, and spread the word among their broad constituency to jump ship from your treacherous ass.

Endorsement interviews are like job interviews. You have to impress the interviewer with in-depth knowledge of the organization's top priority issues, even if they may bore the crap out of you. You had better be 100 percent supportive of the organization's positions on those issues, because you know damn well other candidates will be only too happy to suck up big-time if you won't. Sometimes, you really can buy in wholeheartedly to the organization's mission. Other times, be ready to pander, or at least equivocate or obfuscate, or kiss your chance for an endorsement goodbye. Endorsing organizations have little interest in endorsing candidates who don't swallow their agendas whole.

For example, the National Active and Retired Federal Employees-Maryland Federation made clear its lack of tolerance for compromise between two competing sides of an issue in its letter prefacing its endorsement questionnaire, dismissing consideration of context, complexity and nuance: "With all due respect," the group's legislative director wrote, "we are not looking for 'maybe' or 'it depends' responses."

But there's so much more to piling up endorsements—especially the ones that have the most influence and pack the most potential votes—than being the consummate yes-man. You have to prove you are a "viable" candidate. And that's where the whole ritualistic, relentless rigmarole of running a political campaign feeds on itself in a tornadic cyclone, and if you build up enough centrifugal force, you can suck ever more benefits into your campaign's vortex. Success in one area of a campaign begets an advantage in another facet, which leads to attainment of additional assets in another component, with the whole cycle ultimately and continually compounding the gains in all areas. It's a game of accumulated wealth with compound interest, and endorsements are prime assets augmenting the growth of power.

Suppose that, once elected to represent District 12, I considered a bill that pitted the interests of the endorsing organization against the interests of my constituents. Would I be influenced, even subconsciously, to vote in favor of the endorsing organization? After I promoted myself as a standard-bearer for the endorsing organization and its loyal members, could I politically afford to cross this organization for my constituents' sake? If I knew this organization carried the influence to help me win election, would I stand up against the organization to do what is right for my constituents? I'd like to think yes. But human psychology dictates that the realistic answer for me would likely be no, as it is most assuredly for politicians universally.

A candidate for mayor in Ferndale, Michigan, a small Detroit suburb, expressed this dilemma of endorsement-scrounging and allegiance-owing on his blog.

"What I didn't expect were letters I received from special interest groups and political action committees asking me to complete a questionnaire to test if I qualify for their endorsement. If sufficiently impressed I may also have received contributions to the campaign," wrote candidate Thomas Gagne.

"While I was filling out the forms a curious thought came to me...The only entity that represents all of a voter's interests is the voter...

"I've decided not to seek any special interest group or PAC's endorsement. If I can't raise the money I need from Ferndale businesses and citizens there's little reason to sell a piece of my office to special interests for a mere couple thousand dollars."

Gagne sent a letter to organizations seeking to make endorsements:

*"I've decided not to seek any special interest groups' endorsements to avoid the appearance of impropriety or suggest I may need to return the favor of the endorsement after elected to office...Sure, I may regret not having multiple Good-Housekeeping®-like Seals of Approval on my website or campaign literature and their contributions in my committee's bank account, but I won't be obligated to, or need to excuse my actions as Ferndale's mayor to anyone other than Ferndale voters."*

I admired Gagne's principled stand for the good people of Ferndale. But this is politics. Gagne lost. Principles: 1. Gagne: 0.

Like Gagne, I was inundated with questionnaires and meeting invitations from PACs, unions and other endorsing organizations, more than 40 in all, most of which I responded to. It was enough work to warrant hiring a campaign sub-contractor to fulfill. The organizations that contacted me to solicit responses for official endorsement, or some other form of public support from their constituency, ran the gamut, from motorcycle riders to doctors to tax reformers to gun club enthusiasts to marijuana advocates to farmers to animal-lovers.

# Viability: The Goose That Laid the Golden Eggs

I looked forward to the Maryland chapter of the Sierra Club and the Maryland League of Conservation Voters endorsement interview because I had a long-running interest in environmental issues, including completing graduate-level courses in ecology and environmental law and covering environmental issues as a county government reporter for the *Baltimore Sun*. To prepare, I met with a friend who was a PhD environmental scientist and an advocate on county environmental commissions to discuss a range of concerns and priorities.

But I left the interview feeling flat and disappointed. I felt the two interviewers were disengaged. It didn't help that I was the last interview at 8 p.m. on a frigid winter night. It was a one-way conversation. The interviewers looked at me blankly, seemingly disinterested and burned out. They asked an occasional rote question, but never engaged in conversation. Perhaps they had heard the same answers repeatedly throughout the day, and I didn't break new ground. Maybe they had already decided upon who they would recommend for endorsement.

The interviewers peppered me with questions about viability. How much money had I raised? Was I satisfied with my fundraising? How would I spend the money to get my campaign messages out? How many campaign mailings would I distribute? What were my media strategies? The interview became less about the issues and more about viability and tactics.

A few days later, at a Maryland League of Conservation Voters event, I talked to a Sierra Club member who usually sits in on endorsement interviews but missed mine. I asked for insight on what the organizations looks for in an interview.

He said the endorsement interviewers look for a compelling reason for why a candidate is running. They also look for a factor called "viability"—how much money a candidate has raised, how much he plans to raise and through what tactics, his strategic plan, how many volunteers he has recruited, and what other endorsements he has obtained. Viability, however it's measured, is a pervasive marker about whether you're worth a damn as a candidate. Without viability, you likely won't get an endorsement, and without a foundation of initial endorsements to beget more endorsements, you may just be spinning your wheels.

He told me that for the delegate race, $20,000 is not enough to be considered viable, $40,000 would be possibly viable, and $60,000 would equate to viability. Under that definition, I knew I wouldn't attain "viability." The Sierra Club member explained that the environmental groups didn't want to waste an endorsement on a "non-viable" candidate they pegged as having a slim chance of winning because of a lack of money.

The member laid out how the whole system feeds on itself from the perspective of endorsing organizations. If you don't have enough money, or prospects of raising enough, you won't get an endorsement. If you have more money, you are "viable" and can get an endorsement. Endorsements beget other endorsements. Each new endorsement increases your chances of getting more money, from the endorsing organization itself and from its individual members and supporters. With those contributions, your viability continually increases along with your bank account.

When endorsers asked how much money I had raised, and all those that interviewed me did, I felt like reverting to my inner child and saying: "None of your beeswax." Or, more adult-like: "If you really want to know, check the public record." They wanted to endorse a winner, so they will have a friend in office. And money equals viability equals electability.

But this question about money accumulation involves many factors for a new candidate: How much money did a candidate loan himself? Does the candidate have a large, extended family that donates big money? Is the candidate in a professional field or social circle that provides connections to wealthy associates and big-money businesses and PACs? (For example, attorney Next Big Thing raised about $10,000 from about 40 contributions from his law firm associates.) For a new candidate, "heat-and-serve funders" is where the money is going to come from—the majority likely from outside the election district—especially earlier in a campaign, not from constituents.

I had the palpable feeling that the scorekeeping associated with the fundraising game was a reflection of society's attitudes and skewed values on the whole. If one didn't have the money, he was looked upon as lesser, weak, incapable, unsuccessful, a loser, unworthy, unpopular, not a leader others would want to follow or connect with.

Conversely, the candidate who had the money, and could convince individuals or corporations to donate more, would be viewed as powerful, successful, influential, an achiever, a leader who was exalted in the public's eye, a winner. People want to connect themselves to winners.

Just look at sports, and the basking in reflected glory (BIRG) phenomenon, research that shows that an individual's self-esteem often is tied to associating with a winner. Why were the NFL's Dallas Cowboys dubbed "America's Team?" They weren't through the mid-1960s when they were losers. Once they became perennial winners with a Texas-sized swagger, they became popular far beyond their britches.

In an abstract way, because of the campaign's excessive focus on candidates' political bank accounts, ability to raise money and comparisons to others' treasuries, I got a sense of what it might be like to be poor in society, overlooked and cast aside. Could I do just as good a job protecting the environment and advocating for labor issues as others? Yes. Did they want to back somebody who sucked at fundraising? No.

## An Ethical Dilemma: Can I Have My Cake and Eat it Too?

The firefighters with whom I met for my endorsement interview with the Howard County Professional Fire Fighters Association were gregarious and self-effacing, poking fun at each other as I imagined they did at the fire station, in contrast with the stone-faced and humorless teachers. One young firefighter joked that he was labeled a "late bloomer" by his parents, and the others playfully mocked him. He said he wanted to be a firefighter from as young as he could remember, the classic case of the little boy enamored with the red fire engine and fire hat and men in gear who grew up to be just like his heroes. Several others started in other careers—construction, sales, business management, outdoor adventure—and gravitated to the profession through chance encounters or long-held interest. They all professed a love for their profession, and exuded an unmistakable camaraderie and brotherhood. They even offered me the chance to be a firefighter-in-training for a day.

I asked them what inspired them to become firefighters, and they enjoyed telling me their personal stories. They gave me extra time in the interview; I didn't feel like they were trying to rush me out the door to get to the next waiting candidate. From jaw-dropping stories I had heard from my Baltimore City fire chief friend and my natural curiosity, I probed the group about their profession, feeling truly engaged. I asked whether there was a challenge in recruiting firefighters, women in particular. There was one woman in the group, who said she used to cringe when seeing any injury, and kept pushing herself to become accustomed until she entered the profession. In fact, the firefighters told me, it was nearly impossible to get into the unit. A recent firefighters' class had 30 slots and more than 1,000 applicants.

I believed the Howard County firefighters would be one of my best chances for endorsement, and I really wanted it. I emphasized my union involvement and leadership position as the elected vice chair of the union executive committee at my employer, the health care professional association. I hoped my volunteer union service would distinguish me from all the other District 12 candidates, none of whom held a union leadership position.

Again, the issue of fundraising came up. The firefighters asked me how much money I had raised, how much I wanted to raise and how much I needed to win. This time I exaggerated my goal, pegging it at $25,000.

The firefighters knew that I had advocated a ban on corporate, union and PAC contributions. They asked me if I were endorsed, whether I would accept a contribution. The question posed an ethical dilemma and a challenge to my credibility. I wasn't sure what I would do, because I had yet to be offered a corporate contribution. I responded that I would accept a contribution from a union, because that was the way the political system was constituted, and it was tremendously difficult if not impossible to compete if one didn't solicit or accept money from these sources.

Acceptance of such donations wouldn't mean that I wouldn't still pursue banning them if I got elected. Or at least that's the pretzel logic I used to justify accepting a union contribution. Maybe I was fooling myself. Maybe I was already unwittingly becoming a rationalizing, compromising politician willing and determined to do whatever was most expedient and beneficial personally. What the hell, I reasoned, I would never have the opportunity to pursue change from the inside if I stood no chance of getting elected, and money was the "hall pass" for the State House. At least that sounded legitimate—a form of self-deluding reasoning that politicians no doubt engage in routinely.

After the interview, I thought about whether the firefighters would endorse me if I refused to accept a contribution. Part of their endorsement process is using the PAC money they raise from members to support a candidate. So why would they support a candidate who refuses monetary support? Politics are full of torturous contortions serving as justifications, so I thought of my own: If I were to receive the firefighters' endorsement, I would accept the contribution as proof, then turn around and refund the money. I never had to make such a compromise of principles. I didn't get it.

## Another Dilemma: How to Play the Game When You Aren't Allowed on the Field

Sometimes endorsing organizations don't even bother to consider all the candidates in their endorsement process, concluding some aren't worthy without even having met them. As positive as I felt toward the Howard County Professional Fire Fighters Association, that's how negative I felt toward its cross-border counterpart, the Baltimore County Professional Fire Fighters Association.

At a candidates' forum in February, I was surprised to hear Anointed One and Next Big Thing proudly announce they had received an endorsement from the Baltimore County firefighters. I had never been contacted by that union to fill out a questionnaire or interview for an endorsement. I wondered how Anointed One and Next Big Thing had already gotten the nod. In Next Big Thing's case, it wasn't hard to guess at least one reason why: Delegate Fireman, who publicly supported

Next Big Thing at his campaign kickoff, was a career Baltimore County firefighter.

I wasn't the only one to notice unions that sacrificed fairness and impartiality to play political favorites. "[W]e are disappointed that some unions chose not to do interviews with all candidates and that some insider connections played a role in some endorsements being handed out," wrote the Baltimore County Blue blog.

I could have shrugged it off as just another biased game in the crooked process of politics, but I decided to stand up for myself and challenge the firefighters union for an answer for its biased and deficient process. What I found was a gutless union that didn't have the integrity to respond to a candidate about its corrupt practice.

I wrote an e-mail to the president of the firefighters union saying that I had never been contacted about its endorsement process, expressing surprise that several candidates had announced endorsements, and noting that I had been officially registered as a candidate since Oct. 3, 2013, months before it had apparently made its endorsements. I noted that I was the only candidate in the race who was an elected representative for a union, and that I soon would be representing my union members in collective bargaining with my employer for a new contract. I requested that the president outline the organization's endorsement process.

Receiving no response over three days, I called the union's president and got his assistant. The assistant confirmed she had received my e-mail and had forwarded it to the president. She said the president had been in and out of his office, and that there had been a death in his family. She said she would leave a message for him to call back.

Five more days, and still no response. Now I was feeling insulted and disrespected. I persisted with one more attempt to goad or guilt the president into a response. In an e-mail, I offered to meet with a union leader at an upcoming forum to learn more about the fire department and its concerns, since I had not had an opportunity to interview. It didn't work; I was stonewalled.

## You Didn't Get Endorsed, But We Can Outfit You with Concrete Boots

The AFL-CIO labor organization of the Washington-Baltimore region also made endorsements without contacting me. But at least I can give credit to that organization for responding when I called to challenge its process.

The AFL-CIO regional president called me back promptly, sounding gruff and unapologetic, like I would expect from a prototypical union boss. Even his name sounded like a union heavy: Trucco. I asked whether their endorsement process had concluded.

"We've made our endorsements. You didn't get endorsed," he told me, nonplussed.

"The AFL-CIO never contacted me by e-mail, mail or phone. How could I have been considered?" I protested.

The president claimed notices about the AFL-CIO endorsement opportunity were sent to candidates by e-mail. He apologized if I didn't get one, but it was more like, *Sorry buddy, you lost, stop whining*, rather than, *Gee, I'm really sorry you didn't get to participate, we would have loved to hear from you.*

"I definitely would have responded if I received it, I've responded to many questionnaires and interview requests," I said.

"Are you a Democrat or a Republican?" the president asked.

"Why would that matter?"

"A lot of candidates don't respond to us because they don't want a union endorsement for their campaign. Sometimes Republicans want to distance themselves from unions."

"I'm a Democrat, and that's not the case with me," I replied.

"You didn't get endorsed," he repeated, accepting no accountability and growing testy. Point made, I dropped my challenge, wary of ending up at the bottom of the Potomac River wearing concrete boots.

## Screwed!

While some endorsements may have little impact on an election outcome, sometimes an endorsement can be an irrefutable smack in the face for a candidate and serve as an undeniable harbinger that all may be lost. That was the case in Howard County's District 9 Democratic primary, District 12's neighbors, where 31-year Howard County Public Schools math and computer science teacher Robert Corbin battled lawyer and community activist Tim Callahan.

The Howard County Education Association (HCEA) endorsed Callahan, screwing one of its own. The teachers' association's justification for their choice seemed spurious: Callahan's experience on community nonprofit organization boards.

In a contest of political neophytes, it was hard to fathom how a union of teachers could endorse Callahan over a colleague who had devoted his life to teaching, who knew the challenges of education, who had worked in the trenches every day. I couldn't imagine how Corbin felt about the betrayal of loyalty.

Truth be told, Callahan was the more impressive candidate, more dynamic, polished, articulate and seemingly knowledgeable. The younger Callahan connected well with audiences, while the less-refined Corbin seemed more uncomfortable and unnatural.

This race presented the classic case of a high-profile, influential endorser wanting to go with the more popular candidate, the likely winner. The education association didn't want to waste an endorsement on a primary loser, risking that the ultimate winner wouldn't owe the group any allegiance once in office and even could pursue retribution if he wanted to play hardball politics.

The education association likely concluded that Callahan was the more appealing candidate to voters, and that if Callahan were elected, he would owe a debt to the education establishment. If Callahan were to fail to do everything in support of the teachers' agenda, the teachers could take away its endorsement and rip its "Teacher-Endorsed" red apple off his signs real fast.

## Take a Walk on the Wild Side

The Columbia Democratic Club held forums for all elected offices in the winter. In the spring, the club gave candidates one minute to make a final pitch for endorsement at a meeting featuring about 80 candidates ranging from Congressman John Sarbanes to Orphan's Court Judge candidates. I decided to go bold and challenge conventional thinking in an attempt to distinguish myself among District 12's Ten Little Indians.

> *"You can be safe, you can be predictable. You can endorse people who will be likely not to rock the boat. And you can be pretty sure they'll be there for 20 years.*
>
> *"Or you can be bolder, take a risk, and endorse me. I'm the only one who supports a single payer health care system, a ban on corporate and PAC campaign contributions, a middle class income tax reduction and an increase in the minimum age to buy a rifle or shotgun. Will all this be hard to do? No doubt. But that's what makes this campaign worthwhile.*
>
> *"So play your cards close to the vest. Or, in the immortal words of Lou Reed, 'Take a Walk on the Wild Side.'"*

The reference to singer Reed drew chuckles; it was a non-conformist line in an evening marked by conventional spiels. But it wasn't enough. Frontrunners Anointed One and Zelig got the endorsements.

## Bagging a Big One?

I read in the community newspaper that longtime Baltimore-area Congressman Elijah Cummings, my district's congressman, had endorsed Syed Hassan for delegate in District 13, which adjoined my district. Hassan, a last-minute entry in the race replacing his wife, who inexplicably dropped out *(see chapter on Shenanigans)*, had only been a candidate about a month before receiving Cummings' endorsement, an obvious case of a personal connection and a political favor. Hassan's website featured a photo with Cummings and Gov. O'Malley.

If Rep. Cummings could endorse an unknown candidate not only with no political experience, but who had never been a candidate for any office, I reasoned, why couldn't Cummings endorse me? I knew it was a goose chase, even a lark, but I wrote to Cummings seeking his endorsement. It bothered me the way a politician could throw his influence around willy-nilly to confer advantages to allies, even though, I knew, that's politics.

> *Dear Rep. Cummings:*
>
> *I heard you speak at the Columbia Democratic Club candidates' forum and was very impressed with your passion and support for working people and people struggling to make it. I am a Democratic candidate for Maryland state delegate in District 12. I believe my positions supporting regular people, like a single payer health care system, align well with your passions. I noticed in the Columbia Flier that you endorsed Syed Hassan in District 13. I was interested in whether you will make any endorsements for District 12 candidates. If so, I would be honored to be considered for your endorsement...Keep fighting for things that matter for the residents of Baltimore and the surrounding areas. I will be voting for you come election time.*

Unsurprisingly, I never heard from Cummings, despite my closing suck-up line.

## Duh

Sometimes, endorsements come as no surprise. Anointed One was the only District 12 delegate candidate endorsed by the Thurgood Marshall Democratic Club of Howard County, founded for promoting the political empowerment and advancement of African-Americans. The club's founder and original president? Anointed One's mother. Was Anointed One a strong candidate? Yes. Did the Thurgood Marshall club's endorsement of only one candidate, Anointed One, in the primary where three can advance to the general election raise a specter of impropriety, or at the least, favoritism? Yes.

## Doubly Screwed

If Corbin got shunned by teachers for endorsement despite education credentials that were unmatchable, gubernatorial candidate Heather Mizeur, Maryland's first openly gay candidate for governor and who is married to a woman, was downright disrespected by Equality Maryland, the state's largest gay rights organization. The lesbian-gay-bisexual-trans-gender (LGBT) group made the safe choice by endorsing Lieutenant Governor Anthony Brown, who was all but anointed Maryland's next governor. Mizeur, if elected, would have been the first openly gay governor in the country, a fact one would think would have been compelling enough to warrant endorsement by a gay rights advocacy group. But it wasn't. Brown had the money, endorsements, name recognition and political support as The Establishment's choice.

Equality Maryland selected Brown because he would be the "most effective" ally as governor, said the group's executive director in the *Baltimore Sun.*

The director noted that the group is distinct from the Gay & Lesbian Victory Fund, which supports the election of gay and lesbian candidates nationwide. "Our goal is to elect fair-minded individuals. That is regardless of their sexual orientation..."

In a statement, Mizeur called Equality Maryland's endorsement of Brown "a puzzling choice."

Not really, Heather. The political group calculated that you couldn't win the primary election, and that therefore, despite your bona fides through real-life experience, not to mention your unquestionable support of civil rights and courage to come out in the public arena, even bringing your spouse and talking warmly about her at campaign events, you weren't as valuable to them as a man who could only imagine what it is like to be gay in America in theoretical, abstract terms, but who had political relationships up the wazoo. But that's politics.

## November 13, 2013 – Bringing Nothing to the Table in Fireman's Kitchen

The second time the full District 12 crew appeared together was a forum organized and sponsored by retiring 20-year Delegate Fireman, the lifelong Arbutus resident and career Baltimore County firefighter. The event, where each candidate introduced themselves, explained their reasons for running and responded to nine issue questions, was held at the Arbutus Fire Hall, Fireman's home turf. With Fireman as host and moderator, and with his strong and loyal following, this was a can't-miss event for anyone who wanted to attract a portion of Fireman's votes and succeed him.

It was an unfortunate day for an accident on my way home from work. Out the bus window, I saw red tail lights illuminating a ribbon as far up the road as I could see. Emergency vehicles passed my bus every 30 seconds. It took 30 minutes to get through the accident zone, putting me home at 6:30, with the Fireman forum starting at 7. With no traffic, it would take about 25 minutes to get to Arbutus. It was already dark and I still had to battle the interminable Washington-Baltimore rush hour.

The drive took 45 minutes, and I walked in 20 minutes late after the forum had started. I knew Fireman might attract a crowd, but I still was shocked to see that 300 people had packed the huge fire hall.

I was frazzled. I walked around the edge of the audience and took my seat with fellow candidates at the front table, knowing my tardiness was conspicuous and an immediate black mark. I had to figure out what was going on midstream while one of my competitors was speaking, and be prepared to speak at a moment's notice. I noticed that nearly the whole front row of the audience directly in front of the candidates on my side of the moderator's dais was filled with Zelig supporters wearing color-coordinated purple and yellow "DR. Zelig for Delegate" shirts, a coordinated show of force. I was just beginning to realize the awe of the well-oiled Zelig campaign machine.

Without knowledge of the questions ahead of time, we fielded inquiries on controversial and divisive topics: the death penalty; minimum wage; state funding for abortions, and for certain private school costs; police speed cameras; hydraulic land fracturing, or "fracking," for gas; decriminalizing marijuana; offshore energy wind mills; and property levies to protect the Chesapeake Bay.

I had firm positions on some issues, general thoughts on others, and no idea on a couple, at least not based on any research. In a form of political blasphemy, I told the audience the truth on a couple of issues: I needed more study and had not reached conclusions.

I wanted to tell the audience, *Hey, give me a break! I registered just six weeks ago and I had no idea what Fireman was going to ask. And, you know, I have to work a full-time job for a living and I'm going to graduate school. How would you like to cram on 50 topics and be questioned on any one of them in such a short time?*

## Political double talk

I wasn't alone in struggling to sound like an Encyclopedia of knowledge; I noticed my competitors' tentativeness in responding to some of Fireman's questions.

In his memoir, *The Speechwriter*, about writing for former South Carolina Gov. Mark Sanford, who disgraced himself and his office when he tried to hide his extramarital affair sojourns to Argentina by saying he was hiking the Appalachian Trail, Barton Swaim described the phenomenon of politicians pontificating on everything under the sun, regardless of their actual knowledge, expertise or interest. Swaim said it is folly to expect politicians to have a well-informed position on every issue, and explained how politicians become masters of faking it, not so much out of duplicity but out of necessity.

"It's impossible to attain much success in politics if you're the sort of person who can't abide disingenuousness," Swaim wrote. "This isn't to say politics is full of lies and liars; it has no more liars than other fields do. Actually one hears very few proper lies in politics. Using vague, slippery, or just meaningless language is not the same as lying: it's not intended to deceive so much as to preserve options, buy time, distance oneself from others, or just to sound like you're saying something instead of nothing."

Swaim explained that politicians feel compelled to make statements that say "something without saying anything" to put themselves on record without committing to any particular course of action. They and their staffs become experts, Swaim said, at crafting statements loaded with "rhetorical dead weight," phrases such as "we are looking closely at the situation" and "the remarks raise troubling questions" and "avoid rushing to judgment."

*"Many people take this as evidence of duplicity or cynicism. But they don't know what it's like to be expected to make comments...on things of which [politicians] have little or no reliable knowledge or about which they just don't care. They don't appreciate the sheer number of things on which a politician is expected to have a position. Issues on which the governor had no strong opinions, events over which he had no control, situations on which it served no useful purpose for him to comment— all required some kind of remark...Commenting on that many things is unnatural, and sometimes it was impossible to sound sincere. There was no way around it, though. Journalists would ask our office about anything having remotely to do with the governor's sphere of authority, and you could only offer so many minimalist responses before you began to sound disengaged or ignorant or dishonest. And the necessity of having to manufacture so many views on so many subjects, day after day, fosters a sense that you don't have to believe your own words. You get*

*comfortable with insincerity… Sometimes I felt no more attachment to the words I was writing than a dog has to its vomit."*

. . .

In his closing remarks, Fireman told the audience that all of the candidates were "winners" by putting themselves on the line to run for public office during a time when the national political environment was so partisan, toxic and divisive.

But while Fireman included me by default in the category "winner," that certainly wasn't the opinion of the Marshmallow Man blogger.

Reading the Marshmallow Man's analysis of the Fireman forum was my first experience as a candidate with the Wild West world of bloggers, where anyone with a computer, Internet access and an opinion has a megaphone to spew unfiltered judgments with impunity. With bloggers, there is no review process or editor to provide a check on obnoxiousness, sarcasm, meanness or partiality. In the social media age, snark and outrageousness have been accepted as part of normal discourse, and politics is one of the arenas where this coarsening of society is playing out in full public view, so much so that it was considered not only acceptable, but righteous in 2016 for Republican presidential candidate Donald Trump supporters to wear t-shirts with huge lettering shouting, "TRUMP THAT BITCH!" referring to Democratic candidate Hillary Clinton.

As examples, in one grenade-heavy post previewing the primary nearly 100 days out, Marshmallow Man referred to me and Spare-A-Dime as "fifth-tier candidates in the three-tier race, so they don't count," and made the obtusely poetic reference to Ballerina and Joker as "gossamer fallacies, foisted upon the electorate under a facade of false hope."

Soon after the Fireman forum, a local political activist sent me an e-mail with a link to the Marshmallow Man's analysis of the forum. I wished he hadn't sent it. It was like a car crash—I knew I shouldn't look, but I felt compelled. I didn't sleep well that night, because of Marshmallow Man's screed:

"While I recognize that running for public office is such an investment of someone's time, energy and life, I think at this point two candidates should truly rethink the existence of their candidacy. Adam Sachs brings nothing to the table that would even suggest that his campaign would become interesting in time."

Marshmallow Man delivered a wakeup call that let me know I would have to develop a thick skin to continue competing without worrying what others would say. As much as I tried to steel myself for these inevitable shots, it was hard to know the thickness of my armor until I had to absorb this first bullet.

As a former journalist, I was familiar with the rough-and-tumble world of the media covering politics. But this wasn't media. This was one man's opinion. Still, I was rocked by Marshmallow Man's brick that clocked me between the eyes.

*What do you mean 'brings nothing to the table?' I'm rattling the monkey cage. I'm bringing a complete change in Maryland's health care system that could save $1,000 per person in health care costs and cover everyone, and boot the greedy private health insurers out of the game. Is that nothing, loudmouth? What did any of the other candidates bring that was more consequential? I heard the usual blather about better education and more jobs. You think they'll really have any impact among all the other politicians hollering in that echo chamber?*

Hard to admit, but the Marshmallow Man's caustic comment cut to the core of my self-knowledge and insecurity—that I was an amateur, unpolished political candidate, not high-powered or moneyed or connected to insiders; that I was having difficulty raising money; that I lacked a broad cadre of supporters and volunteers; that, in political parlance, I had yet to "gain traction;" and that I was only able and willing to work so hard for this office, a level that certainly would fall short of Marshmallow Man's expectations.

# November 17, 2013 – An Unholy Alliance?

Since I had become so attuned to Maryland's political scene as a candidate, I had heard about longshot gubernatorial candidate Mizeur early in the campaign. Female, openly gay/married, outspoken, grassroots-oriented, unpretentious, lacking wealth and elite, big-money, corporate connections, and *genuinely* honest and authentic, Mizeur shattered the mold of the prototypical Maryland candidate. I liked what I knew about her. I could identify with her candidacy. Soon after the Fireman forum, I had a chance to meet Mizeur at a "meet-and-greet" at a supporter's house.

When she finished her speech and took questions from the audience, I asked how she would respond to critics who charged that her plans, like significantly increasing the minimum wage, instituting universal pre-K education and legalizing and taxing marijuana, were too liberal, Pollyanna and politically unrealistic.

Later, I introduced myself to Mizeur personally as a candidate for delegate in District 12.

"I hear there are a lot of people running," Mizeur said.

"Yeah, lots of competition. You need a scorecard."

"How's it going for you?" Mizeur asked.

"I'm learning a lot and working hard, trying to meet more people at events like this. I really like what you said tonight."

"Thanks. I appreciate you coming out. Good luck in your race."

I noticed immediately that Mizeur had the singular talent of truly gifted politicians: She could make you feel like you really mattered, that she really cared and was listening, like you were the only one in the room, even though 10 other people were lined up for a chance to greet. And you actually got the sense it was *completely authentic*, not phony. We had a lot in common—and nothing. We were both progressive-minded, non-partisan, unimpressed with entrenched power structures, dismissive of status quo politics, and big underdogs. However, she was adept at policy-making and politics, with demonstrated achievements, such as election to the Maryland legislature and passing laws expanding health care for kids and low-income women and developing policy for U.S. Senator John Kerry; I was a rank amateur, with no political accomplishments to my name.

I also met several members of her campaign staff, and later e-mailed Mizeur's political director asking about Mizeur's position on single-payer, universal health care, and whether I could promote her plan for a middle class income tax reduction through my campaign.

Another high grade for Mizeur: her director replied. On single-payer health care, the director said Mizeur would "absolutely be open to Maryland moving in that direction" and that single-payer "is certainly the best long-term solution to our health care woes." He also gave me the green light to discuss Mizeur's tax plan in my campaign as long as I gave the Mizeur campaign credit.

I was excited about making the connection with Mizeur. But my attendance at the event didn't escape the critical eye of the Baltimore County Blue blog and its followers. The blogger revealed that Man of the People and I were the only District 12 candidates to attend Mizeur's event:

"You would think that Man of the People and Sachs would be careful of too closely affiliating themselves with Mizeur." Blue's sequential logic, a virtual genealogy and extrapolation of political relationships and territoriality, went like this: 1) More than half of District 12 was comprised of Howard County; 2) Howard County Executive Ken Ulman was running for Maryland lieutenant governor; 3) Ulman was the running mate of current Lieutenant Governor Anthony Brown; 4) Brown was far-and-away the leader in the Democratic gubernatorial field and a near shoo-in for the Governor's Mansion; 5) Ulman was "wildly popular" in Howard County; 6) The Brown/Ulman ticket was expected to dominate in Howard County; 7) Ergo, why would any Democratic candidate from District 12 be so self-destructive and foolish so as to risk being seen as not aligning with Brown/Ulman?

Blue also warned that "Man of the People and Sachs should watch out considering Mizeur isn't expected to prevail (recent polls have her last with barely any name recognition) and her liberal tendencies may not be popular in Southwest Baltimore County, an area populated by conservative Reagan Democrats." This Blue statement perfectly conveys the social psychologists' theory of "basking in reflected glory (BIRG):" Why damage your public image by associating with a loser when you can boost your self-esteem by tagging along with a winner?

I didn't care about BIRGing with Brown/Ulman; I was way more impressed with Mizeur. Still, just by appearing at a Mizeur event didn't mean that I had endorsed her or rejected other gubernatorial candidates. I was simply curious, and opportunistic.

Blue readers took notice of my appearance, which I guess was good that I was on their radar at all. As a longshot, they theorized, perhaps I had nothing to lose by showing up with Mizeur.

"Apparently, Sachs is super liberal with his single-payer health care plan for Maryland and doesn't have a shot in this race. But who knows what Man of the People is thinking aligning himself with her," wrote one commenter.

"Since Sachs is running, if we're being honest, just to prove a point and get his issue out there, I don't think he minds being associated with Delegate Mizeur," said another commenter, who got it right.

# Basking in Reflected Glory

*"I should be a coach, because when my players win, I win. But when my players lose, what a bunch of losers and hey, don't blame me, because I wasn't playing."*

Jarod Kintz, Author

When you have the aura of success and winning attached to you, like Lieutenant Governor Anthony Brown for Maryland governor, and Anointed One and Zelig early in the District 12 race, people want to connect with you and be a part of you so they can feel better about themselves, like they are winners as well. It's human nature. It's as true in politics as in other walks of life such as sports, entertainment, technology, investing and business. It's all about creating an aura of popularity, achievement, success, coolness and inevitability. Remember actor Charlie Sheen ranting nonsensically about, "Winning!" after getting dropped from the TV comedy *Two And A Half Men*, and soaring in attention and popularity? Maybe not exactly parallel, but you get the drift. In social psychology, this phenomenon of attaching ourselves with "winners" to protect and enhance our own public image is known as "basking in reflected glory," or BIRG.

In a groundbreaking 1976 study of students from universities with powerhouse athletic programs, researchers observed students' clothing in large lecture halls following big football games and found that students tended to wear more apparel associating themselves with their own university when the football team won compared to when they lost. Researchers also found that people tended to use the pronoun "we" more to describe their team when they won and "they" more when the team had lost.

Studies have shown that ardent fans become so emotionally invested in the success of the teams they root for that they experience hormonal surges and other physiological changes while watching games, such as testosterone increases and decreases in males, and that their self-esteem may raise or fall depending upon a game's outcome. For some fans, their teams essentially represent themselves, penetrating to the core of their being.

As politics have become competitions more like sports—the political arena often is described as "blood sport" or "horse race"—with endless polls declaring the leaders and trailers, pundits declaring debate winners and losers, rankings based on fundraising hauls and opponents trying to figuratively bludgeon each other into submission, BIRGing has become more common in campaigning and elections.

BIRGing has an opposite reaction: "Cutting off reflected failure" (CORF). When people cut off reflected failure, they desire to disassociate from lower-status individuals or entities because they do not want to harm their reputations by associating with "failures" or "losers." An illustration of this concept, albeit in an intentionally self-mocking way, is when fans of a winless NFL football team attend the game with paper bags over their heads.

A 2002 study of an election in Flanders, Belgium demonstrated the phenomenon of BIRGing and CORFing in the context of politics, showing that people like to flaunt their association with victorious political parties, and try to conceal their association with defeated parties. Researchers surveyed several regions two days before a general election, documenting homes that displayed lawn signs or posters supporting a particular political party. The day after the elections, the observers checked whether the homes still displayed their poster or lawn sign.

Homes that displayed signs and posters for the winning party kept their advertisements up longer, showing the tendency to BIRG with the triumphant party, and to CORF with the defeated party.

If a constituent wanted to BIRG for the District 12 race, he would have hitched his cart early to the Anointed One and Zelig Clydesdales. I was much more likely the CORF candidate headed to the glue factory.

## NOVEMBER 21, 2013 – POWER PLAY

Soon after he entered the race, consummate insider Joker held a fundraiser in November 2013 at a steakhouse in which he listed 10 hosts, a lineup of heavy-hitting and influential attorneys, investors, bankers, Realtors, property managers and developers from Baltimore—all outside of District 12—who were high-ranking executives of their firms. These were the type of gold-plated business moguls—CEOs, managing partners, presidents and the like—with the Roman numerals II and III and Jr. after their names, such as Fred Allner III, and who used first initials instead of first names, such as H. Dean Bouland and M. Neil Brownawell, II. That's who Joker ran with, people accustomed to the beneficial mechanics of money, influence, relationships, deal-making and high social standing. My only hope of getting access to such people would be to get a job as a caddy at an exclusive country club.

My Uncle-in-Law Ted Levin, who served as a delegate on the Baltimore County delegation with Joker from 1987 to 1990, warned me that Joker would be a "formidable candidate" based on his ability to raise money and his business and political connections. Joker's fundraiser "hosts" were a good indication of that formidability.

In an article about the fundraiser in the *Maryland Reporter*, Joker claimed he had already raised $60,000 in his two months as a candidate and predicted he would have $100,000 by January 2014. That turned out to be misleading bluster. Joker's 2013 campaign finance report showed he raised roughly $32,000 entering 2014. Another $35,000 came from a Joker self-loan.

I believe Joker touted his campaign bank account to send the message that he was a rainmaker to be reckoned with, because money equates to power and influence and popularity on the campaign trail, and money begets more money. I found such talk insufferable—not only because I was virtually destitute as a candidate, but because such braggadocio says nothing about one's integrity, intentions or positions, what one would actually stand for or do in office. It's just playing a juvenile, illusive game.

Why did Joker feel compelled to boast about how much money he had? It reminded me of a tot's simplistic, absolutist assertion of superiority: *My dad has more money than your dad,* or *I have more toys than you.* I believed Joker's money talk was deliberate to craft a narrative to the electorate: "I'm powerful, I'm popular, I'm loaded, I have influence, people want to donate to me, people admire me. I can outmuscle the other candidates. If you are smart, you will contribute to me and be counted among the powerful."

Joker's money prediction also was calculated to send a message to the other candidates that he was the Alpha Dog with the connections and the influence to crush the amateurs under a pile of money.

# JOKER

Everyone who runs for public office has to have at least a little narcissism. Joker took the crown for narcissistic tendencies among the field. He claimed to be the "frontrunner" in his campaign mailings though he had no such evidence. He consistently and presumptuously offered to take the two neophyte candidates who would ultimately join him as elected representatives under his tutelage and school them in the legislature.

Joker, a former Maryland delegate who was trying to reclaim a seat and the glory more than two decades later, played the villain in the District 12 race. A (disbarred) lawyer, businessman and Maryland State House lobbyist who had many "friends" in the Maryland legislature and its sycophantic orbit, Joker presented himself as the ultimate insider who had valuable knowledge and connections none of us others did. He routinely dropped names at forums to show he was on a first-name basis with elected officials and Maryland's leaders.

While winning would have been great, beating Joker would have been almost as sweet and more realistic. The deeper the campaign went, the more that became my goal. Like a National Football League team whose progression of goals would be a winning record, winning a division and winning the Super Bowl, mine were: avoid finishing last, beat Joker, and place in the top three.

Ken Stevens certainly viewed Joker as the antihero, and if Stevens drew that conclusion, there had to be merit. Stevens, a progressive-minded political activist in Howard County and frequent letter-writer to the community newspaper, was so disenchanted with Joker's candidacy that he wore homemade "Defeat Joker" buttons to campaign forums—and he didn't even live in District 12.

I attached validity to Stevens' opinion because of his passion, knowledge and background as an activist. Stevens, who is white, served as the political action chair of a National Association for the Advancement of Colored People (NAACP) chapter, supported the Equal Rights Amendment as a National Organization for Women (NOW) member and advocated for Maryland's gay marriage law.

## You, Sir, Are No Progressive

Stevens stood for fairness, justice, equality and integrity, and judging from Stevens' actions and words, he smelled a rat—or at least a feckless opportunist—in Joker. Why else would an engaged political observer with no previous ties to Joker and who could not even vote in Joker's election go to such lengths to identify Joker as the one candidate out of 10 who merited particular voter wariness?

Stevens expressed his disdain for Joker in a letter to the editor, noting Joker was a carpetbagger and a disbarred attorney who was trying to buy the election—facts and claims that dogged Joker's candidacy—and concluding from his research on Joker's votes during his House term that he was "no progressive."

Stevens wasn't the only citizen who singled out and blasted Joker with a letter to the editor. Jan Bowman of Columbia wrote that she found Joker's bid "offensive."

"It is insulting to our previous delegates and voters that a disbarred attorney...and an avowed special interest lobbyist...would have the gall to say he's going to represent the people of District 12," Bowman wrote.

And the three main political bloggers covering the District 12 race— 53 Beers on Tap, Baltimore County Blue and Spartan Considerations—all expressed a dim view of Joker's candidacy. None was more critical than Spartan Considerations blogger Jason Booms, strategic communications and opinion research consultant and former political advisor and pollster.

In a post titled, "Joker Gets…What Exactly?" Booms opened, "A one-time lawmaker should be expected to know and follow the law. That is a reasonable enough starting-point." He referred to Joker's slogan on signs and direct mail pieces, "Joker Gets It Done," and asked, "So what has Joker gotten done lately?"

Booms unloaded on Joker's direct mail piece, "Report from Annapolis!" calling it "further evidence that Joker has lost the plot. Running as an uber-insider, especially when one is a non-incumbent, is rarely a sound idea."

Three weeks before the primary, Booms wrote: "This blog has taken a firm stand against the ridiculous candidacy of disbarred attorney Joker, and he deserves it." In a subsequent post, Booms pleaded, "I am still hoping that progressive voters…coalesce around one quality, viable third option to prevent the election" of Joker.

Marshmallow Man wrote: "For the love of Pete, don't vote for Joker." He noted mega-billboards he observed at shopping centers screaming, "Joker Gets It Done." "But the sign is a lie," said Marshmallow Man. "He doesn't. He can't."

## A 'Formidable Candidate'

Despite inspiring critics, Joker, 63, stocky, bushy eye-browed, square-jawed and clad in dark business suits, was a force to be reckoned with. He had political experience as a delegate and legislative counsel, well-placed connections and the resume of a fast-riser in his career and Maryland politics. In quick succession by 35, he served as counsel to the majority leader of the Maryland Senate; worked for the Baltimore County executive in state legislative affairs; gained appointment to the Maryland Governor's Housing Task Force; and won election to the

Democratic State Central Committee and Maryland state delegate in his first run in 1986.

I likely would not be writing about Joker's long-delayed, out-of-the-blue comeback attempt after a quarter-century away from public limelight had he not finished a heartbreaking fourth (the top three vote-getters won seats) in his 1990 re-election bid, falling just 161 votes short. That loss almost certainly changed the course of Joker's life and quashed a likely seat in perpetuity in the legislature and ascent in politics.

After his loss, Joker established a real estate title company. Later, he became what he called a "trusted advisor and consultant"—a euphemism for registered lobbyist—for businesses and organizations advocating in the Maryland legislature, including housing-related groups such as the Maryland Multi-Family Housing Association.

## Carpetbagger Squared

Like Next Big Thing, Joker fit the prototype of a "carpetbagger"—a political candidate who seeks election in an area where he has lived for only a short time—to a tee. He had represented Towson, a separate legislative district in Baltimore County, during his stint in the Maryland House.

The blogger Baltimore County Blue reported Joker put his residence in the tony Roland Park community in Baltimore City on the market in 2013 and moved 12 miles south to Catonsville in District 12, renting a house within about a year of the primary election. The timing of Joker's rental in a new legislative district coincided with the three long-time District 12 delegates announcing their retirements. Joker said he moved because his wife grew up in Catonsville. While that may be true, it seemed an odd reason to move from one of the most desirable, upscale neighborhoods of Baltimore just 30 minutes away with no discernable upgrade in quality of life.

Joker's "sudden relocation when three delegate seats opened does explain why some are labeling him as a carpetbagger," wrote Baltimore County Blue.

## Disbarred: 'One Thousand Dollar Mistake'

What was worse for Joker's candidacy than the perception of being a carpetbagger was the fact of Joker's disbarment from the Maryland Bar.

His downfall came in 2008 when a couple who were his real estate clients reported Joker to the Maryland Attorney Grievance Commission for signing and depositing a $1,000 check into his own account that was made out to his clients. The incident resulted in Joker's disbarment in 2009 by the Court of Appeals of Maryland for "forging the endorsements" and "misappropriating the funds."

In a cautionary tale to other attorneys, the Baltimore law firm Belsky, Weinberg & Horowitz, LLC wrote, "The bottom line is that an attorney may never sign a client's name to a check or legal document without their express authority. That is basic law with a little common sense mixed in. This action was viewed as theft, as it very well might have been, and is just another example of how some will risk their careers over money."

Joker called the incident a "one thousand dollar mistake," a "misunderstanding" and "the worst thing that ever happened" to him.

The Court of Appeals did not buy Joker's contentions that the incident was a simple mistake or misunderstanding. The court found that, by "clear and convincing evidence," Joker violated several Rules of Professional Conduct for attorneys. In its findings, the court concluded that Joker "engaged in conduct involving dishonesty, fraud, deceit and misrepresentation."

But that wasn't enough for the judge who wrote that the court was "disheartened" by Joker's "rather cavalier attitude towards the facts, circumstances and these proceedings." Joker's apology to his clients, said the judge, was "late coming and appeared to be conditioned upon their forgiveness of him." The judge wrote that Joker "did not truly express any contrition or self-awareness of what had occurred in this matter" and that Joker complained about his clients as if they were conduct-ing "virtually a witch-hunt "against him. "These observations," the judge concluded, "are as disheartening" as Joker's inappropriate conduct with his clients.

As letter writers Stevens and Bowman alluded, it took hubris for Joker to run for office after his disbarment. After all, what level of self-confidence and desire for self-glorification would it take for a disbarred attorney who the court said was engaged in "dishonesty, fraud, deceit and misrepresentation" to ask the public to trust him as a lawmaker who will act in their best interests? Even if the court doled out an overly harsh judgment and punishment, wouldn't such a career and personal embar-rassment dissuade one from displaying their failure for all the public to judge in an election? I was amazed Joker would enter the race.

But in politics, where arrogance, deceit, self-aggrandizement, self-importance and extroversion are winning qualities and the rule, no indiscretion is insurmountable or discrediting. In fact, these days, politicians can wear their disgrace and demise as a badge of honor and claim it irrelevant to their commitment and ability to "fight" and "get things done" for "The American People." There is no com-punction for running again and asking for the public's support after dishonor and shame of even much higher magnitude than Joker's. Witness former South Carolina Governor Mark Sanford, who suppos-edly had disappeared from office to hike the Appalachian Trail when in actuality, he was indulging in an extramarital affair in Argentina, who went on to win a seat in Congress; or Eliot Spitzer, who was caught arranging a dalliance with a high-priced prostitute while on a business trip as governor of New York, who later ran for comptroller of New York City.

Joker was arrogant from the campaign's outset. He declared he was the "only one running with any experience" in the *Baltimore Sun*, which was true in the narrow sense of serving as a delegate in the legislature, even though I'm not sure how much advantage that would have conferred given that a generation had passed since his service.

He emphasized on his website, signs, billboards and campaign mailings that "Joker Gets It Done." Knowing how to "get things done" strikes me as one of the most overused, vague, annoying and meaningless political clichés designed to make the speaker appear competent and effective. What *things*? Whatever actually might have "gotten done" often might have had little to do with the claimant's efforts, ideas or initiative. How about all the things that don't get done in politics? Who accepts accountability for that?

I can't recall Joker ever emphasizing any one consequential thing he actually "got done" during his four years as a delegate. More accurately, he may have meant he knew how to manipulate the corrupt system and apply his influence and connections as a lobbyist to "get things done" for clients.

• • •

The *Maryland Reporter* displayed more boasting from Joker at his Alpha Male Fundraiser. The publication reported Joker said that Maryland House Speaker Michael Busch "wants me to win because he says I know how to count votes," an insider phrase presumably meaning that Joker would be a good henchman for the Speaker in influencing other legislators to line up behind the Speaker's agenda. That claim turned out to be dubious. In a follow-up, the *Maryland Reporter* quoted a Busch spokesperson confirming that "the Speaker has not endorsed anyone in District 12, nor will he before the primary."

One other obnoxious statement in the *Maryland Reporter* turned me off to Joker. Joker was quoted saying, "There are nine strong candidates. I think at least six are working hard."

Who was Joker, I wondered, to be the evaluator of who was "working hard?" Was Joker checking up on what each of the candidates were doing? Who were the three candidates who might not have been work-ing hard? I tried not to be offended, but I assumed I was likely one of the three slugs Joker considered a malingerer. The veiled Joker slight served as the proverbial throw-down on my coach's chalkboard. Like letter-writer Stevens, I was all about "Defeat Joker."

# November 28, 2013 – Spare-A-Dime Joins the Fray

We spent 2013 Thanksgiving at the house of my Uncle-in-Law Ted Levin, the five-term former Maryland state legislator who was running again to reclaim his old seat. Uncle Ted told me his independent law practice office suite mate and former campaign treasurer J. Bradley Goldberg was planning to run in my contest. He mentioned that Goldberg liked to talk about gun owners' rights.

The next day I campaigned door-to-door. I came to a voter listed as "Jerome Goldberg." An elderly man answered the door and I introduced myself as a candidate for delegate in District 12.

"I'm running against you," he said, eyeballing me from a step above.

I hadn't made the connection between the "Jerome Goldberg" on my voter registration list and the feisty "Brad Goldberg" to whom Uncle Ted referred. As soon as the man at the door threw down the gauntlet, I realized this was J. Bradley Goldberg, the new candidate.

## Tea Party Democrat

Goldberg, aka Spare-A-Dime, was a blessing or a curse—I couldn't predict which.

Spare-A-Dime was the 10th and final entry to the field, and another underfunded, unconnected longshot like me. Like me, he lived in Columbia, so his entry cut both ways. It diminished my chances of doing better on my home turf, because now Columbia residents who didn't support either Anointed One or Zelig had another choice of a local underdog. And as an 80-year-old who railed against government intrusion and high taxes that were driving businesses and retirees out of Maryland, Spare-A-Dime had an entrée to win support among his cohort of senior citizens, a big voting bloc, and libertarian-leaners. But I also realized that Spare-A-Dime would be the candidate easiest to beat, bolstering my chances to avoid finishing last, a prospect I simultaneously dreaded and used to fuel motivation.

I couldn't point to any of the other eight contenders and realistically say, "*I should beat that candidate.*" They all were stronger on paper, measured by their resources, experience, connections and endorsements. Spare-A-Dime I could point to as a fellow laggard with confidence. In fact, *I knew I should beat him,* and would be embarrassed if I didn't.

But who could say for sure? Spare-A-Dime staked out the far-right position of the Democrats, sounding positively Tea Party Republican, his anti-government, pro-business, pro-gun rights platform delivered in a cranky, folksy, unvarnished, unpolished style. I knew there would be a core of conservative Democratic voters—the old Reagan Democrats—attracted to his core principles.

Spare-A-Dime spoke often about working since he was 11 delivering newspapers (I delivered the *Washington Post* when I was 13 on dark, icy winter mornings, but I never mentioned that as a biographical asset!) and continuing to work as a lawyer when others his age were long into retirement, his implicit message that he resented government dipping into hard-working people's pockets overzealously to redistribute wealth and prop up bureaucracy.

Spare-A-Dime played the crotchety old candidate to the hilt with a mix of humor and old-fashioned sensibility. In response to a question about how the candidates would become familiar with such a diverse district, Spare-A-Dime pledged to give his cell phone number to anyone.

"Call me anytime," he told the audience. "Or you can text or e-mail me, but I won't answer, I'll only talk. But don't call me when I'm sleeping because I won't answer. Or if I do answer and talk to you, I won't remember anything anyway."

Speaking at a forum at a continuing care retirement community, Spare-A-Dime connected with the audience by saying he was as old as they were, but then added to laughs, "but not all of you."

In a newspaper interview introducing his candidacy, he declared that he was "not a 'yes man' and that "one of my problems is that I tell it the way it is." Spare-A-Dime spoke his truth—that is, when he showed up at campaign events.

Blogger Spartan Considerations highlighted Spare-A-Dime's unpredictable attendance and eccentricity in his analysis of a televised forum.

"Of course Spare-A-Dime was a no-show," Spartan wrote. "In substantive terms, that might have been the case had he occupied a chair on the stage last night...but writing that seems mean-spirited. I just haven't seen a legitimate rationale for his candidacy."

Even though Spare-A-Dime appeared the *far outlier* in the field—I also considered myself an outlier, but believed I still blended in more with the field—he did have bona fide credentials. He had been a lawyer for more than 50 years. He served as an Internal Revenue Service field agent, which perhaps explained his antipathy toward government taxation and intrusion. He was elected as judge of the Howard County Orphans' Court, which oversees the probate process for wills and estates.

· · ·

A t his door, I could tell that Spare-A-Dime was a big talker who offered opinions whether you wanted to hear them or not.

"What do you think about gun rights," Spare-A-Dime asked.

"I believe in reasonable gun controls," I responded.

"The Nazis made their own gun laws and confiscated all the guns from the Jews," Spare-A-Dime said. "Are you a Communist or a Socialist?"

"I wouldn't say either. How 'bout you?"

"I'm a *real* democrat, a 'small "d" democrat,'" Spare-A-Dime said. Spare-A-Dime told me he was just going to have fun during the campaign and he wasn't going to raise any money.

"When I ran for judge of the Orphans Court," Spare-A-Dime said, "somebody asked me how much money I was going to spend. I told him, 'Why would I spend any money?' He said you have to spend money to win an election. So I spent 10 cents, a dime, and I still won."

We walked together to visit a neighbor raking leaves.

"We're both running for delegate," Spare-A-Dime said.

"Oh yeah?" the neighbor responded. "That's great."

"Yeah, and I'm not going to spend a dime," Spare-A-Dime said, and launched into the story of his Orphans Court run.

Someone should have informed Spare-A-Dime that District 12 delegate was no obscure Orphans Court race.

## December 2, 2013 – Cold Reception for the Sachs for Delegate BikeMobile

With a Monday off from work, I took the Sachs for Delegate BikeMobile for its inaugural advertising ride. It was a dreary 30 degrees. I hit the road during morning rush hour and immediately felt under siege, naked and exposed on a bike with single-minded, stressed out, aggressive commuters roaring by me on busy roads with two or three lanes in each direction, with no shoulders or bike lanes in many places. It was treacherous; I felt I was risking my life. I rode on main commuter arteries and through neighborhood connector roads for an hour-and-a-half, arriving home wet and cold, with nearly numb feet and hands. I knew Columbia's roads were not cyclist-friendly—the town's architects planned for cyclists to ride on Columbia's network of paths through the woods, not on its main streets—but my ride was eye-opening for its danger and reminded me why I had always avoided cycling in the area. It was good fodder for my published letter to the editor to the *Columbia Flier*.

"In such a progressive and environmentally-conscious community, cyclists shouldn't have to take their life in their own hands," I wrote. "Columbia should be a model along with Seattle and Boulder, encouraging cycling for recreation and as a commuting and transportation mode to reduce vehicle congestion and pollution. More cyclists would travel by bike for errands and to visit Columbia's amenities if it were safer."

# December 6, 2013 – Energy of the Party

The Southwest Baltimore County Democratic Club Holiday Party provided a chance for all the candidates to take a break from battling each other and get to know each other better as real people, not just rivals, in a more relaxed and social environment.

I talked to Energy, and learned that he was a fiddler who played in a local band at neighborhood pubs and street festivals. The fiddle seemed the right instrument for Energy; I could envision Energy working the bow frantically across the strings, beads of sweat forming across his brow and steaming his glasses.

## Erik Everson: Erik Energy

Throughout my two kids' elementary school years, I attended several educational assemblies where an energetic science whiz would perform interactive, cool experiments with dry ice, air blasts, pressurized containers, lasers, and electricity to the beat of pulsating music that taught the kids about heat, cold, light, sound, pressure and energy. He went by the name Eric Energy.

Flash forward, I found myself running against another Erik Energy, who went by the name of Erik Everson. Energy was Energetic and Engaging. The 55-year-old lifelong Catonsville resident was an Educator, a 33-year high school math teacher. The mathematician opened his speeches, naturally, with numbers, telling the audience there were two meaningful ones in his life: 55 (years living in the district) and 33 (years teaching in the district). Apparently he took delight that they were each divisible by 11.

Energy had an affinity for *Es*. In his campaign materials and speeches, Energy emphasized that his focus was on Education, Economy, and Environment. His handout literature trumpeted "Elect Erik Everson." Expanding on the alliteration, Energy proclaimed at forums that his guiding political principle boiled down to one word: Equity. What an Egalitarian!

Energy had a touch of 'gee whiz, Wally' boyish charisma of a grown-up Beaver Cleaver. Another word reflective of Energy: Earnest.

Energy, who held a master's in math Education, taught at three high schools in Howard County, including District 12's premier school. The math teacher got a big boost in his campaign not only from his wife, a PhD Educator who was always by his side, but from his trio of kids in their 20s. His son served as campaign manager, and daughters as campaign treasurer and field organizer.

Energy called his campaign "a family affair," with its evident Esprit de corps. His son said the team Effort "proves you can affect government in a positive way." Sounds like Energy approached his campaign like a collaborative Experiential learning school project, with his family members taking what they had learned in an Advanced Placement classroom and applying it in the field. I was Envious of the Effort of Energy's family Entourage.

Another of Energy's big advantages was his involvement in both District 12 counties. That "dual citizenship" was crucial for the crossover votes all candidates needed.

Energy was nearly my Equal in several ways—age, fatherhood, political inexperience. But as for the race, we were far from Even; Energy had a big Edge.

• • •

At the Democratic Holiday Party, I struck up a conversation with Next Big Thing's wife.

"Do you have a campaign manager?" she asked.

"No, I'm just trying to figure it out as I go," I said. "Are you going to a lot of the campaign events?"

"I'm going to as much as I can," she said. "People don't understand how grueling it is to be a candidate. You take a lot of abuse on yourself and your relationships. People don't know how much work and time goes into it."

"Yeah, really, it's hard to know unless you're in it," I said, appreciating her empathy. I liked her right away, which only strengthened my positive intuition about Next Big Thing.

Next Big Thing came by and shook my hand earnestly and we shared a few words as he and his wife got ready to leave. That meeting in a more sociable environment confirmed the impression I had made of Next Big Thing at the forums. He was approachable and didn't seem maniacal or cutthroat about the campaign process, though I knew he was going all out to win and playing the game.

• • •

On the other hand, I still couldn't crack Zelig's competitive and driven shell. Zelig walked past me a few times around the food table at the party and didn't say hello or acknowledge me. Neither did I him, playing the competitive game also. At one point when we were both in each other's space and not moving anywhere, we each said hello and shook hands. Zelig quickly moved on. Zelig seemed goal-focused and intent on scoring points no matter where he was or what he was doing. Everything, every encounter and every place had a purpose.

My first impressions of Zelig after I had become a candidate and we appeared at several events together were decidedly chilly, at least in our interpersonal interactions, which were minimal. There's no rule that competing candidates have to be friendly. Still, I felt more connection to some other candidates and more good will coming from them.

I knew Zelig was smart, knowledgeable, diligent and well-prepared, and had observed he had abundant capacity to be sociable and conversational—just, apparently, not with me. To me, he seemed aloof and unfriendly. Maybe that was because, even though I was a big underdog, any votes I could muster from our mutual home territory potentially could take away his.

# ZELIG

**Z**elig, a 33-year-old physician, campaigned longer and harder than anyone. When popular Delegate Drummer announced her retirement in 2012, two years before the next election, Zelig was already on the radar, along with Anointed One, as a possible successor.

Zelig was like Leonard Zelig, the title character of the Woody Allen "mockumentary" *Zelig* about a person who shows up everywhere at historical events and with famous people, ingratiates himself with everyone, and blends in with any group in any circumstance.

Zelig was the classic overachiever and over-doer, the type who left no stone unturned and nothing to chance. He was thorough, relentless and indefatigable. I could swear he was cryogenically frozen for preservation every night so he wouldn't have to waste time sleeping. He had the zeal of a missionary.

I was seeing a therapist during my candidacy as part of my master's degree in counseling. I often talked with Counselor Bob about the highs and lows and indignities of the campaign, and how I didn't have the level of dedication, determination, or desire that made Zelig a frontrunner.

"Zelig came to my house and talked to my wife," said Counselor Bob. "Then he came back and met me, and he told me about concerns my wife had told him. I was really impressed he not only visited a second time, but he remembered what my wife said."

"Yeah, sounds like Zelig," I said.

"He's damn tenacious," said Counselor Bob. We laughed at his apt description.

Just after the primary election, Counselor Bob volunteered that the Zelig campaign had returned to his house the day before the election and left a "Remember to Vote" card. We shook our heads and chuckled. Tenacious indeed.

It wasn't only my therapist who vouched for Zelig's tenacity and comprehensiveness. My former neighbor Peggy said Zelig asked her if he could put a sign in her yard. Peggy agreed, even though that was their first meeting. (If you want to win bad enough, you ask *everyone for everything*—lawn-sign postings, money, volunteer work, sign-wavers, in-kind services, phone-banking, donuts and coffee, back rubs, whatever winning calls for. That was a shortcoming of mine—*asking*—but not of Zelig.)

Peggy said Zelig returned to the neighborhood on his Segway, visiting her a second time, just like he did Counselor Bob. I can only wonder how many times the Zelig team double-dipped.

Zelig used Twitter to document his event appearances, describe the importance of each activity, announce endorsements and highlight his canvassing prowess. Such self-promotion wasn't unique to Zelig. Candidates for all levels of political offices glommed onto Twitter as their campaign diary and photographic journal, no matter how obscure the event or trivial the accomplishment. Some just milked it more than others, and Zelig was one who squeezed hard from Twitter's teat. One day at a math festival, the next at a dog park opening, with a watershed stewards' meeting in between. It exhausted me just to review his Twitter feed. The Spartan Considerations blog determined Zelig "must have a teleporter" because he was ubiquitous.

It was a great strategy but hard for mere mortals to execute: get to know everyone, take an interest in everything and be everywhere. That's the mark of a good campaigner. I didn't have time—or more honestly, didn't want to make the time—to show up as consistently as Zelig did. It's not logic or rule that is best applied to these political matters; it's emotion. And if you're there, by default, you care about the same things your constituents do. That's "retail politics" at its finest. And that's one big reason why Zelig was always a frontrunner, and would never relax enough to let someone catch him or outwork him.

If he wasn't cryogenically frozen nightly, Zelig couldn't have slept more than three hours a night with all of his volunteer and political activities, not to mention his day job as director of the preventive medicine residency program at Johns Hopkins University (though a Zelig campaign insider confided to me that Zelig didn't actually work full-time as a physician during his campaign. Apparently, Zelig was not exempt from the laws of time.)

Zelig was typical of state legislators featured in *First Person Political*, who demonstrated a "deeply felt commitment to civic engagement" and "were already dramatically different from most other citizens; in civic terms, they were already carrying a much larger size bucket of the public's water."

Zelig's bucket might as well have been an above-ground swimming pool.

While in medical school, Zelig interned in Congress, working on health oversight investigations. A common slacker may reasonably ask, "Was not medical school enough? Too easy? Time to kill?"

"Enough" was not in Zelig's vocabulary. He multi-tasked by serving in volunteer leadership positions with the Democratic Central Committee, a Young Democrats club, a Community Action Council, a state Asian-American organization, a health care program and his village association—*simultaneously!*

Topping off his eye-popping, multi-dimensional resume, Zelig served on the legislative staff of Maryland Delegate Daniel Morhaim, a physician like Zelig.

Zelig played up his experience as a legislative assistant, telling audiences that he worked for "Delegate Doctor Dan Morhaim," Every time he mentioned it, I couldn't help but think of legless, alcoholic, whore-mongering Vietnam vet "Lieutenant Dan" wobbling around and falling overboard *Forrest Gump's* shrimp fishing boat.

## Insiders' Strut

I saw Zelig at several early campaign season fundraisers for the most popular Democratic candidates. He always dressed the part, sticking to his campaign hue palette of purple and yellow shirts with lettering identifying himself as "DR. Zelig, Democrat for State Delegate," and jackets emblazoned with his campaign insignia and black pants, or dark suits.

I observed Zelig felt comfortable and familiar with the insiders. He smiled and laughed a lot, like the politicians I observed, and was always engaged in conversation. Yes, he had already perfected the confident Insiders' Strut, doubtless from all the practice he had accumulated from years of attending community events where insiders, movers and shakers congregated.

Zelig was a prolific recruiter and door-to-door campaigner, with an army of volunteers and a high-tech approach. He used an I-Pad for his walking list, and cruised neighborhoods while canvassing on a Segway Human Transporter. One older woman, in a stereotypical and politically incorrect comment, told me that Zelig had visited her, riding his Segway. "You know those Asians," she said. "They love technology."

Even Zelig's volunteers were high-caliber, high achievers. One weekend morning, when I had just gotten out of bed around 11, I answered a knock at my door. It was a Zelig volunteer, canvassing with an I-Pad. The Zelig Team made my method of scribbling notes on Steno Notebook paper look positively primeval.

The Zelig volunteer, a woman of maybe 30, was an OB/GYN doctor at Johns Hopkins Hospital who had met Zelig in medical school. The OB/GYN's visit illuminated a major difference in our campaigns: Zelig was getting people who deliver babies for a living to go door-to-door for him, and I was struggling to recruit my daughter's friend a year out of high school.

Competing against a real-life avatar like *Zelig*—everywhere, with everybody, doing everything, all the time—would be, I knew, damn near impossible.

# DECEMBER 8, 2013 -- A DRIVING TOUR: BALTIMORE COUNTY'S LEVITTOWN

*"Don't Come Around Here No More."*

TOM PETTY, ROCK MUSICIAN

With 40 percent of the nearly 40,000 Democratic registered voters in District 12 living in Baltimore County, I had to familiarize myself with the area, so I took a driving tour with Amy. What I saw were older neighborhoods that were probably bright and shiny and full of the promise of suburban prosperity, homogeneity and security in the 1950s and 60s—closeby havens from the growing ills and advancing decay of Baltimore City for the working class—with a preponderance of pickup trucks parked in the driveways, and plastic Jesuses and Marys and nativity scenes and blow-up plastic Christmas lawn decorations lining squared front yards and cookie-cutter homes. Since more than 40 percent of houses in the 21227 ZIP Code were built between 1940 and 1959, the concepts guiding the inner suburb's growth probably were similar to those of Levittown, the Long Island, NY community built for returning World War II veterans that is considered the first veritable mass-produced suburb and is widely regarded as the archetype for 20th century American suburbs and a symbol of the "American Dream."

Route 1, with its inescapable schlock, mish-mosh of building styles and uses, pockmarks of vacant properties and soul-deadening, cluttered aesthetics, bisects the area, so we cruised it several times, finding all that makes Route 1 iconic from Maine to Florida: an impromptu Saturday flea market selling furniture, paintings and lawn equipment fronting a Burger King and an Auto Factory; several abandoned houses, garages and businesses looking lonesome in a row across from a 16-gas pump Royal Farms convenience store; and a full range of consumer options, from Bad Boys Bail Bonds to the Beltway Motel to Chappie's Diner Bar & Grill.

At the end of our tour, Amy gave me her blunt opinion about my chances to make deep inroads in Baltimore County's 21227: "Don't even bother campaigning in this area at all," she advised. "Please don't go door-to-door here. It's just not your place, you're not going to get anywhere. You have enough to cover in Howard County."

Amy is a safety freak; she always thinks of dangers that never occur to me. She was worried for my safety going door-to-door in this area. She subscribed to my firefighter friend's assessment that some neighborhoods were "raw." However, nothing about the neighborhoods worried me at all. It looked like throwback American bedrock. Even though I knew Amy was right that my campaign wouldn't even be able to adequately cover my home turf and that I was a mismatch in the 21227, I was annoyed by the insinuation that I couldn't connect with the 21227's people. Wasn't a good politician supposed to be able to connect with anyone and everyone, like a Mother Teresa or a Mahatma Gandhi in a dark suit with an American flag on the lapel? When politicians pronounce what "The American People" want and need, and that they will "fight for you" to "get things done," they are including the residents of 21227 also, aren't they?

I wasn't just going to give up because this area would be a harder sell. I would immerse myself more in the community's culture and ambiance a few weeks later.

# December 14, 2013 – Maybe I Should Run for Dog Catcher

Sometimes, just by campaigning door-to-door and being on the streets, you may observe something that helps out a stranger.

That happened on the same wintry day I found myself trailing Zelig. By the time I finished canvassing and was pedaling the Sachs For Delegate BikeMobile home, I was caught in a heavy snow. As I took a shortcut through the 7-Eleven parking lot, I noticed a black dog wandering and preoccupied with scavenging for food. I concluded he was lost but not a stray, because he had a collar and seemed docile and friendly. I dismounted my bike and tried to get him to come to me, but he wouldn't.

I called 911 and asked for animal control. The dispatcher said she would send police. I tracked the dog around the 7-Eleven for 15 minutes, but police didn't show up and the dog wandered away to the adjacent elementary school, then ran away.

I rode my bike in the direction the dog headed. I located him a quarter-mile away at a condo complex, rummaging around a metal trash bin, enclosed on three sides with a wooden fence. There was a big tube TV outside the bin. I moved the TV to block the opening and trapped the dog.

With the police nowhere in sight, I called Amy, asking her to go home and get a leash and dog food and come to meet me. I calmed the dog enough to get his collar off to find a rabies tag number to give to animal control. Animal control found the dog owner's phone number.

I called the owner and described my location. She arrived 10 minutes later.

"You crazy dog," she barked at the dog, like the dog disappeared on a regular basis, and ordered him in the car. The dog complied. The woman thanked me, but did not seem upset that the dog went missing in a snowstorm, and drove away.

Still, I felt I had done a good deed for the day. Because I was campaigning, I was in the right place at the right time to save a dog from possibly being hit and killed by a car on a slick road, or going lost. Amy showed up a minute after the dog owner left; all I could offer was a heartwarming story for her effort.

# When One Door Closes, Another Door Opens (or, Remembering UNICEF Days)

*"Pretend that every single person you meet has a sign around his or her neck that says, 'Make me feel important.' Not only will you succeed in sales, you will succeed in life."*

Mary Kay Ash, founder of Mary Kay Cosmetics

Politicians love to say how much they enjoy knocking on doors and talking to constituents on their doorsteps about their hopes and concerns. They're lying. Nobody likes it. One could say the politicians are the same as the youths who do the low-paid grunt work for home improvement, vinyl siding and window replacement companies by drumming up sales door-to-door, or the religious missionaries, Jehovah's Witnesses, Latter Day Saints Mormons and the like selling salvation on the doorstep through Jesus Christ pamphlets: Politicians are seeking an exchange of money for potential future political services and trying to persuade a conversion to their ideological denomination.

But politicians have to say they love going door-to-door, because they have to love people, and if they love people, that means they have to love meeting *all people* and listening to *everything* people say. And it's a rare bird who could say they love that.

There are rare birds who are exceptions, who truly do enjoy trudging through dull, repetitive suburban landscapes like the mailman in freezing temperatures, rain, snow, ice, heat and humidity to knock each door, and wait with a pleasant smile plastered on their face and an out-stretched hand carrying the "lit drop" campaign material, for whoever may answer, if anyone.

I did not know Wendy Royalty well, but she may have fit in this "rare bird" category. Royalty was a candidate for Howard County Council who I met at several political events. She seemed perky, energetic and posi-tive, and couldn't ask for a name better suited for a position of political power than "Royalty."

On one of the first days of spring 2014, she posted to Twitter a photo of herself in sunglasses and smiling, opening a storm door on the preci-pice of meeting a potential voter. Her message said: "I think my two favorite things about campaigning are the canvassing and the house par-ties. I love meeting people at their doorstep…"

I wanted to puke. While Royalty's pronouncement may have been authentic, I would bet that the politicians that secretly hate going door-to-door the most are the ones who go overboard by maintaining a ma-niacal door-to-door schedule and who publicly announce scorecards, revealing how many doors they've knocked on and how many people they've talked to over what period of time, even how many days and hours they've spent doing it. They approach it like a machine, an as-sembly line worker making a quota or a workaholic alone in a darkened building, office light on. They wear their home-visitation prowess as a candidate's badge of honor, an indication of how badly they want to succeed and achieve their goal, like the people who offhandedly let the world know how busy they are by describing their incredible volume of activities that the lesser among us couldn't juggle, or how hard they work by noting their 60-hour work weeks in a way that makes the 40-hour worker seem a slacker.

# Trailing Zelig and Likely on My Way to Slaughter

None other than Zelig made me feel like a door-to-door slacker with his high-volume production. During a series of candidates' forums in winter and early spring 2014, when the weather was miserable, Zelig would announce that he had increased his door-knocking count by an increment of 1,000. So at each successive forum over a two-month period he would say, "We've knocked on 6,000 doors," then 7,000, 8,000 and 9,000 until he announced the 10,000 milestone. By the time Zelig hit 9,000, like a goosed stock on the New York Stock Exchange, his predictable and regimented increases had become a running joke with Amy. When he announced that nice, round next thousandth, I glanced at Amy in the audience from the candidates' dais and we both grinned.

On one of the first decent weather weekend days in March 2014, Zelig took to Twitter to post a photo of himself walking between houses wearing his purple "DR. Zelig for Delegate" shirt, and announced "500+ voters canvassed this weekend by our amazing team of campaign volunteers: Katrina, Scott, Jeff, Eric, Ken, & Sarah." Five hundred voters equaled a strong two months of winter canvassing for me. In another post, he rattled off four communities his team had canvassed in one day, essentially comprising all the major communities in both the Howard and Baltimore County portions of the district. In other words, he was everywhere. Zelig.

Hey, I knocked on a lot of doors as a third grader just before Halloween, carrying my orange UNICEF Fundraising box to collect dimes for starving children in Africa. Did I feel the need to announce my dedication and production to the world? Well, maybe to my teacher.

I have no doubt that Zelig was not exaggerating his accumulation of doors. I saw Zelig, or evidence of his and his many volunteers' presence, a number of times and more than any other candidate during my door-to-door forays. Of course, I was always a few steps behind him.

On one cold, wintry Saturday with snow in the forecast, I went canvassing on the Sachs For Delegate BikeMobile. At one house, a man mentioned that another candidate had just come by. The next house I visited, I found a brochure in the door with a note: "Bowen Family— Sorry I missed you—Zelig." I was on Zelig's trail. That had to be a good sign. At several more doors I found Zelig's brochure with a similar individually tailored note to the occupants. Of course, I was being outdone by Zelig. I wasn't bothering to spend the time in sub-freezing temperatures to write personalized notes to those who weren't home. I just placed my small card in the storm door, in proximity to Zelig's, and hoped people might think we were running as a team.

On another outing, as I approached a neighborhood, I saw numerous dreaded purple and yellow shirts, foot soldiers of the Zelig Machine, and several Dr. Zelig lawn signs being erected for an event. Of all the neighborhoods in District 12, with a total population of 120,000 and about 40,000 registered Democrats, what were the odds that I would come across Team Zelig on multiple occasions?

On Mother's Day 2014, I was on Zelig's trail again. This guy was always a step—more like 10 giant leaps—ahead of me. I arrived at my target neighborhood around noon. Of course, Team Zelig was on the job ahead of me, oblivious to Mother's Day breakfast in bed. One of the first houses I visited had a Zelig pamphlet in the door with a note saying, "Sorry I missed you, hope I have your support on June 24."

My next stomping ground was about two miles away. To my simultaneous consternation and amusement, I spied Zelig himself in his campaign uniform of black pants and purple monogrammed shirt, canvassing the neighborhood. He was stationed outside one house writing a note while I cruised in on my bike and quickly out again to an adjacent neighborhood to stake out my own territory and avoid direct competition. Maybe that was chicken-ass, but as entertainers say about superior performers, Zelig was a tough act to follow.

• • •

Starting before Thanksgiving 2013, as the weather was turning its ugliest, I walked and biked over the next seven months to 1,307 homes to greet potential voters, some days bundled in boots, long johns, and ski jacket, hat and gloves over ice-covered streets and driveways, others in shorts in 90 degrees and humidity, sweat-soaked shirt plastered to my back. Of the 1,307 homes I visited, I made contact with a human at 678, or 52 percent. So essentially, if you're a candidate who has a goal of *actually meeting* a certain number of voters at the door, you have to double the number of homes you will visit to hit your target. Unfortunately, I didn't have an army of volunteers to multiply the impact of my efforts, like Team Zelig.

I wanted to visit 2,000 homes, but a combination of failure of will, lack of time and energy, and the early darkness that fell for most months of my canvassing conspired to keep me short of the goal. Truth be told, if I were more driven and wanted it more badly—in other words, if I had more Zelig in me—I would have easily cleared 2,000. But it would have required me to double my average of two to four hours per day, not including travel time from home to and from my target area when I canvassed by bike. Taking into account that you can't bang on doors too early on weekend days unless you want sleep-deprived, hungover or irate residents to answer, such an increase in time would have accounted for all the daylight hours from winter through early spring, which I wasn't willing to give over to wandering desolate suburban streets to meet strangers.

Knowing I could only personally visit a small percentage of the 40,000 registered Democratic voters in the district, I narrowed my target list to those who had voted in the previous two gubernatorial primaries, assuming those who had voted most consistently in non-presidential election primaries in 2006 and 2010 would be the most likely to come to the polls for the 2014 primary. That strategy also meant that homes on my list were further apart, requiring more travel time to reach fewer homes rather than just banging on every Democrats' door.

Still, I was proud of my effort and production, given the daily motivation necessary to hit the bricks when I could have been sitting home on the couch under a warm blanket eating chips and salsa and watching NFL games or the NCAA basketball tournament. I made 65 door-to-door outings, usually reaching between 20 and 40 homes per trip, depending on what percentage of residents were home, the length of conversations, and the distance between homes and neighborhoods.

There were times I found my encounters with voters at their doors uplifting and entertaining, certain conversations where I connected immediately with somebody and enjoyed their company for a fleeting time, or came across somebody with a similar passion for one of my core issues or principles. I recognized that nothing may persuade a voter more than showing up at their door. However, I wondered: How many homes did I visit whose occupants didn't bother to vote?

## Where's the 'Hail Fellow Well Met?'

Going door-to-door was drudgery, a chore, busywork, a "should." Apparently, I was unable to hide that well, wrote the former political strategist Booms on his Spartan Considerations blog. Booms captured the feelings and spirit of my door-to-door journey— indeed, the whole campaign adventure—so well after my visit at his door on a dreary March afternoon, I couldn't have written it better myself.

Booms began his post about our encounter: "You have to have a certain admiration for the well-intentioned doomed."

Booms said he recognized me on his welcome mat:

> "He greeted me with a wan smile. There was a mixture of nervousness and hope frozen on his face... an expression that would not be out of place on the countenance of an inexperienced and introverted missionary.
>
> "He started winding up, about to launch into his elevator pitch, when I told him that I had seen him speak a couple of times and was familiar with his platform. That seemed to drop his anxiety level down a notch. However, his visage sagged when I told him I wouldn't be voting for him...Nothing personal, strictly the business of democracy.
>
> "We exchanged thoughts on the campaign for a moment and I wished him well with his door-to-door efforts. He flashed a seemingly sincere grin, waved goodbye and began the trudge over to the neighbor's house.

*"He was not a natural candidate by any means. There was little sign of the 'Hail fellow well met' spirit in him...that sense that he enjoys the campaign process: talking with strangers, listening to their hopes and fears, and asking them for their support. Perhaps he did, but if so, he hid it well. And if he was hiding it...why choose that mask?*

*"Of course that is exactly the point. It wasn't a mask. It was, or appeared to be, his authentic self. He was running for the cause, not for self-aggrandizement, not as a stepping-stone to even higher office. That last point is key because he has almost no chance of winning. Importantly, I believe he knows that too.*

*"Yet in the face of that...he chose to subject himself to the rigors of electioneering. He chose to give up his weekends and evenings to lurch from one doorstep to the next, gripping and grinning...All because he wants to advocate for a set of public policy solutions that fit with his conception of how best to promote the common good.*

*"The good news is that such people choose to seek elective office. He isn't alone...Some will win, he won't.*

*"As I look back on that conversation...I believe what impressed me most was his respect for the democratic process. He was willing to endure the discomfort of campaigning and the near-certainty of defeat because of his belief that reform is possible...It may not happen soon, but perhaps in the future. And that is enough for him to knock on doors...*

*"You have to respect that."*

## A Box of Chocolates

Campaigning door-to-door reminded me of the pearl of wisdom from *Forrest Gump*: "Life was like a box of chocolates. You never know what you're gonna get."

My most bizarre door-to-door encounter actually came during my 2006 county council race. An elderly man, around 75, answered the door shirtless. Even though his address was listed in my voting records as a Democrat's, the man asked whether I was a Democrat or

Republican and seemed perturbed when I answered Democrat. The man came out of the door menacingly toward me as I backed down the steps and into the driveway. Then, to my amazement, he challenged me to a fight, and put up his dukes in a Muhammad Ali-like pose. I thought he might have been kidding, but he wasn't. Mental illness? I wasn't taking any chances. I kept backing up, and tried to calm him down. "Hey man, I'm just running for county council," I said. "No need to fight about it, I'll just move on to the next house. Take it easy, man." I was half-laughing at the sight of the shirtless, sagging old man with fists at the ready, and a little shaken. You never know what's behind closed doors.

Some people you meet at the door believe anyone running for any office is omnipotent and can and should fix any problem, oblivious that there are different levels of representation with jurisdiction over different matters. When I asked one couple about their concerns, they didn't bring up taxes or education or crime. *But they did give a crap.* They complained vociferously about the Porta-Potties clearly visible behind their house, placed there for a school renovation project, and just what was I going to do to get them removed, or at least redecorated in more pleasing architectural design and color.

There were several other unusual occurrences during my door-to-door travails, like the time I almost found myself arrested.

## Criminal in the 'Hood

I was in a neighborhood full of politicos, including retiring Delegate Drummer, District 12 frontrunner Anointed One, the former Howard County schools superintendent and the president of the Columbia Democratic Club. I couldn't have been in safer territory for political activity.

I was campaigning on bike, entering a group of townhouses at the end of the street, when I noticed a police car coming behind me. I thought it odd for the cruiser to be heading to the end of a street with no outlet. I parked my bike, preparing to walk to a home. The police car stopped alongside me.

"We got a call about you."

"What? About me?" I responded. Then it occurred to me that I wasn't wearing a bike helmet. I had left it in the bike trailer while I was in the neighborhood visiting homes. I thought that might have been why the officer stopped me. I pointed to my helmet, but the officer wasn't interested.

"Have you been going to people's doors?" he asked.

"Yes."

"Have you been asking for money or soliciting?" the officer asked, explaining that people who solicit door-to-door need county approval and must carry identification.

"No, I'm a candidate, I'm campaigning. I don't ask for money. Someone called?"

"Yes," the officer said. He showed me the computer screen in his car indicating the address from which the police call originated, a home that I had visited within the last 15 minutes.

"People in this neighborhood are sensitive. The area around this neighborhood has had some problems," the officer said. "They're worried about robberies. They think you might be casing their homes and coming back later to rob them."

He said I needed a better way to identify myself as a political candidate.

I pointed to my bike, with big yellow signs attached to the trailer on three sides with the blue lettering announcing "Sachs For Delegate."

"Doesn't that identify me?"

"They might not see that," the officer said.

I didn't know where this was going, whether I had broken any laws of which I was unaware or whether this officer, pleasant and respectful to this point, was about to crack down on me like a hard-ass cop, drop me face down on the asphalt, cuff me and step on my back (Political Candidates' Lives Matter Too!). I started to mollify him more.

"My wife ordered a candidate's name badge, but I haven't gotten it yet in the mail. I also have a delegate t-shirt, but it was too cold today."

"A badge would be better," the officer said. "Do you have any identification?"

My worry meter spiked.

"Well, I didn't bring my driver's license because I was riding a bike. I have an ATM card. Will that work?"

"No." The officer studied me.

Sure, a name badge might have offered more identification. But it's still unofficial. Any simpleton thief could make up a badge and a t-shirt and pretend he's a candidate while casing a joint to rob it later. If law enforcement really wanted candidates to be identifiable, why wouldn't government give us a form of official political candidate identification that would be hard to fabricate so doubters would have more faith that we were legitimate when we showed up at their door?

Concerned I might be nailed as part of a counterfeit candidate sting, I made a final plea to the officer that I wouldn't be out in the cold going door-to-door on a bike with signs if I weren't a candidate. To my relief, the officer appeared to believe me, and was probably more annoyed by the callers who wasted his time.

When I felt more assured that I wouldn't be spending the night in a jail holding cell for suspicious electioneering, I told the officer I was planning to go to three more houses on my list, then leave the neighborhood, and asked if that would be alright. He gave me the go-ahead. I approached a house with the police car still lurking by the sidewalk, feeling like a criminal, or that the person answering might think I was there to rob them. I had observed enough in my canvassing outings to know that many people truly are scared and distrustful.

After I finished visiting the three homes, I checked out the address the officer had shown me and remembered the encounter. It turned out that the house that made the police call was one of my more friendly and conversational encounters of the day. Perhaps I appeared to the resident to be trying to get too much information about their names, and she got spooked. I had intuitively sensed that the people listed as residents no longer lived there and that I was talking to a new dweller. But I had no indication at the door that the resident was worried or thought I was a criminal. In fact, as I left, I offered, "And thank you for being so friendly."

## Fear and Loathing

We live in an age when many people are afraid to answer their door, when people are isolated more than ever and live their lives almost entirely inside—in homes, cars and offices—interacting with technology much more frequently than with people and the natural world. Suburban neighborhoods today are veritable ghost towns compared to the way previous generations grew up.

I experienced that isolation and lack of activity outdoors during my door-to-door travails. It was normal to walk or bike through neighborhoods for two or three hours and barely see another human outside.

Many times, residents would yell through a closed door as a preferred method of conversing or talk to me through an open upstairs window when I came to introduce myself. One older woman opened her door only a crack, telling me normally she wouldn't answer at all because it wasn't safe. She snatched my card quickly and closed the door.

Some neighborhoods in Columbia that were once recognized as fine communities when they were built in the 1960s and early 1970s had become rundown, and were considered mini-ghettoes. There certainly seemed to be more suspicion and caution in these neighborhoods that had seen better days. One was across the street from the community where I was stopped by police—the kind of neighborhood from the proverbial "wrong side of the tracks" that the officer said residents feared because of crime. In this downtrodden neighborhood, an older woman opened her door and immediately waved me away through the screen door and closed the door in my face. This type of greeting wasn't common, but happened often enough to be disturbing and to signal an increasing distance, distrust and disconnection in our communities.

It was understandable that some people would be reluctant to answer their door, bombarded as we are with telemarketers, sales pitchers, fund-raisers and proselytizers. They're tired of interruptions and shaking their head no. I felt the brunt of their annoyance regularly during my canvassing, not only from the "Don't Knock, He's Dead" woman.

One woman, as soon as she opened her main door, said through the screen door she wasn't interested in tree service, lawn care or siding, trying to cover all the bases of frequent solicitors.

One home I visited had a note on the door saying, "We do not buy from door-to-door salesmen. We do not sign petitions." I knocked anyway. Ironically, this homeowner was the only one who invited me inside to talk on a day with blowing snow and a foot on the ground.

That man's warning note was rather tame compared to another one I encountered, deciding in this case that discretion was the better part of valor and leaving without knocking. A yellow sign in the door's window frame read: "NO soliciting, NO canvassing, NO petitioning, NO begging, NO witnessing...You get the idea."

Another house had a homemade note on the door that said "Nap Time." I didn't ring. I treasure a solid nap also.

A door slammed in my face was a relatively rare occurrence, the reaction of the downright rude and nasty.

One of those jerks was a man with a goatee and big turkey wattle hanging from his neck. I introduced myself at his doorstep as a candidate for delegate.

"Good for you," he said.

I thought he might have been dripping with sarcasm, but I pressed on. I wasn't going to leave any potential votes on the street, given all the time and energy I was spending wandering through the suburban wilderness. I briefly explained my purpose in running.

"There's more information about the ideas I'm supporting on this card and my website," I said, and offered it to him.

"I don't need it," he said, and shut the door.

Another woman simply held up her hand, palm open, arm outstretched, in the universal symbol for "STOP" as I was introducing myself, as if I was a kindergartner crossing the road without looking both ways, and without saying a word, closed her door.

One time I decided to see how far I could get through persistence with a dismissive person. When I rang the doorbell, a lady barked at me through a closed window. I tried to explain who I was through the glass and showed my new candidate's badge to prove my legitimacy. Then I just stood there, wouldn't leave. My persistence broke her down, but apparently didn't win me a vote. She finally opened the door, but refused to take the card from my outstretched hand, saying, "I'm really not interested." Refusing to take no for an answer, I asked if I could give her my card. "No," she replied, and went back inside. I lost the battle of wills.

Some people just had no appreciation for the drudgery that's required on the candidate's part, and the toleration required on the voter's part. Yes, dear constituents, we do need to bother you because that's how American politics works, that's the American Way. So buck up, *take my card*, and go back to sipping your coffee!

## You Just Owe

When you are in the midst of it, weeknights until dusk and weekend upon weekend, you sometimes wonder if banging on all these doors is really worthwhile. One constituent told me in no uncertain terms it wasn't.

I knew this constituent's husband from my days covering Columbia for the *Baltimore Sun*. He was a government and politics professor and a village board member who frequently commented on Columbia's unorthodox governance by homeowners' association.

His wife bemoaned why anyone would want to subject themselves to a political campaign and involvement in politics and expressed sympathy for my endeavor.

"In politics, you owe, you just owe," she said. "It's pounding your head against a brick wall. All this time and energy you put in to go to people's houses and all this stuff you have to do just to run and earn loyalty is wasteful. Instead of knocking on doors, you could really get stuff done."

There was truth in her viewpoint. Trouble was, to get any "stuff" done in politics, you had to get on the inside. And for an outsider to get on the inside took a Herculean effort of doing lots of "stuff" over and over, and doing significantly more and smarter "stuff" than your opponents. And in my case, I knew almost all of my District 12 opponents were doing tons of the "stuff" you need to do to get elected. And that included pounding the "stuff" out of doors.

## Familiar Faces

Occasionally I ran into people I knew, and sometimes didn't even know that I knew. One woman recognized me, but didn't know from where. I couldn't place her either, though she looked vaguely familiar.

"Do you have a son?" she asked.

"Yes." Still no idea.

"Did he attend Phelps Luck Elementary School?" she asked.

Bingo! It was my son Daniel's third grade teacher from seven years previous.

Another house on my canvassing list triggered nostalgia. It belonged to former National Basketball Association sweet-shooting All-Star Phil Chenier, who I idolized as a fan of the Washington Bullets in the 1970s. When I was a seventh-grader, Chenier appeared at a basketball camp I attended, and took a photo with me that I kept for decades. Now I was visiting my boyhood idol's home as a 50-year-old to seek his vote.

When I encountered someone I knew, I had to be prepared to spend more time than normal. That happened when I came upon the Silvers.

I was going to skip this house because there was a large porch that blocked access to the front door. But then a woman came through the door. Reflexively, I said, "I know you," but I couldn't recall how. Then it clicked. Mrs. Silver was the grandmother of my daughter's friend since kindergarten. Mrs. Silver, a psychiatrist, invited me in, gave me biscotti and seltzer water, sat me down and called for her husband, another psychiatrist. For 45 minutes, two highly intellectual doctors who had much more experience with the health care system than I ever would grilled me on my ideas for universal health care coverage and its potential impacts. They made me work hard for votes, but it was good preparation.

## Keep on Fighting

Sometimes, encouragement came unexpectedly, a jolt of reinforcement to provide inspiration when I was dragging after numerous mundane and superficial encounters. When Ms. Wall emerged from her garage instead of the front door, I thought that was an indication that she was in a hurry to go somewhere and wouldn't want to spend much time, so I introduced myself quickly and gave her my card.

As I was walking away, she called out, "I stand for everything you have on your card."

I stopped. "Great. A lot of people agree with health care for all, campaign finance reform and cutting income taxes for the middle class, but they say it's too hard to do," I said.

She answered, "It's hard to do but you keep on fighting for it."

Ms. Wall made me feel I was on the right track, that there were many others like her, if I could just reach them.

## Prayers Also Accepted

Sometimes you may not get a vote or money by going door-to-door, but you find something even better. That's what happened when I met Mr. Kline doing yardwork outside his house. I had actually come to meet his mother but she had died. Mr. Kline said he was home after doing missionary work in Nepal, where he ran a hospital. We talked about the 13 Nepali Sherpas who had died while on expedition in an April 2014 Mount Everest avalanche. Mr. Kline talked about the people of Nepal and how little they had and the primitiveness of the nation's economy. When we finally got to the main point of my visit, Mr. Kline told me he was not affiliated with a political party, meaning he could not vote in the primary.

"But I'm going to pray for you," Mr. Kline offered.

After another minute of small talk, as I departed to move on to the next house, Mr. Kline called after me: "You'll be in my prayers."

Mr. Kline was the only one to offer a prayer for me on my door-to-door journey. *Maybe I could use his prayers more than his vote anyway,* I thought.

## Prayers Accepted, but Money Would be Better

In my door-to-door strategy, I should have been more like Tyler Benson, the young, hungry, energetic delegate candidate in nearby, affluent Montgomery County, Maryland, bordering Washington, DC, with whom I corresponded during our campaigns and met just afterward. Benson asked everyone he met at the door for a donation, and succeeded in getting many contributions.

Before I knew of Benson's aggressive approach to door-to-door fundraising, I realized that my indirect, passive approach of encouraging donations through information on the back of my handout card would yield nothing, no matter what type of connection I made on the doorstep.

Contributions weren't going to rain down on me like manna from heaven or mysteriously materialize through mental telepathy. I had hoped not to focus much time, energy and effort on fundraising, but that was misguided thinking, a fool's errand. There's just not enough you can do to build name recognition and get your messages disseminated without sufficient funds. Political campaigns form a cottage industry—printers, sign manufacturers, direct-mail houses, novelty makers, caterers, political strategists, marketing and image/brand consultants, data specialists, social media mavens, media experts, advertisers, fundraising advisors, pollsters and the like. And that industry exists for a reason: All those things packaged in the right formula help produce a winning candidate.

Around mid-campaign, I seriously contemplated doing what Benson did, asking for a donation of each person who answered their door after the formalities of the greeting, a campaign "elevator speech," and an opportunity for questions, even though I felt uncomfortable and smarmy about asking strangers for money.

I discussed how to get contributions at the door in a chance meeting with a seasoned politician from Montgomery County, Cheryl Kagan, who was running a fierce race for state Senate. Kagan advised me that such a request could be made with finesse, and success, once a connection was developed, and that I would sense such opportunities intuitively.

I ran the idea by Amy, and she shot it down as too desperate. I agreed with her that the purpose of going door-to-door was to meet people, listen, engage in conversation and tell them about myself, not to ask for money. But it was a Catch-22: I would never make it into a position where I could advocate for the ideas that these constituents supported if I couldn't raise the money.

Despite my misgivings, I decided to pilot the more aggressive approach to fundraising while going door-to-door in my neighborhood, where I already knew people. My pre-existing relationships would make the solicitation more palatable, I reasoned. During my meetings with several neighbors, I mentioned that one of the most challenging parts about being a candidate is raising money, and asked if they would con-sider making a contribution. In so doing, I was reminded of another les-son that people in sales know well: Close the deal on the spot. Once you let a prospect think and decide later, the opportunity is lost, especially for something they don't need.

I didn't employ this more aggressive fundraising strategy again on the door-to-door circuit. I wasn't intrepid enough, didn't want to face rejection or want it bad enough. I understood that if I was confident in myself and knew I would represent constituents well, I should feel confident about asking constituents to help me get into office through financial support. I just couldn't escape the feeling of groveling. That was one of my shortcomings as a candidate, and in retrospect, a mistake, a copout. Benson's fundraising strategy told me I missed an opportunity I could have grabbed, if I had only been willing to expose my pride.

## December 16-20, 2013 – Let It Ride

O n a week off work, I rode the Sachs for Delegate BikeMobile every day, for an hour or more, trying to get as many eyeballs as possible, returning home the first morning after nearly two hours with frozen feet and switching to afternoon rides for the rest of the week, even cycling the shopping mall ring road amid Christmas shoppers.

I did not encounter cyclist-haters. People did not blow their horns obnoxiously, yell out the window, or throw anything at me. On the other hand, it was surprising—and maybe a sad commentary on busy metropolitan society—that nobody was friendly either. I got few waves or acknowledgements, nods or thumbs up. Even when I was stopped at a red light with backed up traffic, motorists mostly ignored me.

During my rides, I saw few people outside walking, playing or connecting in any way. Everyone was inside, or buzzing around in their cars, closed off from the world. Obviously conditioned by their daily environment, I observed motorists driving with a steely determination and tunnel vision, their unifying, unspoken mission: *I've got to get where I'm going and get there fast. Nobody will stand in my way. There's a candidate on a bike with signs? Invisible. I shall not smile or make a human connection.* From house to car to day care to battling through congested roads to office parking lot to sterile office building to parking lot to congested roads to day care to garage to home. That's the day for many people. And somewhere during that drudgery, they lose some humanity and ability to find joy in their daily travels. I began observing the faces of the drivers, and many looked miserable, faces clenched, expressions anxious. I looked, and many didn't look at me at all. They purposely looked away.

# DECEMBER 26, 2013 -- TRIPLE L'S: AMERICANA LOST

As part of my campaign fundraising outreach, I got in touch with an old reporter friend Jill from Baltimore. We arranged to meet for lunch, and I suggested convening in the heart of Baltimore County's District 12, so I could become more familiar with the region and soak up the ambiance. So we reunited at a place Jill recommended as quintessential Arbutus, Leon's Restaurant and Bar, also apparently known as Leon's Triple L Restaurant, in the heart of downtown on the main drag in a commercial district that stretched just over a quarter-mile. Leon's was a step back in time, indeed the whole area rekindled images of the 1950s and 60s, probably its heyday.

Leon's, which included a mysterious component billed as the Triple L Lottery Room, featured an old-fashioned diner room with a bar on the other side, connected through a kitchen doorway. Something seemed amiss to have a place that served your regular American breakfast fare attached to a bar, where eight people sat rather forlornly in front of the booze in the early afternoon in the dark, staring at screens. I quickly passed through the bar and retreated to the restaurant.

The place was plastered with Maryland Lottery and Keno gambling game ads and screens. The clientele was old—geez, I was 50, and the patrons all could have been my parents. I made a big mistake with my order by getting lunch instead of the all-day breakfast. It's hard to ruin eggs or pancakes, but once you turn that menu page, it can be anybody's guess. Let's just say my lunch entrée was not exactly haute cuisine—my pulled pork barbecued sandwich consisted of squared chunks of meat reminiscent of Alpo (Leon forgot to execute the "pulled" step of the recipe), slathered with a bland red sauce that I'm certain came straight out of an industrial-sized plastic container like the kind supplied to school cafeterias. The cole slaw's soggy cabbage swam in mayo soup. I tried to fill up on the fries. Chef Gordon Ramsey would have had a mega-tirade at Leon's for a *Kitchen Nightmare* episode.

Never mind the meal; I was there for the environment. I was experiencing Arbutus and my future constituency, like a true politician should, like all those presidential candidates who overrun the homey diners in small-town New Hampshire and Iowa with their entourages and media tag-alongs, chatting with impoverished waitresses and interrupting the local retirees mid-coffee sip for a handshake and photo op.

Sadly, I learned later that Triple L himself, Leon Leroy Lineburg, the restaurant's founder and proprietor since 1959 who was known by Arbutians as the unofficial "mayor of Arbutus," died four months after my visit. Jill picked the right place to experience local flavor. "Leon's restaurant is an institution. Everyone associates Arbutus with Leon's," the Baltimore County councilman representing Arbutus was quoted in Leon's obituary.

Leon apparently represented many citizens in the area in his parochialism. "I think I can count on my two hands the number of times my father has left the area," Leon's son said.

Leon's Triple L Restaurant closed a month after Triple L's death, three weeks before the primary, taking a little piece of Americana with it.

Like Leon's, the five-block long downtown Arbutus probably thrived decades earlier when housing was newer and malls had yet to dominate the suburban landscape and squeeze out small-town merchants. After lunch, I took a walking tour of the town to familiarize myself and talk to potential voters on the streets. However, the place was a ghost town—the malls and strip centers had won out.

# Cigarettes, Bologna and the Lottery

What I found was a central district of two-story red brick buildings dominated by convenience and Dollar stores and a "superette" advertising
Marlboro, Pall Mall and other brands of cigarettes, Esskay Bologna
Lunch Meat and Land O'Lakes Yellow Cheese outside the building; con-
signment stores/junk shops; pizza joints; nail salons; restaurants, pubs
and liquor stores with manly names such as Mike's, Paul's and John's; a
pawn shop for gold and silver with a sign proclaiming "Public Auction/
Real Estate;" a throwback movie theatre billed as "historic;" and a preponderance of cigarette, alcohol, lottery, and bankruptcy lawyer advertisements. Odd for a downtown business district were the Cigarette
Outlet, plastered with Maryland Lottery and Keno signs in the window
and the No Limit Bail Bonds, advertising, "We Make House Calls."

Symbolic of a bygone era, downtown Arbutus also featured the
Arbutus Social Club, Inc., dating to the 1950s and billed as the "best kept
secret in Arbutus." I had no idea what the "secret" was; it was firmly hidden. The membership club, which hosted events such as Monte Carlo
Night, Bull and Oyster Roast, Shrimp Feast, and Easter Day, had officers
and an executive board, and nine "chairmen" of functions such as hall,
social, kitchen and liquor. All positions were filled by males in 2013, but
I couldn't say whether it was an all-male social club.

A new millennial addition to downtown was the Habibah Café &
Hookah Lounge, where patrons smoked herbal shisha and purchased
flavored tobacco, played pool and arcade games, and surfed with Wi-Fi
under red-tinted lights.

The plethora of lawyer offices and legal advertisements aimed at the
distressed, and the pervasive, seemingly indiscriminately placed lottery
advertisements—a huge Lotto banner was hung on the back of nondescript two-story office building—gave me the distinct impression that
Arbutus and some nearby areas had seen better times.

Silberger & Silberger Attorneys at Law displayed a large sign in its
window beckoning: "BANKRUPTCY. Chapter 7 and Chapter 13. Keep
your House." The Law Offices of Terrence M. Nolan placed a folding

billboard a half block from its headquarters in front of the Krusty Krab shack that blared: "Are you drowning in debt? Foreclosure? Repossession? Bankruptcy?"

Standing in the looming winter darkness outside the dimly lit, red-tinted hookah lounge, having talked to just a handful of people on my downtown Arbutus expedition, I thought about Amy's admonition on our driving tour that I previously had shrugged off, that I abandon Baltimore County as a lost cause, and consider whatever votes I would get from there as gravy. She was right. My time for campaigning was limited. I was an outcast here. Hell, I was an outsider in my own county. And truth be told, I just didn't like much of the Baltimore County portion of District 12—I'm not talking about the people, but the environment, the aesthetics, the *feng shui*, the vague sense of dread that better days were not ahead but behind, symbolized by Leon's death and the closing of Leon's Triple L Restaurant. I would cut my losses with 2014 approaching and the primary six months away. Baltimore County would only see me when I had to be there, for candidates' forums or politically-motivated purposes, such as Democratic club parties, community events or appearances by gubernatorial candidate Mizeur, whose coattails I was hoping to ride. A "man of the people," at least Baltimore County people, I admittedly was not.

## December 27, 2013 – Encounter
## with the Inspiration

**A**s I rode the BikeMobile on the sidewalk of a busy parkway, I came upon The Columbia Bike Guy. He had his back to me, facing a busy intersection. He was straddling a kid's bike, with small wheels and a high seat, eating out of a plastic container, with a bunch of plastic grocery bags holding items, probably litter he picked up, spread on the sidewalk. I turned the corner behind him, looked back and saw him waving. I stuck up my arm in a triumphal pump as I turned back around to face forward.

The chance encounter with the model for the Sachs for Delegate BikeMobile was the highlight of my Holiday Week of campaigning on the streets. I doubted I would become as well known as The Columbia Bike Guy. He had cycled these streets for years, probably daily, and for purer reasons, because that's what he does, who he is. We were both riding out of a love and spirit for cycling, but unlike The Columbia Bike Guy, who selflessly does a public service by cleaning the streets, I was cycling for personal gain, through a form of subtle manipulation designed to attract attention to me, like a real politician.

# Campaign Finance: Politics' Rocket Fuel

*"This fundraising is consuming us. It's impossible to overstate... what it's doing to members and their ability to just focus on the job that they were elected to do. The collective concentration of the institution is being undermined every day by the need to fund-raise."*

U.S. Congressman John Sarbanes, D-MD

Politics and political fundraising is an incestuous business. Everybody is in bed with somebody else. Once you make it into office, you consolidate your power and influence and protect your position by forming alliances with others with similar power and positions and sycophants within your spheres of influence that have something to gain through their attachments. You build a fortress with others in your ranks with stacks of currency as a bastion against outsiders and newcomers crashing the party.

That's what political slates are all about. Politicians who already have influence and fundraising prowess multiply their power exponentially by pooling resources, strengthening all the insiders with their combined name recognition, political and business connections, powers of incumbency, campaign staffs and other resources.

Even in my race, in which no one except Joker had even run for a state office before, many candidates still were pulling in contributions of $250, $500, $1,000 or more (the Maryland legal contribution limit from any one individual or business entity was $4,000 from individuals for a four-year election cycle, and $6,000 from a PAC or another candidate committee or slate). Early on, the large contributions most likely came from the candidates' relatives, friends and acquaintances and well-placed business associates and connections. Later in the campaign, they also came more frequently from PACs, endorsing organizations and candidate transfers.

I didn't have friends, family members, acquaintances or career connections willing or able to make such large donations. I maxed out at $100. Usually when I asked my wife Amy for advice on whether I should ask a certain family member or friend for a contribution, she would respond, "They don't have any money" or a cruder variation, like, "She doesn't have a pot to pee in."

"What do you mean?" I'd reply. "They must have *some* money. I'm talkin' $25 here."

For example, I asked a friend from high school, who it turned out was on a run of bad luck.

"Hey, it would really help for my campaign if I could put you down for a small contribution."

"You know I would like to help you, but my budget is really tight right now. You know I lost my job, and I don't even know if I can work any time soon because of my back surgery, I can't even sit in a seat without pain. I've even gone to the food bank. Sorry."

Even with people I knew—family, friends, work colleagues, graduate school classmates—I had to walk the line on a continuum from passive to suggestive to assertive to overbearing. With many people, I made a request for a contribution multiple times. Think about it: How often do you put off someone when solicited to make a contribution for something by giving a non-answer or indirect answer? The more I followed up, the more I felt like a money-grubber, even though I knew it was what I had to do to run a real campaign. After all, the seasoned pros, such as the gubernatorial and attorney general candidates, asked for a contribution in every online communication they sent. Some people, however, had never donated money to a political candidate before, just like the vast majority of potential voters, and were uncomfortable with the idea.

Some candidates in District 12 received virtual windfalls in contributions from family members. Next Big Thing received $8,000 from his parents. Energy received nearly $10,000 in cash contributions and in-kind services from family.

I received $410 in contributions from family. But one of those contributions of $20 meant more to me than a $4,000 donation would have. I called my father, who lived in Oregon, to talk about the campaign. My father, in his mid-70s, was dealing with financial challenges. When I asked him if he would be able to make a small donation, he got choked up.

Through a voice muffled by tears, he said, "You have to have a lot of courage to be doing this, son, to put yourself on the line and face rejection. It's got to be tough, really tough. I'm proud of you. Sorry, I get more emotional now." I was glad he understood so viscerally. It touched me. To hear that compassion was way more valuable than his $20 check.

## Where's the Money Come From?

As part of the overarching theme of my campaign, "Placing People Above Corporations," I proposed a ban on corporate, PAC and union contributions to state candidates and implementing a public financing system, or state matching funds, for state elections. The goal of the proposal was to rid the system of the undue influence of corporations, PACs and unions, reduce legislators' dependence on certain industries and organizations as big-money donors, and restore more power to voters.

What I proposed for Maryland was not unprecedented or even unusual. As of 2015, 22 states prohibited contributions by corporations to political campaigns, and 15 states prohibited contributions by unions. PACs, organizations that pool campaign contributions from members to support candidates, were different. No states prohibited

PAC contributions, and 13 states allowed PACs to contribute unlimited amounts of money to state campaigns.

To support my proposal, I did a painstaking analysis of campaign contributions in 2012 to all 11 state legislators representing Howard County, resulting in a report I called, *Where's the Money Come From?* A press release resulted in an article in the *Columbia Flier* that quoted me saying:

> *"There's no denying that money from businesses, corporations and special interests has an influence on the legislative process, whether through securing more access to legislators, getting a key provision in a bill or keeping one out, preserving the status quo or potentially even swaying votes. I want to ensure that legislators' dependence on certain industries and organizations is reduced and influence is returned where it appropriately belongs, with residents, the true voters."*

My report didn't directly link any actions or votes of Howard's state legislators to the sources of their campaign contributions. Rather, it was to highlight the degree to which legislators relied on corporate and PAC contributions to fund their re-election campaigns.

According to my analysis, nine of the 11 Howard County legislators received at least 50 percent of their 2012 contributions from PACs and business-related entities, such as corporations, unions and special interest groups.[1] Five legislators—including Senator Career Pol and Delegates Cop and Fireman from my District 12—raised at least 70 percent of their money from business entities and PACs. Five of the 11 legislators received at least one-third of all their contributions from PACs, including Career Pol, Cop and Fireman.

---

1 Categories of contributions from PACs and business-related entities: alcohol, automotive, general business, development, education/social services, financial/consulting, gas/fuel, health care, hospitality/entertainment, insurance, labor/union, legal, political, public safety, science/technology/engineering, tobacco, transportation, unknown, utility/energy.

The District 12 Maryland Senate race demonstrated the overwhelming advantage incumbents enjoy for re-election when they have established tight relationships with perennial PAC donors. In the 2011 to 2014 election cycle, Career Pol raked in about $70,000 in nearly 140 PAC contributions. In the 11 weeks before the general election alone, 33 PACs[2] flooded Career Pol's campaign with $21,500 in an effort to ensure that he would keep his prominent spot as chair of the powerful budget committee. Career Pol's Republican newcomer opponent, Jesse Pippy, a car dealership manager with no political experience, received nothing from PACs.

I found it was routine for Howard County's state legislators to accept contributions from industries over which they had direct influence through legislative committees. For example:

Career Pol received contributions from horse racing and breeding PACs. Career Pol chaired the Senate Budget and Taxation Committee, which considered casino gambling legislation, including proposals involving horse race tracks. Career Pol also received contributions from Lottery Agents Association PAC of Maryland. The lottery is a source of state revenue considered in his committee's deliberations.

Fireman received nearly $11,000 in contributions from trucking, towing, scrap metal, and auto repair, dealership, leasing, donation, and parts companies. Fireman chaired the House Motor Vehicles and Transportation Subcommittee. Of the 14 entities that contributed at least $1,000 to Fireman in 2012, eight were in the automotive, scrap metal/recycling or transportation business.

Six utility companies and PACs representing the Allstate, GEICO, Nationwide and State Farm insurance companies contributed to Delegate Warren Miller. Miller served on the Property and Casualty Insurance Subcommittee.

---

2  Career Pol's PAC contributions represented a broad array of industries and occupations: pilots, trial lawyers, police, alcoholic beverage distributors, power/utility, banks, health insurers, physicians, car rental, medical institution, law firm, nursing homes, horse breeders, lottery agents, petroleum distributors, truckers, teachers/public education, Realtors, restaurants, gas stations, law enforcement, firefighters, thoroughbred horse owners, state troopers, telecommunications, railroad workers, engineers, apartment property developers/managers, and commercial real estate developers/managers.

Delegate Susan Pendleton received about 60 percent of the $27,000 she raised in about 60 contributions from a broad range of health care and health insurance interests.[3] Pendleton occupied several leadership positions on committees dealing with health care and health insurance.

## Money's Outsized Impact

Researchers say wealthy, special-interest donors have an outsized impact on state legislation and elections. In *The Influence of Campaign Contributions in State Legislatures*, University of Rochester political scientist Lynda Powell contended that seeking to establish a direct connection between money and legislative outcomes does not provide the true picture of the more subtle or covert influence of campaign contributions on the legislative process.

"What voting studies cannot detect are the important, but less observable, pathways where money is more likely to shape legislation," Powell wrote. "Members have many opportunities, especially in the committee process, to structure the details of legislation to a donor's advantage. Often subtle changes, even altering the wording of a single sentence, can matter to a contributor. Equally important, studying votes ignores the opportunities lawmakers have to kill a bill quietly and prevent it from coming to a vote."

Concerns have been raised at all government levels that "special interests" are having an undue influence on elections, politics and government. Campaign contributions often are identified as the conduit for political influence and access, and a key ingredient in election dominance.

"I am not arguing that there is much quid-pro-quo influence," Powell wrote. "But even the best intentioned legislator receiving money from an interest group is likely to at least listen to what donors have to say. And if you are

---

3  Health care-related contributors to Pendleton: cardiologists, chiropractors, dentists, health information technology, health insurers, health plans, hospitals, medical devices/consumer products, mental health/therapists/psychologists, nurses, nursing homes, optometrists/vision/eye care, pharmaceuticals/drug stores, physicians, physician assistants, psychiatrists, radiologists, urologists.

hearing much more from people who donate money to you, it is hard not to be swayed by the greater body of argument and evidence from donors."

The National Institute on Money in State Politics' 2012 report, "The Role of Incumbency and Money on 2009-2010 State Elections," said that election ideals of "numerous and diverse candidates, high voter turnout, and…informative debate over issues" is "overpowered" in many instances by incumbency and money. Money is the second most powerful variable behind incumbency in determining electoral success. Legislative candidates who raised more money than opponents had a 76 percent success rate in the 2009 and 2010 elections. Combining incumbency and money advantages delivered an 88 percent chance of victory.

## The Gaping Loophole

I found that businesses are adept at hiding their identities and the true source of funds from public disclosure by creating various names for enterprises operating under the corporate umbrella, or core business name. For example, Howard County Senator Andy Kellerman received large contributions from entities with gobbledygook names apropos of a robot companion to R2D2 in a *Star Wars* movie, such as WT B-2 LLC; 8601 Robert Fulton Dr LLP; KDL Limited Liability Company; M10 Health Care at Turf Valley, LLC; and BD Panama City I, LLC.

I also discovered that the Howard legislators weren't immune from using a well-known, gaping loophole that businesses employed to get around the $4,000 per four-year election cycle contribution limit. Businesses made frequent use of the wink-wink, nod-nod "Limited Liability Corporation (LLC) Loophole" (also Limited Liability Partnership, or LLP) to make contributions through legally-established offshoots of the core business. Under this loophole, one core business could make as many $4,000 contributions to an individual candidate as LLCs/LLPs it had established.

For example, Kellerman received six contributions totaling more than $20,000 from corporations linked to J.P. Bolduc, former President and CEO of W.R. Grace & Co., and Bolduc individually, through his tangled web of interrelated business enterprises, such as JPB Capitol Partners Management Co. LLC; JPB Partners, LLC; and JPB Strategic Advisors, LLC. Kellerman's largesse was legal under the LLC loophole. Still, you know something stinks to high heaven when you need certified public accountants to make sense of it all.

It wasn't just seasoned, incumbent politicians who were taking advantage of that cheesecloth loophole. In my race, Next Big Thing benefited from the porous law to the hilt.

Next Big Thing collected seven contributions totaling $25,000 from the CEO and six alphabet-soup entities, such as ESAACC, LLC, ESCCS, LLC and ESRR, LLC, associated with Ecology Services, a waste management company. Either Next Big Thing had a passion for garbage, or a mighty strong connection.

Man of the People, the champion of the working class, also demonstrated that even a candidate trying to portray himself as an Everyman can fall prey to the temptation or desperation of taking easy money from the wealthy and powerful. Man of the People collected $12,000 in one fell swoop four weeks before the primary election from three LLPs under the control of Stephen Whalen of Whalen Properties, named Catonsville Series V, VIII and IX. Whalen was the prominent Catonsville developer who pled guilty in 2013 to channeling $7,500 in illegal contributions to a Baltimore County councilman, and who was seeking approval to develop the $350 million Promenade at Catonsville to which Gadfly objected. Those contributions, radically uncharacteristic of Man of the People, crushed my image of a squeaky clean candidate who could walk through the mud bog of dirty money and emerge smelling like a daisy.

A 2006 study by Common Cause Maryland, "The Six Million Dollar Loophole: How Money Moves in Maryland Campaigns Through Limited Liability Companies," found that LLCs and LLPs funneled more than $6 million to Maryland political campaigns during the 2003 to 2006 election cycle.

"The campaign funding system in Maryland favors interests with money and encourages candidates to engage in the money chase using all available tools," the report said. "Owners of corporations and LLC/LLP businesses often give several checks to a candidate on a single occasion, hiding from the public the total they have given…If the identity of the owner of the business is not obvious, large amounts of money may be given in support for a favored candidate."

The Maryland legislature responded to such abuse of the spirit of the law by addressing the LLC loophole for election cycles after 2014. But unsurprisingly, the legislature took a timid, half-assed approach, leaving enough space in the loophole for crafty businesses to drive a Mack Truck through it.

The new law still allowed LLCs linked to the same core business to each contribute the maximum amount as long as the "controlling entity" of those LLCs had less than 80 percent ownership. It didn't take long for corporations and their attorneys and accountants to figure out how to sidestep the supposed loophole-closure. In the 2016 Baltimore mayor's race, several developers and contractors flooded candidates' coffers with multiple contributions from business entities linked to the same company, exceeding the new $6,000 contribution limit many times over. The *Baltimore Sun* reported that in one case, contributors with ties to real estate developer Dennis S. Gorsuch, the owner of Maryland Live Casino, had contributed more than $60,000 to a candidate, including six business entities that each listed the business address of The Gorsuch Cos. headquarters.

In April 2016, the Maryland Board of Elections forwarded to state prosecutors a complaint that another developer used several different companies to circumvent donation limits in contributing $36,000 to Maryland Senator Cynthia Peters' campaign for Baltimore mayor, asking prosecutors to investigate possible violation of the LLC law.

## District 12 'War Chests'

According to pure dollar figures, Joker was far and away the champion fundraiser of District 12 candidates, accumulating a "war chest" of

$151,125. But that figure was misleading. Joker loaned his campaign $85,000, or 56 percent of his total.

The prodigious Zelig was second, with $121,784. He also was generous to himself, loaning his campaign more than $37,000.

Anointed One actually was the leading fundraiser from outside sources, collecting $110,966. Next Big Thing was close behind, with $94,000. Those four were way ahead of the pack. Needless to say, I was last, at $2,500, except for the self-declared pauper candidate Spare-A-Dime.

PACs representing health care, labor unions, firefighters, teachers and other groups played a bigger role in goosing candidates' bank accounts as the primary drew near in 2014, helping chosen candidates spread their name and messages and making it even harder for me to compete. Energy received $14,000; Anointed One $12,350; and Zelig $12,550. Zelig banked a whopping $9,000 from the Service Employees International Union. (*Wait a minute…wasn't Maryland's limit on PAC contributions $6,000? Ahh, but SEIU and Zelig found a way around the law: $6,000 came from SEIU New York State Political Action Fund, and $3,000 from SEIU Maryland/DC State Council PAC.*) SEIU's support for Zelig and Energy, and opposition to Joker, would explode into a back-and-forth brawl between the three candidates in the last weeks of the campaign.

And Next Big Thing pulled in nearly $15,000 from the broadest array of PACs and unions[4], at least partly attributable to his connections with Fireman ($2,600 came from five firefighter organizations) and Gov. O'Malley ($4,000 came directly from O'Malley's personal PAC). The white-collar Next Big Thing even scored with truckers, Teamsters, steelworker and ironworker unions (copper workers apparently sat out the Maryland primary).

---

4 Next Big Thing had broad appeal among PACs and unions. Those contributing represented: Accountants, abortion rights advocates, firefighters from four jurisdictions; food and commercial workers, gas & electric, ironworkers, Maryland Congressman Ruppersberger, Maryland Governor O'Malley, paramedics; plaintiff lawyers, police, Realtors, Republican legislators, social services employees, steelworkers, student government, Teamsters, transportation workers, truckers.

## Bless You with Riches

Of course, incumbent politicians also got into the District 12 act, an irksome political ritual that destroys the concept of an even playing field. Those who already have the power of public office, having built overflowing treasuries and accumulated more money than they know what to do with through ties with consistent big donors, take it upon themselves to grace their chosen ones with big bucks. With one stroke of a pen, an incumbent, especially one who has an easy path to re-election, can drop $6,000 into an upstart's account, changing the complexion of a race.

Do the math. A $50 donation to a campaign is a reasonably generous donation from your average grassroots voter. Typically, only those with a particular tie to a candidate or a personal agenda to pursue give extravagantly more. A candidate would have to work his ass off to get 120 contributions of $50 from grassroots donors to equal the $6,000 one incumbent can bestow upon his hand-picked favorite. Looked at another way, if a candidate went door-to-door and asked each person he met for a donation, and received one donation averaging $20 for every four people he met, that candidate would have to visit 2,400 homes to reach $6,000 (assuming the candidate meets a voter at only half the homes he visits).

That was the kind of grassroots campaign run by the young, ambitious Democratic candidate for delegate from Montgomery County, Tyler Benson. The Young Hustler raised more than $12,000 from about 350 small donors in 2013, in addition to the nearly $12,000 he received from family and several larger donors. But Benson barely would have had to lift a finger for that additional $12,000 if two incumbents somewhere had taken him under their wing to the tune of $6,000 each.

These District 12 candidates got a generous boost from entrenched Maryland politicians:

Anointed One: $6,000 from 28-year legislator Career Pol; $4,000 from 20-year retiring Delegate Drummer.

Zelig: $3,500 from his mentor and former boss, 20-year Delegate *Doctor Dan Morhaim.*

Next Big Thing: $5,345 from 20-year Delegate Fireman.

## Spending Blitzkrieg

The candidates with the most money were able to smother the public with a blitzkrieg of spending on strategies to increase awareness and name recognition in the weeks leading up to the primary.

For example, Joker spent $24,000 on outdoor advertising billboards, $47,250 on printing and campaign materials and nearly $8,000 on automated voter phone calls, or "robo calls;" Anointed One and Zelig each spent about $70,000 on printing and campaign materials, and Anointed One $3,000 in consulting fees and campaign workers; Next Big Thing plunked down $15,000 on direct mail.

Unlike my go-it-alone strategy—out of necessity more than desire—other candidates had money to spare for businesses that specialize in providing advice and services to campaigns. Joker paid nearly $8,000 total to an information technology firm and an advertising agency; Zelig shelled out $6,150 to a Democratic political consulting firm; and Next Big Thing forked over $2,500 to a political consulting firm.

## Joker 'Gets It Done'...Tardily and Sloppily

Joker's financial statements deserve special attention. They validated his "carpetbagger" status. In 2013, Joker reported about 100 contributions totaling $45,300. Of those contributions, none was from a person listing a District 12 address as a residence, your average voter. Here's where they were from: More than $20,000 from the development and housing industry, including numerous apartment property managers (Joker was a lobbyist for the Maryland Multi-Family Housing Association); $4,000 from a health club association, for whom Joker was a lobbyist; and $4,500 from the "hosts" of a Joker fundraiser, all executives at Baltimore investment and law firms, banks, and development and real estate companies.

Out of about 150 contributions Joker received throughout the campaign, only three appeared to be from within District 12, each from principals of development, realty and law firms.

It was obvious that Joker was not a "man of the people" of District 12. Joker's campaign, far from being grass-roots, was positively Dust Bowl.

What was worse was that, despite his claims of being the only one with lawmaker experience and his motto, "Joker Gets It Done," Joker was the only one in the field who failed to adhere to campaign finance laws by neglecting to submit his campaign finance report electronically, as required, until a month after the deadline. And even when he did finally submit his electronic report, it was so riddled with mistakes and confusing entries that a reporter doing a story on fundraising in District 12 couldn't figure it out.

Joker made 17 duplicative entries in his report, meaning 17 times he listed the same individual or entity contributing the same amount on the same day twice. Such contribution scenarios—an individual or business giving Joker two separate checks for the same amount on the same day—make no sense and are highly unlikely, and such errors would artificially inflate Joker's contribution total.

In a *Columbia Flier* story, Joker danced around the errors and came up with an excuse right out of a *Mad Men* episode: It was the secretary's fault.

Joker said any double-counting of contributions was "unintentional" or "inadvertent."

He added that mistakes might have occurred while transferring data from the paper campaign finance report his campaign prepared to the state's electronic filing database. Problem was, the state long ago had transitioned from paper to electronic reports.

Joker said his campaign treasurer had filled out his report on paper, and then the campaign hired a secretary from a political consulting firm to transpose the information to file an electronic version (*What efficiency and cost-consciousness for someone who wants responsibility for handling taxpayers' money!*) Joker noted the filing process had changed from snail mail since he served as a delegate 24 years previously. (*C'mon Joker, you want to be a delegate but can't assume accountability to know that the laws have changed since we have entered the Internet Age and use computers? All the candidates received the same information on campaign finance laws and procedures from the state Board of Elections. Nobody else failed to follow them.)*

"If there are any errors they were secretarial errors and we'll correct it," Joker assured. "We clearly raised the most resources…I think it's a testament to a lot of people and organizations who think I'm going to do a good job and support me."

According to Maryland campaign finance records, Joker never did correct his erroneous report with duplicative entries. Joker's reference to the "testament" of support was pure braggadocio. He may have had financial support, but not from any residents who could actually vote for him.

## The Gold Rush

It's all how you play the game.

In an effort to at least give lip service to the potential corrupting effects of big money from special interests on the legislative process, the Maryland legislature prohibited incumbent lawmakers from raising money during the three-month General Assembly session.

So what do lawmakers do? Big surprise. Many schedule big fundraising shindigs just before the legislative session starts, creating a new annual ritual for lobbyists, corporations and legislators to convene in the state capital and make their trades before the deadline, like NFL general managers on draft day. Lobbying firms have reported that 40 to 50 fundraisers take place annually just under the deadline. Of course, the only tangible property that changes hands is the check from the donor to the politician, but who can really say what kind of hidden currency the legislators offer in return.

The ostensible purpose of the restriction on contributions while the legislature is in session is to eliminate the perception—or reality—that donors essentially pay off politicians to cast votes or take other actions to support or kill legislation they are monitoring. If, as any politician worth his salt would contend, campaign contributions have no influence on their actions, then wouldn't it stand to reason that such a law wouldn't be needed? And if, as the law suggests, legislators can be unduly influenced by special-interest contributions during the session, what's to prevent them from being influenced by such contributions over the intervening nine months?

"It's a shark feeding frenzy," declared one of Annapolis's highest-paid lobbyists about pre-Opening Day fundraisers before the 2014 General Assembly session. "It's incredible."

Rock God is one of those legislators who has gathered sustenance during the "shark feeding frenzy" week with fundraisers at the Governor Calvert House, a historic Annapolis inn that was the residence of two former Maryland governors and is described as having a "refreshing blend of 18th century ambiance and modern luxury."

## Anything for a Buck

Some politicians will use any reason as the basis for a donation request, even Divine Intervention. Maryland Delegate Dereck Davis implied he could be the envoy for Pope Francis' messages to humanity—ergo, the surrogate voice of God himself—in an e-mail solicitation during the pope's September 2015 visit to the U.S.

"What brings me the most pride is that this pope has brought with him a message so close to our own: a commitment to social and economic justice is the way to creating real, broad prosperity," wrote the candidate for Congress from Prince George's County, MD.

The e-mail concluded with a link to the delegate's website donation page: "Help us spread Pope Francis' message of hope and dignity by contributing today."

## By the Numbers: David vs. Goliath

A 2011 report by The Center for American Politics and Citizenship at the University of Maryland quantified the huge money advantages of incumbents, how much they depend on corporations and interest groups to maintain their power, and how those money and power advantages translate to electoral success. In other words, it illuminates a corrupt system in which the powerful continually expand upon their power by courting and pleasing special interests, while challengers to the throne face a David vs. Goliath battle that is virtually foolish to embark upon *prima facie.*

The report, which evaluated data from more than 500 Maryland state candidates during the 2010 election cycle, showed that general election winners in House races raised on average $82,000 more than losers, and winners in Senate races raised $157,000 more than losers. Among House candidates, the typical general election winners raised $103,000, between five and seven times as much as the typical general election and primary losers, who raised $21,000 and $16,000, respectively.

The typical Senate general election winner raised $218,000, about four times as much as the typical general election and primary losers, who raised $61,000 and $53,000, respectively.

Both House and Senate challengers raised more from individuals than interest groups.

In contrast, incumbent candidates raised more money from interest groups than from individuals, illuminating the influence of PACs and other "organized interests." The typical Senate incumbent raised $131,100 from interest groups and $84,000 from individuals.

Several public opinion polls show Americans are disturbed with how political campaigns are funded and support significant changes.

In a 2015 *New York Times*/CBS News national poll, 84 percent said money has too much influence on the elections process, and 66 percent said the wealthy have more influence on the process. The poll showed that 46 percent favored completely redesigning the system for funding political campaigns.

And a 2013 Gallup poll showed that a majority of Americans would support extreme campaign finance reform, finding that 50 percent of the country would support banning all contributions by individuals and instead have campaigns entirely funded by the government.

# GOVERNMENT OF THE PEOPLE, BY THE PEOPLE, FOR THE PEOPLE...WHO FORM THE MOST POWERFUL SPECIAL INTEREST GROUPS WITH THE MOST MONEY

> *"A group experience takes place on a lower level of consciousness than the experience of an individual... If it is a very large group, the collective psyche will be more like the psyche of an animal, which is the reason why the ethical attitude of large organizations is always doubtful."*

CARL JUNG, PSYCHIATRIST/PSYCHOTHERAPIST,
FOUNDER OF ANALYTICAL PSYCHOLOGY

In a 2014 study, "Testing Theories of American Politics: Elites, Interest Groups and Average Citizens," researchers Benjamin Page and Martin Gilens, professors at Northwestern and Princeton universities, respectively, concluded that America's government policies reflect the wishes of the rich and of powerful interest groups, rather than the wishes of the majority of citizens. Any connection between public policy and the preferences of average citizens "may be largely or entirely spurious," the researchers said, adding that average Americans' interests may be reflected in policy to the extent that those interests "align with the interests of the wealthy" citizens and business interests.

"Economic elites and organized groups representing business interests have substantial independent impacts on U.S. government policy, while mass-based interest groups and average citizens have little or no independent influence," the researchers found.

The more power that special interest groups exercise in influencing government policy, the more that the government's decision-making process veers away from the interests of the average American, the study said. The researchers go so far as to question whether current American government truly reflects basic principles of democracy, and sound the alarm for the need to restrain the influence of money on public policy decisions, slacken the unbridled power-sharing relationships between special interests, "economic elites" and politicians, and return more power to average citizens:

> "It is simply not the case that a host of diverse, broadly based interest groups take policy stands—and bring about actual policies—that reflect what the general public wants. Interest groups as a whole do not seek the same policies as average citizens do...These business groups are far more numerous and active; they spend much more money; and they tend to get their way.
>
> "Interest groups do have substantial independent impacts on policy, and a few groups (particularly labor unions) represent average citizens' views reasonably well. But the interest group system as a whole does not... The net alignments of the most influential, business oriented groups are negatively related to the average citizen's wishes...
>
> "What do our findings say about democracy in America? They certainly constitute troubling news for advocates of "populistic" democracy... [T]he majority does not rule—at least not in the causal sense of actually determining policy outcomes. When a majority of citizens disagrees with economic elites and/or with organized interests, they generally lose."

The researchers postulate that some believe true "populistic democracy" has a fatal flaw because average citizens are "inattentive to politics and ignorant about public policy." Under that reasoning, it could be beneficial to have economic elites and interest group leaders with more policy expertise driving policy decisions. Perhaps those experts do know better which policies would have the broadest benefits, and perhaps they "seek the common good, rather than selfish ends" through their advocacy.

"But we tend to doubt it," the researchers asserted. "We believe instead that, collectively, ordinary citizens generally know their own values and interests pretty well, and that their expressed policy preferences are worthy of respect.

"Our analyses suggest that majorities of the American public actually have little influence over the policies our government adopts...[W]e believe that if policymaking is dominated by powerful business organizations and a small number of affluent Americans, then America's claims to being a democratic society are seriously threatened."

In his book, *Affluence & Influence: Economic Inequality and Political Power in America*, Gilens found that "patterns of responsiveness," such as in matters of policy decisions, in American government "often corresponded more closely to a plutocracy (rule by the wealthy) than to a democracy."

Gilens presented a view of Democratic and Republican parties not as representative of large swaths of public preferences, but as a "means to an end" for special interests and their activists seeking to control policy-making.

From that perspective, Gilens wrote, "Parties in America have evolved from largely independent organizations run by professional politicians and power brokers to captives of 'intense policy demanders' who view control of government (or influence over policy making more generally) as a means to an end. Parties, by this account, respond to public preferences to the extent that they must do so to obtain or retain power. But once in power, parties seek to maximize the policy gains for the organized interests, affluent campaign donors, and other policy demanders that form their base of support."

Gilens concluded that "the poor and the middle class are already far more likely than the affluent to feel that their preferences and interests are ignored by government policy makers. Further concentration of political influence among the country's affluent threatens both the perception and the reality of a shared political community so central to the health of even the modestly democratic republic we currently enjoy."

# Political Slates: You Scratch My Back, I'll Scratch Yours

Power is in numbers, in banding together for a common purpose. The *Mean Girls* high school clique knew it; fraternities and sororities flaunt it; the Million Man marchers recognized it; the Occupy Wall Street 99 Percenters and Black Lives Matter advocates adopted it to bring about social change; and politicians understand that numbers help them stay in command and ward off aspirants to their positions.

That's the purpose of political slates. Politicians who already have influence, high-placed relationships and fundraising prowess multiply their power by banding together to pool resources, strengthening all the insiders exponentially and shoring up any weaker members by redistributing wealth. And slates throw lifelines to those candidates their clubs deems worthy. A University of Maryland study revealed that slates tend to contribute more heavily to candidates who are in competitive races to increase the probability of a successful campaign.

In the 2010 University of Maryland report, "Slates and the 2006 Maryland State Elections," researchers said slates, which are naturally the province of established politicians with proven fundraising abilities "create a viable alternative for groups of candidates to aid the prospects of their political allies."

For example, District 12's Career Pol transferred $25,000 to the Maryland Democratic Senatorial Committee Slate just more than a month before the 2014 general election to aid his compatriots, and

Rock God transferred $50,000 to the Senate slate, his soon-to-be new home, and $18,000 to the Maryland Democratic House Committee Slate to support his former colleagues in the months before the election.

The focus of slates as a means for incumbents to protect allies can be starkly seen in this telling statistic: Maryland Senate candidates in competitive races (decided by 15 percentage-points or less) received $34,000, on average, from slates. By contrast, candidates running in comparatively non-competitive races received just $4,200, on average.

Almost one-third of all Maryland candidates were members of at least one slate during the 2006 election cycle. The most common slate members included incumbents, candidates with longer tenures in office, candidates who were more electorally successful, and candidates who raised more money.

The study said "the overwhelming majority of contributors to slates were established politicians," noting that about half of all slate funds came from direct transfers from candidate accounts, not from average voters. About 65 percent of the money candidates contributed to slates came from incumbents, and another 31 percent from "politically experienced non-incumbents," such as candidates who held elected office but were running for another one. Incumbents donated roughly $30,000 and politically experienced non-incumbents $48,000 to slates, on average, another demonstration of the incestuous, insider nature of electoral politics.

What it all boils down to, the researchers said, is trading favors, creating debts and bolstering power.

"Altogether, it is clear that funding for slates came primarily from a small set of well-established politicians," the researchers said. "These candidates generally raised large sums of money and were able to dispense some of that money into slate committees to attempt to 'spread the wealth' and aid the election prospects of their colleagues. By contributing large sums to aid their allies, these politicians increase their standing among their colleagues and their power. They make debtors of friends who in the future may be called upon to return the favor or to support them in some other political endeavor."

The study concluded that candidates who are "in need of assistance and could benefit the most from slate membership—typically novices with little political experience—are the least likely to be part of a slate. Ironically, slates appear to be made up primarily of candidates that can bring a lot of money to the table and candidates that already had a strong chance of electoral success."

A subsequent University of Maryland report for the 2010 election found that, on average, the more slates to which a candidate belonged, the more money the candidate raised. Identifying slates as a method for consolidating power, the study revealed 1 in 4 Senate candidates were members of four or more slates, and that Senate incumbents were more likely to have been associated with three or more slates than with no slates.

## Team 13: Who Will Make the Pledge Class?

Rock God was one of those, with memberships in four candidate slates. A look at the finances of Rock God's Team 13 Slate shows how joining forces strengthens election prospects for all members of a slate.

The powerhouse Team 13 Slate included four Democratic candidates running for Maryland General Assembly in District 13— Rock God, the Senate candidate, 20-year delegate incumbents Susan Pendleton and George Mercer, and newcomer delegate candidate Valerie Appleby—and several other prominent local politicians, including the leading Maryland lieutenant governor candidate. With Rock God moving up to Senate, being drafted to join Team 13 would be a coup for whichever newcomer candidate was seeking to fill Rock God's delegate seat. Selection would all but assure the newcomer political victory, by mere fact of the bounty in which the rookie would share and the association with politicians with high name recognition and winning track records.

Joining Team 13, the neophyte delegate candidate would benefit from the BIRG (basking in reflected glory) phenomenon: Voters were habituated to voting for Rock God and other District 13 incumbents, and no doubt liked to associate themselves with voting for "winners." So, naturally, whoever was associated with the Team 13 stalwarts as the third delegate candidate would be considered a winner as well and worthy of a vote.

Team 13 engaged in shenanigans (*for more on the monkey business, see chapter on Shenanigans*) to come up with its ultimate choice for the third delegate member. Team 13 snapped up Regina Hassan, a pediatrician and Howard County school board member, for membership in August 2013 as soon as she entered the race—six months before the February 2014 filing deadline—leaving candidate Tony Eifort, a career grocery store worker, out in the cold. Why mess around with a Giant Food manager when you can have the cache of a doctor and former chair of the county school board who also had connections to Gov. O'Malley and Congressman Cummings?

But when Hassan dropped out at the eleventh hour, Team 13 went into God mode to anoint a winner from among Eifort, a long-established candidate, and two fresh-faced candidates who entered upon learning of the gaping opening at the eleventh-and-three-quarters hour, including Hassan's husband.

It's a maddening and disillusioning aspect of politics to witness how the people in power bestow upon themselves the authority to select who else will rise to power, because that's what they do, how the system is rigged. The slate functioned like a sorority or fraternity during "rush" season, at first jumping the gun and selecting who it wanted, damn whoever else might have entered later. Then, when best-laid plans were upended by The Dropout, interviewing three plebes to see who would make the cut to fit the mold of the group, add value, strengthen the whole, and be the pledge to join the class.

Once Team 13 made its last-minute choice, the other two leftover candidates, forced to run as scrawny individuals against the Paul

Bunyan-esque strength of a four-member team with a combined 48 years in the state legislature and another 16 years on the Howard County Council, and which had a combined $577,640 in their treasuries at the outset of 2014 (compared to less than $1,000 for Eifort), might as well have thrown in the towel.

Several months before the primary, the four Team 13 members running for General Assembly each transferred $15,000 from their own campaign accounts to the slate to promote the team. That allowed Team 13 to smother the scrawny individualist candidates under a wave of slate spending to influence voters leading up to the June 24 primary: $4,200 for yard signs; $2,200 for outdoor billboards; $13,000 for brochures; $19,500 for mailings; and $1,900 for advertising in publications produced by high schools, political organizations, civic groups, community associations, and other county mainstays. And, that was in addition to what each of the Team 13 members spent from their own candidate accounts, producing a multiplier effect.

# Public Campaign Financing: Returning Power to the People

One way to reduce the influence of deep-pocketed special interest groups, businesses, corporations and affluent individuals on the election process and encourage more otherwise intimidated and overwhelmed potential candidates to run is by implementing a public financing campaign system, in which the government matches funds that candidates raise from smaller, grassroots donors under a formula or ratio.

The concept of public financing of elections as a way to improve the conduct of campaigns has been around for more than a century, since U.S. President Teddy Roosevelt said in his 1907 State of the Union Address, "The need for collecting large campaign funds would vanish if Congress provided an appropriation for the proper and legitimate expenses of each of the great national parties."

As of 2016, 13 states provided some form of public financing option for campaigns. However, only five states extended their programs beyond governor to state legislative contests.

Only three states (Arizona, Connecticut, Maine) run a "clean elections" program, in which candidates generate a certain number of nominal contributions from individuals (as little as $5) to demonstrate a show of public support to trigger a public funding mechanism, up to a specified expenditure limit. Candidates participating in the program agree to forego contributions from PACs, unions and corporations. An analysis in Maine found increases in number of candidates running in elections and in candidates choosing to run publicly financed campaigns in the three election cycles after Maine adopted its program.

Maryland Congressman John Sarbanes introduced campaign public matching funds legislation in 2014, The Government by the People Act. Describing the act, Sarbanes said, *"American democracy is under siege. More than ever, the wealthy and well-connected are flooding our politics with big-money campaign contributions. Candidates—dependent on these contributions to run competitive campaigns—are caught up in a bad system. Instead of being able to spend their time talking to their constituents and representing their communities, candidates must court big donors. Too often, this also means that public policy suffers. As a result, the public's trust in government is eroding."*

# Lobbying: Pay to Play?

*"Under a system in which no single question is*
*submitted to the electorate for direct decision, an ardent*
*minority for or against a particular measure may*
*often count for more than an apathetic majority."*

PATRICK DEVLIN, BRITISH LAWYER AND JUDGE,
AUTHOR OF *THE ENFORCEMENT OF MORALS*

Lobbying the Maryland legislature is a multi-million dollar business. Joker was small potatoes as a lobbyist compared to the rainmakers. In 2015, 29 lobbyists were compensated more than $475,000, and eight were compensated more than $1 million. Ten firms reported more than $1.3 million in compensation from lobbying activities. Three of those firms generated more than $3 million.

More than 300 Maryland employers spent at least $50,000 on lobbying in 2015. And lobbyists spent $2.3 million on more than 400 "special events" to wine and dine legislative committees and groups.

It's an incestuous business that's all about creating "relationships,"—the code word for access, face time, influence, inside information, reciprocal favors and annual financial contributions—an activity at which many politicians excel. Ordinary citizens may get occasional face time with legislators on a designated day or two over a 90-day session, but they have to earn a living on the others. Lobbyists *are* earning a handsome living by being in the legislators' faces at the State House all day, every day.

## The Swinging Gate

The career path of former Maryland Senate Majority Leader Rory Garrity shows the intertwined and opportunistic relationship between politics and lobbying.

During his third term in the Maryland Senate, Garrity ran for Congress in 2012 and lost. On September 1, 2013, he announced his resignation from the Senate, more than a year before his term expired, saying his decision was driven largely by his desire to spend more time with his three children, according to the *Washington Post.*

Two weeks later, Garrity announced he had joined a law firm with a major lobbying practice in Annapolis.

Under Maryland law, former legislators are prohibited from lobbying in the state legislature on behalf of clients during the first legislative session after their departure.

But the groundwork had been laid for Garrity to return to Annapolis to influence his former cronies as soon as possible. His new law firm, Alexander & Cleaver, quoted the Senate Lion Miller sounding eager to see Garrity back in the chamber's halls in its news release about Garrity's hiring.

"I was honored and privileged to work closely with Rory as my colleague and the Majority Leader," The Lion said. "He remains my good friend and I look forward to working with him in the future…"

Garrity set about showering politicians throughout the state with gifts from his Friends of Rory Garrity campaign account, which ceased to exist for its originally intended purpose of getting re-elected to the Senate, but remained valuable as a vehicle for currying political favor. From the time Garrity left the Senate in September 2013 through 2015, the candidate-cum-lobbyist transferred about $60,000 from his dwindling campaign account, stretching out the largesse into more than 80 contributions to more than 60 different Maryland political candidates and slates. He covered all the bases, contributing to Maryland candidates for Congress, governor, lieutenant governor, comptroller, attorney general, General Assembly and county executive; and to both the Maryland House and Senate Democratic Slates and several "team" slates by legislative district. He transferred money to 16 of the 33 Democratic senators and 16 delegates. His contributions to two district slates—23rd District Team Slate and Team 30 Slate—appear strategically targeted: A powerful 40-year delegate and 20-year chair of the Maryland House Judiciary Committee was from District 23; and the Maryland House Speaker was from District 30.

Garrity's campaign finance report showed that he opened 2014 with about $47,000. He could have disbursed that money legally to charities as a retiring legislator, but he didn't, not a cent. But he gave $32,375 to politicians during the year. Perhaps he was looking for a return on investment that donations to charities could not provide beyond a warm and fuzzy feeling?

In 2015, the first year Garrity was legally permitted to lobby during the legislative session, he was compensated $1.7 million and represented more than 70 clients. In just a six-month period covering from before to after the 2016 legislative session, Garrity billed organizations for nearly $1 million in lobbying, making him one of 14 lobbyists to bill for more than $500,000 during that time.

I can't say how it really works from an insider's perspective; I'm an outsider. But perhaps this is all I really need to know. Employers representing the insurance, energy, health care, communications, defense/security, gaming, alcohol, technology, real estate, transportation, pharmacy, financial and numerous other industries had so much faith in Garrity's ability to influence his former colleagues that they paid him $1.7 million for his insider knowledge, access, influence and relationships. And the Alexander & Cleaver law firm knew Garrity would be such a hot commodity as a lobbyist with his recent relationships that they hired him away from the legislature and sent him back to the State House to lobby former cronies as soon as he was eligible.

Of course, Garrity's quick switch from legislator to lobbyist is common in politics.

Glenn R. Parker, an author and political science professor, contended in his book, *Capitol Investments: The Marketability of Political Skills*, that
the prospect of a future lobbying career can affect legislators' views and
decisions. Donations from special interest groups can lead to the development of relationships with lobbyists, increasing chances that legislators will come to share the policy positions of those groups. "Legislators
invest human capital in rent-seeking activities [efforts to obtain preferential treatment for special interests by using the machinery of govern-
ment] as a way of dazzling future employers with their adeptness and
effectiveness in these activities," Parker wrote.

In her study, "The Influence of Campaign Contributions on
Legislative Policy," the University of Rochester's Lynda Powell docu-
mented that the access legislators give to lobbyists clearly is biased in
favor of campaign donors. Powell contended that her findings "suggest
the possibility that the access or 'pay to play' model of lobbying may have
some credence."

The 2016 run for Congress by Maryland Delegate Dereck Davis,
chairman of the House Economic Matters Committee, exemplified the
"pay to play" model of lobbying. At the least, many lobbyists were making
sure they were on Davis' radar as contributors.

*Center Maryland*, the online political news outlet, suggested that special interests and lobbyists may have been contributing heavily to Davis'
congressional campaign as much to hedge their bets against the possibility that Davis would lose—and retain his Maryland House chairmanship—
as wanting him to be elected to Congress. According to *Center Maryland's*
analysis, at least $138,000 of the $188,000, or 73 percent, Davis had raised
at one point in his campaign came from industries and entities—and the
lobbyists who advocated for them—that had legislation before his committee. *Center Maryland* identified 26 lobbyists who had contributed $250
or more to Davis's campaign, including 13 who donated at least $1,000.

While Garrity became an immediate uber-lobbyist, he was far from
the only former Maryland legislator to cash in on trading in influence.
For example, Barbara Hoffman, a 20-year Maryland senator, averaged

244

$384,000 in compensation for lobbying activities in 2014 and 2015; former Maryland delegate, senator and Baltimore County executive Dennis Rasmussen averaged $676,000; American Joe Mieduiwski, a 20-year member of the Maryland House and Senate, averaged $340,000; and Gil Genn, a 12-year delegate, averaged $259,000.

Others with strong political connections also cleaned up. For example, Frank Boston III, son of the former chairman of Baltimore City's General Assembly delegation, raked in an average of $756,000 over those two years; Garrity's wife, who works at the same law/lobbying firm as her husband, averaged $565,000; and Career Pol's wife, a principal in a lobbying firm, averaged $622,000.

## All in the Family, In Bed Together

Career Pol and his wife represent the prototype of the legislator-lobbyist power couple, with crossover between the industries and businesses that pay the wife to represent their interests before the legislature as a lobbyist and PACs that donate to the state senator, chairman of the powerful Budget and Taxation Committee. How more clearly can the incestuous nature of special interest money in politics be illustrated than to have the same industries and professions feeding the bank accounts of a lobbyist paid to influence legislation and a politician who uses the money to stay in office so he can to pass, kill or otherwise influence legislation, and who literally go to bed together every night (at least, assuming a good marriage and absence of sleep apnea)?

| Organization Career Pol's Wife Represented as a Lobbyist | PACs Contributing to Career Pol (2011-14 Election Cycle) |
|---|---|
| Baltimore Gas and Electric Company | Baltimore Gas and Electric PAC |
| American College of Emergency Physicians, Maryland Chapter | Emergency Medicine PAC |

| Maryland Motor Truck Association | Motor Truck Association PAC Maryland |
|---|---|
| Maryland State Medical Society | Medical PAC Maryland |
| The Maryland Insurance Council | • Insurance and Financial Advisers PAC Maryland; and<br>• AgentPAC Professional Insurance Agents Association – Maryland PAC |
| Mental Health Association of Maryland | Community Behavioral Health Association of Maryland PAC |
| • Mid-Atlantic LifeSpan (senior care provider association); and<br>• Maryland Association of Adult Day Services | • LifeSpan PAC; and<br>• HFAM (Health Facilities Association of Maryland) Maryland Nursing Home PAC |
| Sprint Corporation | • VerizonCommunications Inc. Good Government Club-Maryland PAC; and<br>• AT&T Inc. Federal PAC and AT&T PAC Maryland<br>• Sprint/Nextel ($1,000 contribution from Phoenix, AZ address) |

So, for Career Pol to take legislative actions against the interests of these industries and professions, he would not only be jeopardizing future PAC contributions to his campaign, but potentially biting the hand that feeds his wife, ergo himself. In the dog-eat-dog, retributive realm of politics and influence-trading, would it really be far-fetched to think that a Baltimore Gas and Electric or a Maryland Motor Truck Association would fire Career Pol's wife as its lobbyist if they deemed that Career Pol betrayed them on key legislation?

Efforts and resources to influence legislation through lobbying are growing, according to Common Cause Maryland, the government watchdog group. Spending on lobbying increased 18 percent over two years, from $16.8 million in 2014 to $19.8 million in 2016 *(see Appendix 2 listing top lobbying interests)*. "The increasing amount of money spent on lobbying represents a challenge to the ability of individual citizens to make their voices heard in Maryland lawmaking," Common Cause's director said. "Most citizens lack the time and resources to compete with professional lobbyists, giving the interest groups—and influential lobbyists—significant influence."

# January 4, 2014 – Beware the Marshmallow Man

At a pre-General Assembly session League of Women Voters legislative luncheon, I sat with Bill Woodcock, aka Marshmallow Man, the 53 Beers on Tap blogger. I knew Marshmallow had already blasted my candidacy as meritless. I introduced myself and we had a friendly conversation. Marshmallow offered to meet for coffee and talk about my candidacy. Marshmallow was highly opinionated and didn't mind ruffling feathers on his blog, but I believed he was committed to knowing his subjects and accuracy. On that day, I had Gadfly to look out for me. Whether it was really for my own good or because of a personal beef she had with Marshmallow or another ulterior motive, I'm not sure.

Gadfly noticed me talking to Marshmallow and approached me later to caution me to keep my distance. She told me that Marshmallow had already gone public about his personal support for and relationship with Man of the People—essentially warning me that he had a bias and implying that he couldn't be objective. At the time, I didn't know that Gadfly also had a history with Man of the People from their 2010 Baltimore County Council race that produced residual antagonism.

# GADFLY

Gadfly and her husband Pest were known as rabble rousers in Catonsville for their long-running battle against development plans being pursued by an influential developer, dating to her 2010 council run.

Developer Steve Whalen was pushing plans to redevelop part of the grounds of a 200-acre state psychiatric institution into an estimated $350 million development of housing, office and retail/hotel called The Promenade at Catonsville. Gadfly and Pest led an opposition group called Catonsville PromeNOT. PromeNOT leveled accusations that the deep-pocketed developer was swaying Baltimore County's District 12 Delegates Fireman and Cop, and County Councilman Tom Quick to grease the skids on a development deal. The Promenade proposal became controversial during Gadfly and Man of the People's primary race against Quick for the Baltimore County Council seat in 2010. Opponents of The Promenade contended that such a large-scale development would undermine the small businesses that formed the core of Catonsville's downtown charm and that resources should be directed to redeveloping downtrodden commercial areas.

In that contentious 2010 council race with Man of the People, Gadfly argued that residents felt "shut out of the process" and that developers were "calling the shots" in Baltimore County government. She testified against state legislation targeted to redeveloping state hospital properties that laid the foundation for The Promenade to move forward.

Gadfly's PromeNOT prodded the development's supporters, posting an animated parody video on YouTube with the faces of the developer and politicians Fireman, Cop and Quick atop elves' bodies dancing together, as if in cahoots, to a hip-hop version of the Nutcracker Suite.

Gadfly, it turned out, had good reason for concern. The developer pled guilty to funneling $7,500 in illegal campaign contributions through three surrogate "straw men" to Councilman Quick, concealing the true source of the money. Before the developer's guilty plea, Gadfly and Pest had gotten under the politicians' skin like poison ivy. "They continue to engage in petty personal attacks and I resent it," Councilman Quick said.

Gadfly and Pest, however, had the last word after the developer's guilty plea. Pest penned an op-ed to a Catonsville online news outlet, which expressed Gadfly's future persona as a delegate candidate as well as the couple's persistence in scrutinizing authority.

"Many Democrats refuse to be cogs in the machine and are disappointed in the status quo in local politics," Pest wrote. "My wife and I are Democrats because we believe in protecting the vulnerable and disenfranchised. We believe in sticking up for the little guy. I'm proud to be part of a family that hasn't been afraid to speak truth to power."

. . .

One other maneuver in Gadfly's 2010 Baltimore County Council race prompted Man of the People to cite it in retrospect, four years later, as a sign that Gadfly was duplicitous. Other observers suggested Gadfly was involved in a deceitful ploy to make voters believe that she was on a candidates' ticket endorsed by President Obama.

For the 2010 primary election polls, Gadfly positioned herself with a life-sized cardboard cutout of President Obama. Perhaps coincidentally, a mailing had been sent to Maryland voters by a PAC, headed "Team Obama" and listing candidates at all government levels representing Baltimore County. Gadfly was not named on the misleading mailer's "endorsed" list—Obama made no such endorsements—but some observers like Man of the People still linked Gadfly with the political trick because of her Obama cutout and accused her of pandering to get African-American votes.

. . .

G adfly appeared the modern-day, versatile, do-everything Super Woman: Mother of three school-aged children fighting for safer neighborhoods and against school overcrowding; independent small-business owner who managed workers, set a budget and met payroll; principled community activist battling moneyed developers to preserve Catonsville's character and defeat greed; environmentalist with a biology degree; and philanthropist assisting domestic violence victims.

Gadfly and I had a similar outlook; we ran left of center. I found her personable and friendly—opposite how some business and political targets of her community activism experienced her. We were close in age—Gadfly was 46—and surprisingly, we were the only two candidates who had children in public schools. She was an attractive and poised woman, and attracted a strong following of women and people who opposed the mega-development Promenade plan to her camp.

Gadfly was one of two candidates—along with Energy—who had roots in the disparate Howard County and Baltimore County sides of the district. Gadfly grew up in Howard County in a prominent family. Her father was involved in local politics. A main road in the county carries Gadfly's maiden surname as does an historic house, granary and environmental preserve. Gadfly and Pest operated a catering company from their Baltimore County home and rented business space in a Howard County community center.

With her bona fide county "dual citizenship" and appeal to women in a majority male field, Gadfly was as well-positioned as anybody to slip into third, if not to challenge frontrunners Anointed One and Zelig.

# January 25, 2014 - Terror at the Mall

A teenager entered The Mall in Columbia with a backpack and sat in the food court. After an hour, he climbed the stairs, entered a skateboard and surf shop, unpacked and assembled a shotgun and shot and killed two young store employees before shooting himself. The incident caused chaos and panic throughout the crowded mall, ignited a massive law enforcement and emergency services engulfment and struck fear in the community.

I learned that only a few states required a buyer to be over the age of 21 to purchase a long gun. The 19-year-old had purchased the shotgun legally. I was incredulous: You need to be 21 to have a beer in a bar, yet you can buy a deadly weapon legally at a gun store as a high school senior.

# February 19, 2014 – Deadly Combination: 18-Year-Olds and Guns

Three weeks after the mall massacre, I was the only District 12 candidate to address the tragedy and lax gun control at a Columbia Democratic Club forum:

"You can buy a shotgun or rifle at the age of 18," I told the audience. "I would propose raising that age to 21. An 18-year-old's brain is not developed fully. They're emotionally not able to make rational decisions. They don't have the maturity. They make rash decisions. I think it's ridiculous to have an age of 18 for a person to be able to go in and purchase a shotgun. You know what I'm referring to…"

Despite the tragedy occurring in our district, no other District 12 candidate committed to changing the law. If two senseless murders and a SWAT team shutdown of a crowded commercial center weren't enough to warrant a sensible change to help prevent a reoccurrence, what would be? I had to wonder: Where was the backbone among these candidates to actually *take a stand* on something specific and controversial, instead of pontificating on vague generalities and playing it safe?

## Most Admired Politician

At that same forum, the moderator asked, "What politician do you most look up to and why?" Several candidates answered that they admired Rock God. Though Rock God was widely admired and engendered loyalty, the more I observed him, the more I believed he may be growing too comfortable as an entrenched politician.

When I had one minute to make an opening statement, I had to immediately connect my background and experience with the audience's, clearly articulate why I was running and why I was the best person for the position, deliver my messages in a succinct, understandable and compelling way, and try to make an indelible impression and distinguish myself from my competitors.

It wasn't like that for Rock God. At the forum, Rock God wandered through his minute, seemingly unfocused, recalling how he appeared in that same community center before an election 20 years ago as a political rookie, omitting discussion of his core issues. When the timer rang the bell, Rock God joked with the timer about how quickly the 60 seconds flew by, and the audience chuckled, the good will palpably filling the room. Rock God was given special dispensation by the moderator to speak free-form for two more minutes, the time allotted for other candidates to answer a question later in the forum. Rock God's next two minutes weren't much more noteworthy, except for a pat line: "Some people go to Annapolis to make a point and some go to make policy." Rock God's message was clear by inference: Some politicians are show-horses, full of bluster and style and sound-bites but short on substance and desire or ability to do the nitty-gritty policy work. Rock God, on the other hand, is the workhorse, bringing people together, working through differences and crafting solutions to complex problems.

I'm sure Rock God felt more compelled to do what I felt I had to do at these events earlier in his political career—get to the points, make them strong, and make an immediate impression. But it didn't appear he had that same sense of urgency anymore. He could afford not to, the dues he had paid allowing him some luxury of indulgence. He was like Tony Montana in *Scarface*. He had built his empire from nothing; now he would defend it while enjoying its privileges (minus the cocaine and palatial digs). Discipline and passion in his presence and delivery would have been a bonus, the cherry on top of the gooey hot fudge sundae, but it wasn't necessary. Like a gifted comedian with a buzzed audience, he held the politically engaged in the palm of his hand, seemingly effortlessly. He was a master of the craft.

# Shenanigans: Everyone in (or out of) the Pool

*"The conscious and intelligent manipulation of the organized
habits and opinions of the masses is an important element
in democratic society. Those who manipulate this unseen
mechanism of society constitute an invisible government which
is the true ruling power of our country...In almost every act of
our daily lives, whether in the sphere of politics or business, in
our social conduct or our ethical thinking, we are dominated
by the relatively small number of persons...who understand
the mental processes and social patterns of the masses. It is
they who pull the wires which control the public mind."*

Edward Bernays, Austrian-American "father of
public relations," author of *Propaganda*

Politics are rife with shenanigans. What would politics be without shenanigans? It would be like a Chinese dinner without a fortune cookie;
a county fair without farm animals; a James Bond movie without a beautiful
love interest. It just wouldn't be complete. It would be missing its essence.

Nowhere was that more evident than in District 13, Rock God's king-
dom adjacent to my District 12, in cunning maneuvering around the
February 25 candidate filing deadline.

Here's the anatomy and chronology of a sleazy political circus full of
Machiavellian scheming, backroom handshakes, cloak-and-dagger plot

twists, opportunism, manipulation, nepotism, fudging the truth and insider intrigue:

On June 13, 2013, District 13 Delegate Rock God officially announced at his annual pizza party fundraiser that he would vacate his seat to run for District 13 Senate to replace retiring Senator Jerry Ruley. Lo and behold, two days later, Howard County Board of Education member and pediatrician Regina Hassan announced she would be running for Rock God's seat. Backroom Exhibit #1.

Never mind that Hassan still had two years remaining in her term on the elected school board. Apparently, in politics, why bother keeping a commitment you made to voters, even the *most important* commitment: Fulfilling the term to which you obligated yourself, if a better opportunity comes your way? Yet such commitments are broken all the time by political fast-climbers. Uber-lobbyist Garrity broke his to make millions.

Leaving a regular job for a better opportunity is perfectly understandable. The contract is only between employee and employer; legally, it is an at-will arrangement, meaning that either party can end the contract at any time. But when you promise voters countywide all the things you will do to improve education and the school system for four years, and they take you at your word and trust you enough to donate money to you and vote for you, you don't break that contract.

Hassan's announcement obviously had been in the works for quite a while, indicating Hassan and members of Team 13 running for reelection—Rock God and Delegates Pendleton and Mercer—had been caucusing in somebody's trap door basement. Team 13 must have been thrilled to recruit a new member to their club with the status of a school board chairwoman and a physician, who had valuable, influential, well-placed and moneyed connections herself.

The *Baltimore Sun* reported that Congressman Elijah Cummings was among the "numerous elected officials" who attended Hassan's announcement event in support. It was not an impromptu affair; Hassan already had Cummings's endorsement wrapped up from the word go. Backroom Exhibit #2.

In his endorsement speech, Cummings said he would do "everything in my power to get her where she has to go," according to *The Sun*.

"We trust Regina," Cummings said. "We trust that when she says she is going to do something, she is going to do it."

But Cummings was absolutely wrong. [Cummings would reappear later in the dramedy when the plot thickened, forcing him to select from the Politician 101 Bag of Tricks one of the fundamentals they do best for any particular occasion (choose among the entries): backpedal, equivocate, flip-flop, pivot, jump ship, convert, have a change of heart, conform, fudge, obfuscate, hide, drift with the wind, etc.]

According to the article, Rock God, Ruley, and Pendleton attended to "welcome Hassan to Team 13." Pledge Master Rock God extended the sorority rush invitation to Hassan.

"The four of us [Ruley. Rock God, Pendleton and Mercer] were able to work together on so many issues in such a cooperative way to *get real things done* (**My emphasis:** *there's that cloying phrase again!*) for the district and for Howard County. We knew we would have to come together and find someone who could join us in Team 13 to deliver the same kind of service. It's with great pleasure we are welcoming Regina to run with us," Rock God fawned.

*Whoa, slow down Team 13! We're still a year away from the primary, and eight months from the candidate filing deadline. Don't you want to wait and see who else might jump into the race, and then evaluate all the candidates if you really want to recruit one to Team 13?* That would seem logical, but that would be a 'no.' By August 2013, Hassan was registered with the state as an official member of the Team 13 slate.

Team 13's maneuver was the typical political power play. By reeling in Hassan as soon as she entered, they protected her from having to run a potential knock-down, drag-out fight on her own against a potential high number of contenders eager to vie for an open seat, anybody's ballgame, best man or woman wins. By placing her on the Team 13 ticket, they automatically associated her with an avalanche of political and public service credentials (Ruley, Rock God, Pendleton and Mercer combined had 56 years of General Assembly experience, 16 years on the Howard County Council, eight years as Howard County executive, and seven years as county police chief). That's not to mention all the money the individual candidates had stockpiled for years, the Team 13 slate bank account, fundraising prowess, name recognition, advertisements, campaign literature, yard signs and billboards, and political, business and civic connections those four and other local politician Team 13 members could bring to bear on an election. All that amassed force would be enough to scare all but the most hearty—and perhaps foolhardy—newcomers away from an attempt, all but guaranteeing Hassan a victory no matter how well she ran her own campaign or what she stood for.

About a month after Hassan was welcomed to Team 13, another candidate filed for the District 13 delegate race, Tony Eifort, a career grocery store manager and community organizer. Eifort acknowledged that he was a longshot and that he would run a "low budget campaign" in a *Baltimore Sun* profile. That was an understatement. Eifort filed an affidavit with the state declaring he would not raise nor spend more than $1,000; by the end of 2013, Hassan already was loaded with $45,000. "I'll be an underdog," Eifort said, "but I don't think they'll see me coming. That'll be the surprise."

*In fact, Tony, Team 13 wouldn't see you coming or going. More likely, they would squash you under the Team 13 steamroller and never see you at all.*

## Bait and Switch

Everything was going along swimmingly for Team 13, until a funny thing happened on the way to the State House. Inexplicably, Syed Hassan, Regina's husband, filed to run as a candidate for delegate in District 13 *against his wife,* on the day of the candidate filing deadline, February 25, 2014. What was Team 13 going to do with *two Hassans* in the race? Was there an obscure state election law that allowed a married couple to run as one candidate, maybe to promote gender equality so they could split career and political ladder-climbing ambitions with child-rearing and housekeeping duties?

For three calendar days, husband and wife were political opponents. Not even the most voracious political couple ever, Hillary and Bill, ever did that to each other!

"Why the stone cold hell would a husband file against his wife? Well, I know, but I'm talking about elections here," mocked Marshmallow Man's blog.

But Regina Hassan had a quick fix to the messiness: a political divorce. On the second full day after Syed filed, Regina officially submitted her withdrawal papers, on the deadline for candidate withdrawal, February 27. Regina offered a reason publicly for her withdrawal within hours of the deadline to delete her name from the ballot. But whether that is the real reason was anybody's guess, except for the insiders, who surely knew. Backroom Exhibit #3.

According to the *Baltimore Sun,* Hassan said she withdrew after discovering that two particular school board members would not run for re-election, declaring, "I just felt that in that moment it was the right thing to do."

Translated, her reason meant she believed the school board was going to lose too much knowledge or integrity or accountability or some other such value without her diving back into the fray to save the day.

Phony-baloney. There was no guarantee any school board member would run for re-election when Hassan announced eight months previously that she would be leaving the board in the lurch before her term had expired to pursue a higher office. Why would she feel guilty about it now, or suddenly adopt a sense of responsibility that she had willingly shirked eight months before? Or could it have been that she possessed a healthy amount of the personality trait that fills many politicians' tanks—narcissism—and truly believed the school board could not function adequately without her after all. But that doesn't make much sense either. A full-blown narcissist would surely choose the glory of a state delegate position, where you can be wined and dined by lobbyists, feted at community events, vote on the state's top issues and sometimes even have your picture taken with the governor, over the comparative drudgery, obscurity and schoolmarmish aura of school board meetings.

And what about all the people who loaded her campaign account with cash, thinking she was running for higher-profile state delegate? Should an office-seeker have to return such donations for collecting them under false pretenses?

As is usually the case in politics, there was more going on here than the politicians let on. In other words, the politicians had no compunction about hiding the truth from the public and massaging it for appearances sake.

I don't know what the real story was, but I'll venture a guess: Regina Hassan just wasn't cut out for the political game, the rough-and-tumble of it all, the salesmanship, socializing, deal-making, relationship-building and sleight of hand, and realized it well into her campaign, and took cover back in her safe haven, where she felt more comfortable, useful, purposeful and impactful.

I saw Regina speak at a forum. No doubt, she was a smart and competent person, but I was not impressed with her as a candidate. Seemingly an introvert, quiet and reserved, she was not a compelling speaker. She seemed to have difficulty expressing her thoughts and explaining why she was running. She appeared uncomfortable and passionless, and did not arouse the crowd. The bottom line: she was dull, and maybe she felt internally about the race what she showed externally.

She was a doctor who took care of children; of course it made sense for her to serve children on the school board. But she didn't say that. I did.

Addressing the bizarre, husband-for-wife bait-and-switch, Regina Hassan said in *The Sun,*

"It was [Syed Hassan's] decision and I'm really excited about it. I think he will be great; he brings that business perspective."

In a letter to constituents, Regina Hassan wrote: "Due to my commitment to the people and children of Howard County I felt that it was my duty and responsibility to continue on the Board of Education to help maintain stability and direction...With the filing deadline approaching there was only one person close to me who I felt would carry on my vision for Howard County and the State of Maryland, and will be a perfect replacement for Team 13: my husband Syed Hassan. He shares the same values, passion and vision..."

## Curveball

Perhaps neither Syed nor Regina saw the curveball coming. But if they did, they whiffed. Delegate Mercer had some deep undercover intrigue of his own brewing, some clandestine meetings of his own on the third level of an underground parking garage, because there couldn't have been any other way what happened next could have happened without Mercer having a hand in it.

Syed Hassan wasn't the only wannabe candidate from Howard County making a last-minute, desperate 35-mile dash to the state elections office in Annapolis before the curtain fell on the 2014 election registration season, like a heroin junkie who caught wind that his supplier was about to blow town. Maybe unbeknownst to each other, Valerie Appleby was racing Syed down Route 50 on her way to get her own high before the supply was shut down for good. Backroom Exhibit #4.

Where did Appleby materialize from? Wasn't this an inside job implemented with exquisite timing that only the Hassans would know about and execute, with the complicity of Team 13? Didn't they measure it just right, maneuvering so close to the deadline that by the time any other potentially interested candidates learned of the shell game, it would be too late to enter? Was there a mole inside Team 13 who was playing his own game? And what would Mercer have to do with all this?

Turns out, Appleby's mother had been Mercer's campaign chairwoman for his five State House elections. Not only that, but Valerie Appleby was identified as Mercer's niece initially in some media accounts. Valerie Appleby corrected that fact in subsequent media reports, saying she was not technically Mercer's niece, but that she had known Mercer "for my whole life, probably" and that he was a close family friend who had "always been very supportive of me."

*Houston to Team 13 pshhhh: We have a problem. Over.*

Marshmallow Man didn't take kindly to the shenanigans in District 13. *"With all respect to Regina Hassan, it was not for her to decide who else may run for that seat...I will, under no circumstances, support Syed Hassan for delegate. The geometry of this entire exercise of the dual filing and the 48-hour later drop out smacks of favoritism with a whiff of arrogance.*

*If you're part of a 'team,' you don't let your teammates down. You don't line up for a play and then you run another play while the other 10 players run the play that's called...So while Regina's motivations may be noble, her and her husband's actions smack of selfishness."*

This was where the Team 13 politicians should have backed out and let the three remaining challengers—husband Syed Hassan, pseudo-niece Appleby and grocer Eifort—duke it out independently, stand on their own two feet and compete for the open seat without all the advantages of riding the coattails of the incumbents. Prove yourself. Rise above. Outwork and outsmart each other. Win on your own merits.

But Team 13 members couldn't resist the ability to exercise their power and manipulate the outcome. How could either of the two candidates who had been in the race less than a week, and who had never run a successful campaign—though one, Appleby, had run a troubled, error-prone election effort—possibly deserve to be elevated for preferential treatment? If anybody, Eifort should have earned the ticket. Most recently, he had been working as the "community organizer" for one of Columbia's 10 village associations, which put him more in touch with residents than either of the other two. He was a county resident for 40 years, compared to Appleby's two years, and demonstrated himself to be the more committed candidate, having pounded the beat for six months.

But Eifort didn't have the panache or the money, and he wasn't going to get the nod. In contrast, evidence showed that Syed Hassan, the high-tech business owner with the physician wife, and Appleby, an attorney who had loaned her 2010 campaign $113,550 and worked for her CEO father's company, each had strong connections to money and influential people.

But that's politics, the ugly underbelly. Like the Mafia: Using power and influence to choose who gets "made" and who gets "whacked."

I like the concept of fairness. Unfortunately, that makes it hard to abide politics.

Syed Hassan's campaign website said Syed, who holds a master's degree in mechanical engineering, had "worked hard for every inch of his success. His journey has taken him from poverty to owning a prosperous IT firm."

Appleby also had a strong professional background. She worked as corporate counsel in the workforce development firm that her father founded and served as president and CEO. Appleby had run for delegate in neighboring Montgomery County in 2010, discovering how difficult it was to compete against a "team slate" of three incumbents. The three incumbent slate members won, with Appleby finishing fifth out of six.

During that race, Appleby had received a $400 transfer from Mercer's candidate committee and $200 from Mercer as an individual, highlighting their connection.

## Red Flags about More Shenanigans

If the Team 13 members looked, they would have found red flags in Appleby's 2010 campaign. It was marked by flagrant violations of campaign regulations, connections to a crooked consultant and misleading—if not outright deceitful—campaign literature and marketing.

Appleby sent a mailing to voters showing her in the center of a group photo from a Maryland Women's Legislative Briefing that included a host of Democratic politicians, including Maryland U.S. Senator Barbara Mikulski, Maryland Congressman Christopher Van Hollen, the Montgomery County executive and several other elected officials, with the caption, "We all agree that Valerie Appleby is the one." A local political blogger asked politicians who appeared in the photo whether they had endorsed Appleby. They said they hadn't, though several said they had endorsed the state-registered slate of three candidates against whom Appleby was running.

In an article on the Appleby mailer in the (Montgomery County) *Gazette* newspapers, Appleby blamed the confusion on a printing error and mistakes that were not caught by her campaign consultants. "That should not have gone out," Appleby said.

Observers also noted that the Appleby campaign had placed many signs in state and county road medians and other spots that were prohibited by regulations. The Maryland Politics Watch blog took photos of the misplaced signs and posted them online.

The Town of Kensington, Maryland's code enforcement officer advised Appleby that "it is unlawful to display or post any sign in a public right of way," according to the blog.

About two months after that Kensington code violation notice, the Maryland Politics Watch blog featured a post alleging that the Appleby campaign had "resumed her placement of illegal campaign signs all over the district," featuring a photo of a park police officer in a busy intersection, holding several Appleby signs, presumably after removing them.

And then there was Appleby's connection to a shady political operative. The *Baltimore Sun* reported that Appleby paid Julius Henson's political consulting business at least $79,000 during her 2010 campaign. Henson was convicted of election fraud, sentenced to prison and ordered by a federal judge to pay Maryland $1 million for more than 100,000 election-night "robo-calls" his firm made in 2010 on behalf of the Republican gubernatorial candidate that the judge determined were intended to suppress the votes of African-Americans.

Commenting on Henson's tactics in *The Sun,* Baltimore Mayor Stephanie Rawlings-Blake said, «No campaign committee in Maryland should support his brand of gutter politics and candidates should think twice about hiring the likes of Julius Henson.»

Distributing dishonest and deceitful mailers? Violating state and local legal codes? Hiring a consultant known long before the 2010 election fraud charge for dirty political tricks like calling a candidate a "Nazi" and paying a crowd to shout down a candidate? Who cares! Business as usual. Win at all costs, ethics and laws be damned? Join our team!

• • •

With three candidates to choose from to fill Regina Hassan's spot on Team 13—pseudo-niece Appleby, husband Syed Hassan and grocer Eifort—the slate members scrambled to save face. They claimed to interview each candidate, and within a week, selected Appleby, who had been a District 13 and Howard County resident for only two years, to join the team. Team 13 issued a news release saying it chose Appleby because "her experience in business and her advocacy for victims of domestic violence will complement the team's expertise." Backroom Exhibit #5.

Wait a minute. Experience in business? But hadn't Syed Hassan founded and run Scientific Systems & Software International Corporation since 1985, rising, as he claimed, from poverty to successful IT business ownership? Appleby's business experience included working as an associate in a law firm for five years and as counsel in her father's company. Like most candidates, Appleby had her fair share of accomplishments. But if I judged their two resumes based on business qualifications, Syed, business founder and CEO, would be the clear winner. So advocacy for domestic violence victims must have won the day.

Syed was left out in the cold, whacked by the Team 13 Mafia, despite his wife's strong recommendation that he would be an outstanding replacement for her. The ostracized Syed fought gallantly, and quickly.

On May 15, 2014, Syed registered the Excellence for Howard County Slate. Guess which two members comprised the slate? Syed and Regina Hassan.

It would appear the slate was created for one purpose: to fund Syed's election bid. The day after Syed registered the slate, Regina unloaded $30,000 from her now-useless delegate campaign fund into the slate fund.

Previously, Regina had transferred $6,000—the maximum allowed—from her campaign account to Syed's individual candidate account.

Within a month of his entry, before he even had a campaign website to outline his positions or appear at any forums, Syed scored an endorsement from Congressman Cummings, who stayed aboard the Hassan train, just moving to another car. *Who knew it could be that easy to get a congressman to ride your train,* I thought, inspiring my wild-goose chase inquiry to Cummings to consider endorsing me as well.

Within four weeks of his entry, Syed whipped up a fundraiser featuring an appearance by Cummings, requesting $2,000 from "sponsors" and $1,000 from "hosts." A little research showed that the Hassan's had well-heeled friends, running in the circles of doctors and business leaders. The hosts of Syed's fundraiser owned a 5,232-square-foot, five-bedroom, seven-bath house on five acres that was listed as being sold for $1.15 million in 2012. I randomly Googled the addresses of contributors to Regina and found, for example, two homes in Montgomery County valued at between $1.68 million and $1.76 million, and two homes in Howard County valued between $840,000 and $980,000.

With the help of the Hassan's well-heeled friends and associates, Syed ramped up his fundraising in record time, generating $110,000 in less than three months through his wife's candidate account transfers, donations and a $50,000 loan from himself.

He spent more than $20,000 in the last month of the campaign. But none of it was enough to overcome the strength of Team 13 and Appleby's inclusion as a member. As evidence that voters identified with the Team 13 slate, Appleby, Pendleton and Mercer placed within narrow margins, each receiving between 25.6 percent and 27.3 percent of the vote, exactly the result one would expect if voters checked off the slate at the voting booth. Syed was a distant fourth, at 15.5 percent. Eifort, who predicted Team 13 wouldn't see him coming, never came, at 4.5 percent.

# MARCH 6, 2014 – LOST IN LANSDOWNE:
## HANG A LOUIE AT BURGER KING

This admission is anathema for a candidate who needs every vote he can get and must ingratiate himself with every community, but I just wasn't down for Lansdowne. Lansdowne was an old, working-class community bordering Baltimore City that had seen its better days—decades ago. I just didn't jibe with the Lansdowne vibe.

I had no particular interest in representing Lansdowne, but the scheming politicians who drew the nonsensical boundary lines for District 12 ordained I would, voters willing. Also, Lansdowne was the hometown of Man of the People. I would be fine leaving representation of Lansdowne to him; he was a better man for it.

Lansdowne High School was the site of our next forum. I left for Lansdowne from my job near Washington at 5:30, thinking 90 minutes would be sufficient for the 7 p.m. start. The drive normally would be an hour or less without traffic. But this was the notorious Washington-Baltimore rush hour, and traffic on the Washington Beltway and Interstate 95 was nightmarish.

It was dark. I got in the vicinity of Lansdowne in enough time, around 6:40, but I took the wrong Route 1 when it split into "Business" and "Main." I got off track from the directions I had mapped on Mapquest. Once I lost that option, I was doomed. I had no GPS or street map. Compounding the situation, hardly any streets in that area connected because the area is laced with a labyrinth of major highways that ring and bisect Baltimore and connect the United States' Northeast corridor, including Route 1, the Baltimore Beltway, I-95, the I-895 tunnel through Baltimore and the Baltimore-Washington Parkway. These major thoroughfares are spliced by several railroad track lines. The result of the cluster of major transportation arteries is that almost all local roads are cut off at some point by highways and tracks, creating a disconnected network of neighborhoods and local roads.

What did this intricately planned, economically vital transportation network mean for me? It meant that I was screwed and my stress level would increase exponentially with each false turn I made, aimless circle I completed and dead end I encountered.

I drove in circles several times through the neighboring community of Arbutus trying to find the right road to lead me to the Promised Land of Lansdowne. But for all intents and purposes, Arbutus and Lansdowne may as well have been East and West Berlin divided by the Berlin Wall for an unfamiliar driver bumbling through the dark. I finally stopped, desperate for directions, in the heart of the two-stoplight Arbutus commercial district. The memory of arriving 20 minutes late to the Delegate Fireman Forum in Arbutus because of snarled traffic was fresh in my mind, and I didn't want to be noticeably late again, make a bad impression and miss my opportunity to make an opening statement.

I pulled into a colorless gas station/convenience store at 6:55 and ran in hoping there would be someone to give me directions. A nun was in line, in full frock and hood regalia, making a transaction and conversing with the shopkeeper, who was behind a glass partition. I was panicking and the nun was taking too long. But how do you interrupt and jump ahead of a nun without creating bad karma?

A young man had just entered in front of me and was in line for cigarettes or lottery tickets or something else behind the counter. The clock was ticking. I didn't have time to wait to ask the shopkeeper for directions. I took my chances and asked the young man, hoping I'd hit the jackpot just as he may have been with the lottery.

"Excuse me, do you know how to get to Lansdowne High School?" I asked, trying to hide my desperation and secret prayer for knowledge.

"Yeah, man. No worries. Take a left at the light before the movie theater and go under the bridge. Turn left when you come to the Burger King. Then turn right at the Royal Farms. That will be Lansdowne Road, take that and the high school will be on the right."

I scribbled the notes on the back of the index card I was using for my opening speech. Turned out this good Samaritan gave me perfect directions, saving my ass from failure and embarrassment. I arrived in the high school auditorium at 7:07. The forum had just started. I scrambled to the stage during a break in speakers, as quickly and inconspicuously as possible.

## Zelig's Brilliance Shines

Zelig showed his brilliance and research skills in addressing the intricacies of the Cove Point project, a proposal by energy company Dominion to develop the East Coast's first natural gas export facility in the Chesapeake Bay. He presented a rapid-fire, 90-second dissertation dissecting the complexities of the environmental risks, including the likelihood of expanded hydraulic fracturing, or "fracking," to extract gas from underground shale by high-pressure drilling, and economic consequences, predicting that exporting natural gas would drive up U.S. prices. Cove Point was not in my wheelhouse, but Zelig, as always, had it covered.

## Audacity

I was pleased to find a letter to the editor in *The Sun* after the Lansdowne forum from

Michael Abrams of Catonsville, whom I had never met, evaluating the candidates' performances and singling me out for comment.

On "fracking," Abrams wrote that I "boldly noted that jobs in this case might not be the highest priority." On raising the minimum wage, Abrams said I was "uniquely vivid" in my support by stating that businesses with employees earning $7.25 per hour were "arguably not very successful ventures." And on the national educational movement known as "Common Core"—standards designed to ensure high school graduates can think critically and are adequately prepared—Abrams noted that "Sachs added to his colorful remarks by saying much opposition to the new standards was a 'bugaboo' of Republicans."

Finally, Abrams separated me from the pack, for better or worse, by declaring that "Sachs demonstrated the most passion for liberal positions, including for campaign finance reform and single-payer health care (perhaps non-starters, but I do admire his audacity)."

Non-starters or not, I took Abrams' letter as a sign that I was hitting my stride, having an impact, and doing what I needed to do to have any chance of standing out: taking identifiable, bold positions and speaking my mind.

# MARCH 11, 2014 – THE KEY ELEMENT FOR POLITICIANS: PERSONAL CONNECTION

At the Charlestown Retirement Community forum, one of the best attended because of the captive audience living on campus, I eschewed my usual stump speech in favor of an effort to connect with the seniors on an emotional and personal level.

"I have a good idea of the issues you have faced and your current challenges," I told the Charlestown residents, "but not because I read it or heard a policy wonk or a politician talk about them. I know from personal experience, from trying to help my mother with problems the last couple of years of her life before she died, when her health was going downhill."

I told them about my mother's challenges with downsizing and finding appropriate housing; exploring assisted living facilities; searching for viable transportation when she couldn't drive; navigating a poorly coordinated, frustrating health care system; determining finances; and finding social outlets.

I wasn't aiming for sympathy, but nevertheless several of the attendees and my fellow candidates offered me condolences and said my speech was heartfelt afterwards. Once again, I didn't know if my speech had earned me any votes, but I was proud that it was memorable.

In that way, I shared a trait with at least one real politician, South Carolina Gov. Sanford. In *The Speechwriter*, author Swaim said delivering original, engaging speeches was imperative to Sanford. "He hated the thought of being the politician who says the same predictable boring things at every event; he wanted to walk into every speaking engagement armed with a story or fact or witty remark that would make him stand out..."

# MARCH 14, 2014 – YOU WON?
## CONGRATULATIONS. YOU'RE FIRED!

At the last minute of my regular Friday meeting with my boss, she said she had something to tell me. It was in response to the letter I wrote to her and the HR director nearly two months earlier outlining the details of General Assembly service, such as time frames and legislative meeting schedules, and recommending flexible alternatives through which I could continue working part-time while serving during the three-month legislative session.

"We can't accommodate your request," she said flatly. And that was that. No discussion, no negotiation. She handed me a memo:

*"We have considered your request to work out a job arrangement to continue working...if you are successful in your run for election... Unfortunately... [we] would not be able to work out an arrangement that provides the flexibility you need to also serve in the state legislature."*

The flat denial to work out a schedule around legislative service was a punch in the gut, but worthwhile to know. I would be heading into crunch time of the campaign with the knowledge that if my longshot bid was successful, I would have to quit my job. I was concerned about how that would affect my motivation, which I knew already paled compared to certain candidates such as Zelig.

The Maryland General Assembly is made up of people who fall into three categories: those who treat the legislature as their full-time or only job (nearly 20 percent); those who own their own business and can structure their employment (for example, Anointed One, with her own plastic surgery practice); and those whose employers support and work with them to allow them flexibility, calculating that having an employee in the legislature adds value to the organization (for example, Next Big Thing's law firm). With my employer's rejection, I knew I didn't fit into any of those categories. I had hoped my proposal would be the starting point for a negotiation on what type of arrangement could be possible. Instead, it turned out to be my own declaration for what was not possible. No one from my employer ever talked to me again after I submitted my hypothetical proposal, no give-and-take or negotiating on telecommuting or part-time work or experimenting with a one-year trial period, if it came to that. It was a cold shower when I needed to fuel the fire.

It was understandable that my health care organization didn't want to try to fill the gaps of my potential absence. Many employers wouldn't. But it was still disappointing to know that my employer did not take enough interest in me personally to support a personal endeavor that could have been a source of pride for not just me, but for the organization to say one of their employees was advocating as a member of a state legislature to improve health care. No, I was just a replaceable cog, easy to let go if I strayed from the straight and narrow.

# March 19, 2014 – Brother, Can
# You Spare a Dime (Bag)?

I suffered through a Chamber of Commerce forum with a headache, bad cold and exhaustion. The highlight came on a question about decriminalizing marijuana. A bill moving through the General Assembly eliminated criminal penalties for possession of less than 10 grams of marijuana and instead imposed a civil fine of $100 for possession.

This proposal represented typical gutless politics and weasel politicians in action—doing something to claim action and progress without really doing anything at all.

"There are big pros and cons about decriminalizing marijuana that have to be evaluated," I told the audience, "but I don't believe in going part way and saying a nickel bag of dope is OK but a dime bag isn't, or we're going to lead you to believe it's legal to possess marijuana but if we catch you with it, we're going to fine you. That's a confusing mess."

The marijuana proposal demarcating 10 grams as a cutoff between slap on the wrist and criminal repercussions reminded me of a scene in the 1984 movie, *This is Spinal Tap*, a mockumentary parodying a fictitious British heavy metal band. Guitarist Nigel Tufnel explains to Marty DiBergi, the band's documentarian, that heavy metal bands have amplifiers that go up to volume level 10, but Spinal Tap has found the secret to intensify its sound through special amps.

**Tufnel:** …"if we need that extra push over the cliff, you know what we do?"

**DiBergi:** "Put it up to eleven."

**Tufnel:** "Eleven. Exactly. One louder."

**DiBergi:** "Why don't you just make ten louder and make ten be the top number and make that a little louder?"

**Tufnel:** [**contemplative pause**] "These go to eleven."

"So we're going to say with nine ounces of marijuana you're not a criminal but with ten ounces you are?" I continued. "Are police going to carry around little kilo scales? I'm starting to come down on the side of individual liberty: If you want to smoke marijuana, that's your choice. Make it legal. But if we go all the way on marijuana, we better increase our funding for mental health and addiction treatment, because one in 10 becomes addicted."

Feeling miserable by the forum's conclusion, I headed straight for the coat rack, intent on skipping the all-but-compulsory post-event hobnobbing. But as I was gathering my coat, Michael Abrams introduced himself to me. The name registered: Abrams wrote the *Baltimore Sun* letter to the editor that highlighted my performance at the Lansdowne forum, saying that I demonstrated "the most passion for liberal positions" and "audacity."

Abrams told me I was "the maverick" in the field, a good strategy because others were "playing it safe." Great. I could handle losing, but not as a milquetoast.

## April 5, 2014 – Kindred Spirits

Cycling home after a Saturday afternoon campaigning door-to-door, I came to the busy intersection a half-mile from my house. On the other side was The Columbia Bike Guy, plastic bags dangling from his small-wheeled bike. When the light turned green, I rode past him.

"Be careful," he yelled out to me.

"You too," I responded.

Kindred spirits, respecting the dangers each of us faced amid a sea of fast-moving metal and experiencing the joys of powering ourselves along, senses alive with the effort, fully present in the elements.

## April 15, 2014 – Breaking Up the
## Shutout: NARAL Endorsement

I received notice by e-mail that I had earned the National Abortion Rights Action League (NARAL) Pro-Choice Maryland's PAC endorsement. After countless questionnaires, interviews and omissions, I had nearly given up hope on endorsements. I even checked NARAL's website for their endorsement postings to make sure the notice wasn't a mistake.

"We are excited about your candidacy and look forward to working with you as we advance the agenda for reproductive rights in Maryland," NARAL's PAC chair wrote.

Next time I had an endorsement interview, I'd have something consequential to say when asked about other endorsements. Unfortunately, as it turned out, all my endorsement interview opportunities were in my rearview mirror.

# April 27, 2014 – Moxie but No Cigar

After being treated mostly as a punching bag or a non-entity by two political bloggers monitoring the District 12 race, I was happy to see that Spartan Considerations' blogger Jason Booms came close to endorsing me, making me the equivalent of a fourth place Olympian.

"I've been around candidates long enough to sort the wheat from the chaff, the sincere from the phony, and the workhorses from the show horses...I believe that Man of the People is the real-deal...I stand four-square behind Man of the People," Booms began.

Next, he supported Zelig, saying Zelig was a "formidable candidate" with potential for "a distinguished career in public service."

Third, he said Anointed One had "stellar qualifications." However, Booms said, he was reluctant to jump on her bandwagon because of a "reflexive contrarian impulse...when the Democratic Establishment lined up in support" and his "predisposition in favor of insurgent campaigns." But he ultimately landed in Anointed One's corner, saying she was "Harvard smart with an easy-going personality and accessible communications style...ready from 'Day One'"...

Booms could have stopped there, but he didn't. "If I had a fourth vote, it would be for Adam Sachs. A low-key fellow with some bold progressive ideas...with the moxie to quote Lou Reed as he did at a recent forum...it would be interesting to see what someone like him could do in Annapolis."

If there would have been many more Jason Boomses, voters with a "reflexive contrarian impulse" and a "predisposition in favor of insurgent campaigns," I could have been riding a wave. But few pay close enough attention to even know which candidate may be a "contrarian" or have "insurgent" tendencies. I would need a Booms Cloning Machine for his opinion to resonate.

# June 1, 2014 – Crime on the TV News

I was going door-to-door after work when I got a call from Amy.
"There's big news in the District 12 race," she said.

"What do you mean?"

"It was on the TV news."

"What? How did we make TV news?"

"Something about Man of the People being charged with a crime."

"What crime?"

"I didn't catch it all. Something about doing something improper with a campaign ad or website or something. I'm not sure."

"And *that* made the news? What could it be?"

"You'll have to watch tonight."

Whatever it was, it was big news for the complexion of the District 12 race. At the time, I believed Man of the People was a prime contender to finish top three and advance to the general election.

Man of the People was splashed all over the news that evening and the next day.

After an investigation, the Maryland state prosecutor charged Man of the People with a criminal election law violation after finding that a website created by Man of the People's campaign and deployed to criticize Gadfly, Man of the People's nemesis from their 2010 Baltimore County Council race, did not have an accurate campaign authority line required by law.

The prosecutor, who received a complaint about the Gadfly website, said that Man of the People published and registered a website domain name using Gadfly's name in the address (URL), and used the website to "publish derogatory campaign material concerning Gadfly."

Election law requires that candidates apply an "authority line" to campaign material that includes the name of the sponsoring campaign and address. The website created by Man of the People's campaign instead stated that "this message has not been authorized or approved by any candidate," according to the state prosecutor.

In a news release, the state prosecutor revealed that the web hosting company GoDaddy.com supplied records showing Man of the People paid for the website using personal funds and paid an additional fee for private registration of the domain name to protect his identity.

Charges for such an election law violation can be assessed either "civilly, or criminally when we feel it was done intentionally, which we felt it was in this case," the state prosecutor said.

Man of the People responded to the charges by saying that his campaign had "misapplied an inaccurate authority line on a campaign website which failed to properly credit me with ownership and knowledge."

But Man of the People remained defiant and righteous, and attempted to redirect the negative coverage back to the core issues of his campaign.

"I fully stand behind [the website's] contents," Man of the People wrote in response to the media when the story broke. "I won't be distracted from working for middle class families, small businesses, senior citizens, veterans, and for everyday folks, ensuring they receive the representation they deserve and expect."

Gadfly said she was "shocked" by Man of the People's surreptitious ploy.

In a *Baltimore Sun* letter to the editor, Man of the People said he took "full responsibility" for his campaign's "error."

"They say that taking responsibility, honesty and integrity are characteristics of sound leaders," Man of the People began. Then he attempted to divert attention from his campaign's "error" and the shadow it cast over his character and campaign.

"I won't change," Man of the People continued defiantly, steadfastly sticking to his message about fighting for the working class. He touted his endorsements from education associations and qualifications as a civic and political activist, saying that "public service is my calling" and welcoming comparisons of his "proven record" of service against other candidates.

Strategically—or greedily and obliviously—Man of the People turned what began as an apology into an advertisement to vote for him. Constituents throughout the district, he wrote, "want to see their government work harder for them. They want a workhorse, not a show horse, like some politicians out there. I promise District 12 voters that I am up to that challenge. A vote for me ensures you'll receive the representation you deserve and expect."

In a local race, any publicity isn't necessarily good publicity, when many constituents personally know the candidates, and trust, integrity and accountability are big factors. As much as Man of the People tried to play down the charge and refocus on his strengths and passions, the error spelled the death knell of his campaign. His attempts to obfuscate fell flat and smelled of desperation. For many voters who may have been on the fence over their top three candidates, the criminal charge surely was enough to topple Man of the People from their lists. That became obvious when two local political bloggers who were solidly in Man of the People's camp before the criminal incident each announced that Man of the People's transgression was ample reason to disavow their support.

> *"Ambition can change people," Marshmallow Man began. "I believe what we're seeing in this case is one of those examples. I don't get the Man of the People-Gadfly dynamic but Man of the People felt the story needed to be told. Well, now he is paying a price for that... [I]t is with my friend that I have the greatest disappointment. Because he does know better. And because, although he's not showing it, he is better...[T]o continue to challenge people in the public eye to follow their better angels, I need to call out my friends when they stray. And Man of the People, I am strongly and terribly disappointed. You will always be my friend, but I don't think you can be someone who I choose to support for election to political office. Not now."*

Before dumping him, the Marshmallow Man paid tribute to Man of the People, detailing why he had originally cast his lot with him, how he had met Man of the People as a college student when the two had worked together to "save a nonprofit organization" that Marshmallow Man had founded.

"[Man of the People] is one of the most courageous people I have ever known," Marshmallow Man praised. "He looked cancer in the face and beat it...The man has survived a lot..."

I didn't believe Man of the People would survive criminal conduct charges. I felt bad for Man of the People, but also was astonished how he had been blinded by ambition, or possessed by a grudge. Man of the People was the classic case of the man with the imaginary angel whispering in one ear and the devil in the other. He had too many positive attributes and credentials to go down in flames, apparently blinded by an old rivalry or personal dislike. But the bottom line is people often reject candidates who stoop to underhanded and subversive attacks on an opponent. It's what people abhor and drives them away from politics. Locally, such devious chicanery comes off as even more despicable and unpalatable.

The Spartan Considerations blog also provided condolences for Man of the People's likely self-inflicted demise. Author Booms had been a Man of the People supporter upon introduction, as Booms researched candidates in his home district.

Acknowledging he had witnessed "a fair amount of campaign-related foolishness" during his years as a political strategist, Booms said he was still "shocked and saddened" about the criminal charge against Man of the People.

Upon introduction, Booms said Man of the People "came across as sincerely civic-minded and focused on working for the public good," passing his own "fairly well developed bullshit detector."

He also met with Gadfly, describing her as "intelligent and personable." But if he was going to endorse a Baltimore County candidate, he favored Man of the People for his "progressive outlook," "blue-collar background," and community activism.

Booms said he believed Man of the People had a good shot for at least third place and the Democratic nomination for the general election in November, adding, "I marked up my sample ballot with a big X next to his name" just days before the news broke.

But the criminal charge against Man of the People changed everything.

"While I was aware of the existence of bad blood between Man of the People and Gadfly," Booms wrote, "I chalked that up to the emotions that churn up from a hard fought campaign…

"Based on what I know…I can't see myself voting for [Man of the People] in the Primary Election."

Man of the People's gaffe gave me a bump, at least in Booms' assessment.

"I haven't decided about the third slot yet," Booms wrote. "Perhaps I will cast a ballot for Sachs."

Whatever votes Man of the People may have lost in his misguided attempt to impugn Gadfly, voters still had nine other candidates to choose from, so Man of the People's loss probably wouldn't mean an avalanche of votes coming my way. Gadfly, the victim, likely was also the biggest beneficiary.

The post-script on Man of the People's transgression: probation before judgement—found guilty by the judge but allowed to keep the conviction off his record in exchange for probation. Six weeks after the primary, Man of the People received a $500 fine, one year of supervised probation and 200 hours of community service as election participation parting gifts. Bad blood simmering, an indignant Gadfly criticized the penalty as merely "a slap on the wrist."

# Narcissists: The Perpetual Self-Promoters

*"The silent killer of all great men and women of
achievement—particularly men ...Narcissism is the killer.*

James Woods, actor

*"I went from being a senator... to being considered for vice
president, running for president, being a vice presidential
candidate, and becoming a national public figure. All of
which fed a self-focus, an egotism, a narcissism that leads
you to believe that you can do whatever you want. "*

John Edwards, former U.S. Senator (NC) and
Democratic presidential candidate who initially
lied about then admitted an extramarital affair
and fathering a child with his campaign worker

Closely related to the "hubris syndrome" is the personality trait of narcissism—those who exhibit excessive self-love. Some character traits of narcissists are positive, such as high self-confidence, ambition, leadership ability and power. But when those traits become all-consuming, narcissists implode, damaging themselves and others.

"Ambition and narcissism are occupational hazards for all political leaders," said Stanley Renshon, professor of political science at City

University of New York, in a *USA Today* article headlined, "Narcissism Is in the Cards for Many Politicians."

An implicit prerequisite for the job of politician—perpetual self-promotion—would feel abnormal and unnatural to people who don't score high on the narcissism scale, postulated Pepper Schwartz, author and sociologist at the University of Washington in *USA Today*. "Politicians are different. How many of us would have the desire, much less the ability, to promote ourselves ceaselessly? You have to do that as a politician. It's an amazing level of self-love…and a need for affirmation."

Jerrold Post, M.D., described narcissists as "arrogant, vain, egocentric, extremely ambitious, entitled to succeed and to be followed by throngs of admirers, the narcissist believes he is a very special person; he is full of himself."

Post, a George Washington University professor of psychiatry and political psychology, said in his book, *Narcissism and Politics: Dreams of Glory*, that narcissistic personality traits are "abundantly represented (indeed, overrepresented)" in politics. "It should not be so surprising, after all, that narcissism should flourish in the political environment and that narcissistic individuals should find irresistible the attractions of the public life."

In his scathing 2011 essay in *Psychology Today*, "Narcissism: Why It's So Rampant in Politics," writer Leon F. Seltzer, a psychotherapist, deconstructs the weaknesses, temptations and self-delusions suffered by narcissistic politicians.

Some politicians develop an "exaggerated sense of entitlement," Seltzer said. "It's hardly surprising then that so many politicians somehow think they 'deserve' to game the system… In their heavily self-biased opinion, if they want something, by rights it *should* be theirs. So…they take from public and private coffers alike whatever they think they can get away with." Yet, narcissistic politicians feel little, if any, guilt, he said, and only show remorse for unethical behavior when they are caught and denials fail. Such politicians can be viewed as "moral relativists," he said, publicly condemning the same type of immoral behavior that they engage in themselves, like New York's Eliot Spitzer's dual roles in prosecuting prostitutes as attorney general and cheating on his wife with them as governor.

When narcissistic politicians feel comfortably ensconced in office, that's when arrogance, greed and recklessness can take over, Seltzer said.

> *"They may well feel accountable to no one but themselves—free to play their competitive power games with impunity (and frankly, the public be damned). Now perched high above the populace, they're especially vulnerable to the vaguely camouflaged bribes that routinely come their way... And so, with all the perks of office and fawning by lobbyists representing private interests, they can begin to exploit people and institutions with faint awareness that they're doing so unscrupulously. And with their grandiose sense of self fully ignited, they can easily convince themselves that they deserve everything they receive—while experiencing little to no obligation to respond in kind (unless, that is, they've forged a 'privileged' deal to legislate in behalf of their campaign benefactors)."*

Seltzer contended that narcissistic politicians delude themselves into thinking their adoring public needs "their unique talents and skills." However, he said, such politicians are not in actuality motivated by serving citizens. "They've won their position primarily to serve themselves—and they can do so almost obsessively."

# POLITICAL SCANDALS: MEN BEHAVING BADLY

*"But people love a hypocrite, you know—they recognize one of their own, and it always feels so good when someone gets caught with his pants down and his dick up and it isn't you."*

STEPHEN KING, AUTHOR, *THE GREEN MILE*

*"One day, I want enough money to be at the center of a corruption scandal."*

GIL A. WATERS, AUTHOR, SELF-DESCRIBED
"GENERIC MIDDLE-CLASS WHITE BOY"

During my time running for office, there was a perpetual and relentless onslaught of scandals taking place in politics: ethical, moral, financial, sexual, addictions and criminal deviancies of the first order, and judgement lapses that are nearly incomprehensible given the public trust, responsibilities and privileges bestowed on these elected individuals, and the public position they occupy. Or, maybe those are exactly the reasons why such behavior by politicians should be entirely comprehensible and even anticipated, according to David Owen's and Jonathan Davidson's hubris syndrome theory, research that evaluated the behaviors and actions of national leaders.

Hubris, which can develop with the acquisition of power, can lead to dysfunction in powerful offices, the researchers said. Impulsive behavior is the most illustrative example of hubris. Something about attaining power and privilege certainly seems to jolt a few bolts loose in the brains of elected leaders and relax the standards and mores of life that these politicians undoubtedly espoused in achieving their rise to power, the kind of bedrock, noble rules by which to live one's life that were reinforced, for example, by the old-school Catholic nuns through a paddle to the backside or a whack of a ruler on the knuckles of a wayward student.

In *The Speechwriter,* Swaim wrote that philandering former South Carolina Gov. Sanford, caught cheating with his Argentinian mistress, still craved the attention, however negative and embarrassing, in a perverted way.

"[D]espite the fact that most of the media attention was now premised on his fall and not his rise, there was something about it that he couldn't help enjoying. The crowds of reporters, the incessant headlines, the necessity of responding every day to some new self-inflicted absurdity—there was something about it all that made him thrive."

Swaim asked why people trusted politicians who gained their positions "by innumerable acts of vanity and self-will," who built careers by "persuading us of their goodness and greatness?"

*"Successful politicians are people who know how to make us think well of them without our realizing that that's what they're doing; they know how to make us admire and trust them.*

*We go badly wrong when we trust them,"* Swaim asserted.

…Swaim said he was unnerved to observe the "stark difference" between Sanford's public face and the one he presented to his staff. *"[I]t signified something terrible…at least about democratic cultures in which political leaders often function as celebrities and even heroes…Here was a man who shattered his ambitions and humiliated his family and friends by pursuing his own petty, myopic desires. And yet in his ruin he could not find more than the paltriest shred of genuine self-criticism....And if that was true of him, it wasn't true only of him. It was true to one degree or another of all politicians.*

*"I don't say any of this to demean politicians. It takes an able and industrious person to do what they do, and many of them are capable of courage and honorable conduct. But the same can be said of traveling salesmen; it does not follow that we should trust them."*

. . .

The scandals I noticed during my campaign were undoubtedly but a few of countless many that occurred throughout the country. They were sordid and repulsive, a combination of soap opera, trashy Lifetime cable TV movie, *Law & Order: SVU (Special Victims Unit)* and cunning investment tycoon Gordon Gekko's *Wall Street*. Here is but a small sample:

## Greed/Money

In a federal case, **former Virginia Republican Governor Robert F. McDonnell** was found guilty of 11 corruption-related counts for conspiring to sell access to the power, prestige and influence of the governor's office to a Virginia business owner in exchange for favors and paybacks, such as golf outings, gifts, wedding expenses, vacations and $120,000 in favorable loans.

**Former Illinois Democratic Congressman Jesse Jackson Jr.** pled guilty to charges of fraud, conspiracy, making false statements, mail fraud, wire fraud, and criminal forfeiture in connection with his use of about $750,000 in campaign account money for more than 3,000 personal purchases unassociated with his campaigns. He was sentenced to two-and-a-half years in federal prison.

**Former Democratic New Orleans Mayor Ray Nagin** was convicted on 20 of 21 counts of bribery, fraud and money laundering committed while serving as mayor and handed a 10-year federal prison sentence.

**Former Democratic Speaker of the New York Assembly Sheldon Silver** was found guilty of honest services fraud, extortion and money laundering stemming from an arrangement through which he accumulated nearly $4 million in exchange for using the influence of his position to advance businesses' goals.

## Sex

**Former New York City Democratic Congressman Anthony Weiner** was forced to resign from Congress in 2011 after the lewd sexual scandal dubbed Weinergate, in which he admitted using Twitter to send a link to a sexually explicit photo to a 21-year-old woman.

During Weiner's 2013 comeback bid for New York City mayor, he admitted engaging in a series of sexually explicit communications, or "sexting," with a young woman, allegedly involving nude pictures and using the pseudonym "Carlos Danger." The *New York Daily News* reported that Weiner's sexting took place with a porn star named Sydney Leathers, who appeared in a porn movie called "Weiner & Me."

## Substance Abuse

**Former Maryland Republican Delegate Donald H. Dwyer Jr.** lost his bid for re-election in 2014 after pleading guilty to drunken boating charges in an incident in which a boat he was captaining collided with another, injuring himself and six others. Prior to Dwyer's final sentencing in the drunken boating case, he pleaded guilty to a separate charge, driving under the influence.

**Former Florida Republican Congressman Trey Radel** resigned from Congress after pleading guilty to a misdemeanor charge of buying 3.5 grams of cocaine at a Washington restaurant from an undercover agent.

# Misuse of Public Office and Other Deplorable, Unethical or Illegal Behavior

In the Bridgegate Scandal, federal prosecutors brought charges of conspiracy to commit fraud against a high-ranking staff member for **New Jersey Republican Governor Chris Christie**, and two Christie appointees to the Port Authority of New York and New Jersey. The indictment said the officials exploited Port Authority resources for political ends, conspiring to create massive traffic jams in Fort Lee, New Jersey by closing lanes to the George Washington Bridge. Prosecutors alleged a possible motive was retribution against Fort Lee's Democratic mayor for not endorsing Christie.

**Former U.S. Republican House Speaker J. Dennis Hastert** pleaded guilty to attempting to evade federal banking laws. According to the plea agreement, Hastert promised to provide $3.5 million—in small amounts to avoid reporting requirements—to an unidentified individual "to compensate for and keep confidential his prior misconduct" against that individual decades earlier. Prosecutors revealed in court filings that Hastert allegedly had inappropriate physical contact with teenagers affiliated with a high school wrestling team Hastert had coached. Hastert was sentenced to 15 months in federal prison.

# Career Politicians: Why Settle
# for Being a Schnook?

*"The difference between a politician and a statesman*
*is that a politician thinks about the next election while*
*the statesman thinks about the next generation."*

James Freeman Clarke, American theologian and author

Why do so many people take an office that, in Maryland and many other states, is supposed to be a part-time, time-limited job for a "citizen legislator" and hold onto it for ever and ever, term after term after term, until their affixed, nearly mummified bodies are pried from their high-backed chairs?

Henry Hill, the Irish mobster immortalized in *Goodfellas,* who lived the high-life while heisting, racketeering and money-laundering, may have divulged the answer after he ratted out his co-conspirators and was secreted into the FBI Witness Protection Program:

> *Anything I wanted was a phone call away. Free cars. The keys to a dozen*
> *hideout flats all over the city. I bet twenty, thirty grand over a weekend*
> *and then I'd either blow the winnings in a week or go to the sharks to*
> *pay back the bookies... When I was broke, I'd go out and rob some more.*
> *We ran everything. We paid off cops. We paid off lawyers. We paid off*
> *judges. Everybody had their hands out. Everything was for the taking.*

*And now it's all over. And that's the hardest part. Today everything is different; there's no action...have to wait around like everyone else. Can't even get decent food—right after I got here, I ordered some spaghetti with marinara sauce, and I got egg noodles and ketchup. I'm an average nobody...get to live the rest of my life like a schnook.*

Some people who enter the political arena certainly want to engage in public service. But everybody who strives for public office wants to be *somebody*, not an *average nobody*, a *schnook*. If public service was the sincere and legitimate reason for running for office, the politician would not stay in the position forever, because it's not a job, it's a public service, and it does not serve the public for one person to use power, money and relationships to monopolize the office, becoming more and more distant from the people that person supposedly serves while effectively excluding other people who may have fresh ideas and new perspectives and dynamic energy from contributing their talents to public service. Sure, the career politicians can argue that it is up to the voters to put someone in or take someone out. But that argument is disingenuous, ignoring all the facts about the overwhelming advantages bestowed on those who enjoy incumbency, established campaign bank accounts, reliable fundraising sources, slate memberships, high name recognition, powerful allies, and ample time, resources and opportunity to plot their re-election.

For "career politicians," their job is like Groundhog Day. Win election, start executing plans for re-election. Win election, start executing plans for re-election, ad infinitum. Many will become more focused on keeping lobbyists with whom they have formed relationships, large campaign donors, legislative leadership and other power brokers happy rather than making real progress or standing for needed change. The "career politician" becomes a monopoly in the truest sense of the word: By using levers available to him by virtue of his position, he takes exclusive possession or control of the trade in legislating and "constituent service."

The notion of career politicians was not something the nation's founders envisioned, wrote Lawless in *Becoming a Candidate*, but "something against which they warned." Weary of the power of heredi-tary succession and monarchical rule, Thomas Paine, one of America's founding fathers, cautioned in 1776 against a permanent ruling class:

*"Men who look upon themselves born to reign, and others to obey, soon grow insolent. Selected from the rest of mankind, their minds are early poisoned by importance, and the world they act in differs so materially from the world at large, that they have but little opportunity of knowing its true interests, and when they succeed in the government are frequently the most ignorant and unfit of any throughout the dominions."*

In his *Psychology Today* Evolution of the Self essay, "Narcissism: Why It's So Rampant in Politics," writer and therapist Leon F. Seltzer wrote that the insatiable ego of many politicians—their "immense appetite for flattery, praise, and adulation," similar to what Paine cautioned against during the American Revolution—leads them to become "career politicians."

*"Quite independent of professional achievement, they expect to be treated as superior. Their fragile psyche demands being admired and looked up to—and unquestionably holding high office almost guarantees that this ego requirement will be amply met. Such an enormous 'fringe benefit' helps explain why so many of them become 'career politicians,' holding onto such psychological blessings as long as possible. In such instances, the chief reason for remaining an incumbent isn't to fulfill any idealistic aspirations. It's to 'secure' their inflated self-regard.*

*"In fact, much of their pompous demeanor and arrogant behavior is inextricably tied to this inflated sense of self stemming from their political 'tenure.'"*

Perhaps some who enter politics don't originally intend to become "ca-reer politicians;" it's just something that happens along the way. Sure, some politicians are smart as an Einstein on steroids, strategic and deter-mined as Napoleon eyeing a new conquest, and charismatic and socially adept as, well, Bill Clinton (who else?) in a New Hampshire donut shop. But many politicians fall into the trap of believing they are unique and nobody else could possibly work the magic, convey the wisdom or empathize with constituents the way they do. They're wrong. They're replaceable, like nearly anyone else who works a job. What they know best, perhaps their only truly unique knowledge gained through a particular experience from which others are blocked, is how to work the political machinery, the manipulation, relationship-forging, deal-making and rhetorical pretzel-twisting, skills that can be mastered by common boobs, as we witness in Congress.

The thought of becoming just an ordinary citizen again after enjoying an exalted position, after having people coming to *you*, to give *you* money, to stroke *your* ego, to let *you* know *you* have influence and *your* decisions are important and *you* can have impact and make a big difference to them, must be difficult to accept.

In *First Person Political,* Reeher described this dynamic of self-importance and ego-stroking that compels many politicians to all but etch their names into their legislative office desktops.

"Having a firmly held belief...that what they do is important, that it really matters to people's lives, and that they are effectively serving the public, is a powerful source of legislators' gratification."

The feeling of mattering is bolstered by the media and supportive communications from interest groups, organizations and constituents, Reeher said. Finally, Reeher noted, the successful incumbent enjoys the "exhilaration of being re-elected" by fellow citizens. "Indeed, few other occupations offer similar levels of those kinds of positive reinforcement."

## I'm Not a Career Politician, I Just Keep Running and Running

I don't know if that psychology has anything to do with Career Pol's extended legislative run. All I know is that relatively early in his legislative career, he denied being a "career politician." But given enough time to prove otherwise, he became exactly that.

As a reporter for the *Baltimore Sun,* I covered Career Pol's race for the Maryland Senate in 1994. Career Pol had already represented western Howard County as a delegate and senator for eight years, one term each. But in 1990, he lost his bid for re-election to the Senate to a Republican.

Undeterred, he ran again for Senate in 1994, but this time switching districts. During that campaign, Career Pol's Republican opponent charged him with being a "professional politician" and a carpetbagger for moving into District 12 the year of the election.

Whether Career Pol's timely move across district lines was merely happenstance or calculated to position him to run for an open seat in a newly redistricted District 12 instead of against a strong incumbent in his former district, only Career Pol knows.

The Maryland prosecutor's office determined that Career Pol had been a resident of District 12 long enough to legally run for Senate from that district. Career Pol had moved three times since he was separated from his wife in 1990. At the time, Career Pol said he made the moves for personal, not political reasons, ending up in a condominium he owned in District 12 about eight months before the election, squeezing under the residency requirement wire by about two months.

In an article I wrote about the state prosecutor's determination, Career Pol called the investigation "an incredible waste of time and state resources" and punked his opponent for having the gall to challenge his residency, saying, "I was working in the community while [the opponent] was still in school."

At a 1994 candidates' forum I covered for *The Sun* less than four weeks before the election, the opponent accused Career Pol of being a "professional politician" who didn't have the same commitment to the district's residents that he did.

"I believe we're tired of professional politicians," the opponent said.

In an interview with me after the forum, Career Pol called his opponent's comment a "joke statement."

"I don't think serving two terms is being a 'professional politician,'" Career Pol said.

Career Pol won. Flash forward 20 years. Career Pol won in 2014 for a sixth term as District 12's senator. Beginning in 2015, he was serving a second term as chair of the powerful Senate Budget and Taxation Committee. The 2014 election was the ninth consecutive election in which he had run, spanning 32 years. Career Pol first was elected to the General Assembly at age 37; when his 2015-18 term expires, he would be 73. That's half his life running for and serving in public office.

Putting on my objective reporter hat, I'd have to say that Career Pol was correct in rebutting his opponent's charge in 1994: two terms does not a "professional politician" make. But since then, the "joke statement" has turned out to be prophetic; the "joke" was on Career Pol. There's no other way you can spin it other than Career Pol has become a poster boy for "professional politician." For confirmation, one need only look at Career Pol's 2012 political contributions to realize how deep his ties run to special interest groups, corporate entities and businesses that have the most influence over the political process. In that year, Career Pol received nearly 80 percent of his money from PACs and business-related entities.

In 2014, 50 percent of Career Pol's $83,000 in contributions came from PACs and transfers from candidates and political slates, his political allies. Of the $41,141 that didn't come from PACs and other candidates, $35,851, or 87 percent, was identified in Career Pol's campaign finance reports as being donated by businesses, corporations and other formal organizations and the principals who represented them. Such institutional support builds the foundation upon which the career politician can rely for self-sustenance in perpetuity.

Of all the money Career Pol raised in 2014, about 7 percent or less came from what one might call "grassroots contributors"—people contributing presumably for civic reasons without a self-interested business stake. With fundraising numbers like that, would Career Pol even need to relate to and connect with your average voter to stay in office? Probably not.

## Animal House

But Career Pol is far from alone. According to a 2013 Maryland analysis, more than half of the 47 state senators had served at least 16 years in the legislature, and more than one-third had served 20 years or more.

There's another dynamic other than the thrill of power, the feeling of mattering, and the intellectual challenge of tackling complex issues that keeps legislators returning to their still-warm seats like the perpetual high school troublemaker who has a permanent perch reserved in the principal's office. The legislature becomes politicians' primary social life, Reeher wrote in *First Person Political*. It's a lot like college—constantly surrounded by like-minded peers pursuing similar paths and goals, always a pal with whom to chat, commiserate, bond and gossip, learning together in the same rooms, joining the same clubs, participating in the same fraternal rituals, breaking bread together and attending the same parties—only better, because it doesn't have to end in four years. It can go on forever! Like John Belushi's Bluto from *Animal House*, who lamented washing "seven years of college down the drain," why ever leave Faber College's Delta Tau Chi fraternity when you know you'll never dance The Gator on a beer-soaked fraternity floor ever again in civilian life?

> *"Legislators are involved in a collective enterprise, a shoulder-to-shoulder political battle… The social rewards of serving are woven through these shared experiences…they are united by their shared public service…including the shared gauntlet-running experience of the campaign…These kinds of interpersonal bonds are increasingly rare in our society, and increasingly precious. Indeed…these bonds become an important sustaining factor in their legislative service. And for most of them, these relationships and bonds are key elements of the job's most significant attractions."*

## Geezers

Showing the "aging in place" phenomenon used to describe people who won't leave *their own house,* 86 percent of the senators and 59 percent of the delegates in Maryland State House were age 50 or older in 2013. On average, about one in four Maryland delegates and senators turned over in each election from 1998 through 2010.

Political publications called attention to the "old war horses" ruling the Maryland General Assembly in 2014. In a post titled, "Geezer Ceiling," the *Maryland Reporter* wrote, "Anyone in their 30s joining the General Assembly will find a body run by people old enough to be their parents, or even grandparents."

The publication presented a rundown of "legislative leadership" showing elongated tenures by legislators long in the tooth. As of 2014, The Lion of the Senate and House Speaker, and seven of the 10 House and Senate committee chairs were Medicare-eligible (65+), with an average age of 70.4, an average of 15 years in their positions of leadership and an average of 30 years of legislative service each.

## 'What's Wrong with You?'

In an article in the conservative news publication *Human Events,* writer Anthony Furey seized upon an interview conducted by MSNBC's Lawrence O'Donnell on *The Last Word* with Anthony Weiner. Weiner had resigned from Congress in shame after a sexting scandal only to resurface two years later as a candidate for New York City mayor in 2013. Furey credited O'Donnell with one of the rare times a media member called out a politician for his addiction to public life, what Furey labeled "the perpetual political class."

O'Donnell's interview, conducted the eve of New York City's primary, is fascinating for the way O'Donnell cut to the core of the issue: What compels the "career politician," and why can't he give it up?

O'Donnell didn't bother with the usual friendly small talk and laughs among friends in the synergistic businesses, nor did he lob

Weiner softball warm-up, feel-good questions. Instead, he bore in on the career pol like a jail warden apoplectic at seeing a recidivist criminal before him for the umpteenth time. Weiner was caught off guard like a man with his pants down in public...Oh wait. That did happen to him.

**O'Donnell:** "I have really just one basic question for you that I think a lot of people have wondered about for different reasons...For me, it just comes down to this, which is [O'Donnell pauses for dramatic effect]: What...is...wrong...with... you?"

**Weiner:** "I don't understand the question. What is wrong with me that I care so much about the issues that I fight for every day, that I have for my entire career?

**O'Donnell:** "No, what I mean is this: What is wrong with you that you cannot seem to imagine a life without elective office?"

**Weiner:** "That's ridiculous. [Pregnant pause]. Of course I can. [Stutters]. Are, are, are you saying that, that because I have things in my personal life that are embarrassing I shouldn't run for office? OK, that's a fair position to have, some people have it."

**O'Donnell:** "No, let me be clear. I'm not...I have never once criticized you in any way for anything involving your texting...What I find strange about your campaign is what seems to be your absolute desperate need for elective office and what seems to be your inability to live outside of it.

"What did you do, for example, with your time away from elective office? Did you find any problem anywhere in the world that you thought: I think I'd like to apply myself to that and try to help some people who might need my help. You didn't do that! You just set yourself up for running for elective office again."

**Weiner:** "OK, you're wrong, but, I don't know, is there a question I could possibly help you out with?"

The interview devolved into a war of words, with O'Donnell psychoanalyzing that Weiner had some relentless psychological need to assume public office, and Weiner countering that he was fighting for his constituents and following a "noble" pursuit. O'Donnell smacked Weiner for becoming a high-paid lobbyist after he resigned from Congress (which Weiner denied): "You did the classic hack thing," O'Donnell charged, "and you know it."

Furey applauded O'Donnell for taking "a swing at the entire concept of the career politician, at the entire concept of the perpetual political class that views Washington and any other seat of government as a giant trough. It's an indictment on American political discourse that it has somehow become bad form to call out leeches for their leeching."

The bottom line, Furey declared, is "career politicians need to be challenged because they're the true impediment to fighting big government...Got a problem with certain legislation and want to hold office for a couple terms to change it? Come on board. Want to endlessly suck at the taxpayer's teat and see yourself on the cover of the paper to satisfy your ego? Get out of town."

## 52 Years? Maybe it's Time...

In Maryland, nobody sucked the teat longer than Senator Marvin Rockledge.

"I've decided that 52 years is enough," said Rockledge, who began representing his working-class Baltimore County community of steel workers just before Martin Luther King's civil rights March on Washington and President John F. Kennedy's assassination, announcing he would not run for a 14th term. "I think it's time."

Time, already? I guess Rockledge listened for the chant, "Four more years! Four more years!" but just couldn't hear it anymore.

Rockledge got started in the days when "political bosses" asked people to run, and if they asked, like "Iron Mike" did Rockledge, you did. He served in the Senate so long that in 2000, he was bestowed the honorary title of Senate Pro Tem Emeritus, like they confer on a beloved professor in retirement. But 14 years later, Rockledge was still in his seat. Maybe they should have bequeathed him "Emeritus of the Emeriti?"

# I'm Not Saying Goodbye without a Party

Maryland Senator Janice "Never Can Say Goodbye" Foreman from Montgomery County, who served 36 years in the General Assembly, is another legislator who couldn't exit stage left, until she finally did at age 78, when she faced a rigorous re-election challenge.

"I've got a few more things I'd like to accomplish," Foreman said in a newspaper interview, vowing to run again before changing her mind and retiring months later.

Good Lord, Janice, if you couldn't accomplish those "few more things" within 36 years, maybe it's time to stop being Sisyphus pushing a boulder up the hill and give someone else a shot!

I commend Foreman for donating much of the $20,000 left in her campaign account to charitable causes upon her retirement. But one large expense reeks of the entitlement and privilege one might expect of a "career politician." Foreman paid Historic Inns of Annapolis $4,660 out of her campaign account for her own retirement celebration party. By all means, Foreman should celebrate her 36 years of service. But if Never Can Say Goodbye wants to party at elegant quarters, she should do it on her own dime.

# June 5, 2014 – Running along the Roadside

D riving home from dropping off my son at school at 7 a.m., I spotted
District 9 Republican Delegate candidate Pete O'Halloran across
the street on a major commuter artery, standing just past a light for east-
bound commuters, holding up his campaign sign and waving at motorists. Several signs were lined up along the road in front of O'Halloran,
and his car was parked behind him (illegally, no doubt) on the shoulder
with a big "O'HALLORAN" sign in the rear window.

O'Halloran came from the original school of Republicans who
pioneered roadside sign-waving in Howard County. A Harvard and
Cornell Law graduate and former U.S. Navy lieutenant, O'Halloran had
represented Howard County in the House for 16 years before the surprise Republican winner in the 2002 governor's race appointed him as
Maryland's secretary of transportation. O'Halloran got bounced when
the governorship reverted to Democratic hands, and in 2014 he was
making his political comeback.

With such sterling academic, military, political, and government leadership credentials, and at age 68, one may have thought that O'Halloran
could be excused from standing before whizzing traffic at 7 a.m. implor-
ing distracted motorists for votes. But there he was.

And O'Halloran was not just standing there passively displaying his
sign. Nor was he waving mechanically. He was working the corner with
animation and enthusiasm, like a street mime displaying theatrical talents, maximizing the effort in the hopes that passersby would make a
drop in his vote bucket.

Similar to my advertisement exploits by bike, O'Halloran knew that stressed out, tunnel-vision commuters might ignore him as part of the scenery without added gyrations. O'Halloran appeared that he had developed an art for roadside sign-waving through all his past campaigns, performing a dance not unlike the advertising billboard sign-spinners. O'Halloran, dressed in sweat clothes for the workout, would lurch forward toward passing cars, peer directly into their windshields to make eye contact, and do an exaggerated fluttering, waving motion with his hand, making the effort to connect individually with each harried driver.

When the light turned green and I turned left, headed toward home, I wondered if I should be roadside waving at commuters, too. It was one of those tactics I decided I wasn't going to do, not that I was too good for it—O'Halloran had me beat by a country mile for the right to say, *I'm above all those naked, attention-seeking displays that cry out, 'Look at me!'* I just had aversion to the idea of Doing the O'Halloran, standing and waving at passersby, similar to roadside panhandlers except the currency is votes instead of money. His was the more aggressive approach; mine, on a bike, more passive, but for me, more enjoyable and smacking less of prostrating myself. I put pleasure and dignity above monotony and determination, and likely impact and effectiveness also. O'Halloran's gesturing, an act that was more palpably in-your-face, looked more like working hard for votes than my laissez-faire pedaling.

The contrast between my approach and O'Halloran's to generating recognition was another metaphor for my campaign. In a business predicated on tight networks, personal closeness and calling attention to oneself, I was always more comfortable maintaining some distance.

# June 11, 2014 – Proud Dad

I brought my kids, Rebecca and Daniel, 18 and 15, to a Heather Mizeur for Governor rally at a restaurant. Mizeur boldly appeared before enthusiastic supporters hand in hand with her spouse Deborah. She told the crowd that the bonus for Marylanders if the state elected its first-ever female governor would be that Maryland would still get a "kick-ass" First Lady.

I met Steve Chapman, a community gay rights advocate who I had seen at other campaign stops. Chapman told me that if he lived in my district, he would vote for me. He talked to my kids:

"You should be proud of what your father is doing," he told them. "It's not easy in an election to be someone with the courage to say what he believes in no matter what happens, to stand up and have integrity."

My kids didn't know what to say. I think all along they were mostly dumbfounded at why I was putting myself through this colossal and often times bizarre effort. It made no sense in their teenage worlds, doing a lot of work *voluntarily* that no one was making me do. I was gratified that someone I barely knew gave my kids that perspective. Hopefully it will be something they remember when they look back with the perspective of an adult about what it means to take on a daunting challenge, stick to your beliefs, and persevere against long odds. I thanked Chapman for his comments told him they were meaningful.

After the event, I posted to Twitter saying that Mizeur likely earned a vote at the rally from a first-time voter, my 18-year-old daughter. That tweet garnered numerous "favorites" and "retweets." I had learned that I could disseminate my name on Twitter through "retweets" by tweeting as a loyal supporter of Mizeur, whose campaign had been "blowing up" on Twitter with thousands of followers, compared to my dozens. (Perhaps I should apologize here for shamelessly riding coattails, but such behavior is commonplace in politics, so I won't.)

## June 14, 2014 – Frontrunner? You Must Be Joking

I t's on!

The District 12 political embers flared into an inferno, courtesy of the Service Employees International Union, which sought to ensure that Joker didn't crash the party of the three candidates the union was escorting to the State House—Anointed One, Zelig and Energy.

SEIU sent a mailer showing two hands handling paper money, with the words, "JOKER STOLE HIS OWN CLIENTS' MONEY." On the back, SEIU asked, "Why Should a Law Breaker Become a Law Maker?" The mailer outlined Joker's disbarment, saying he "ripped off his clients by forging their names on a check," and highlighted his lobbying activities, saying he "represented big casinos and other gambling interests." It concluded: "Joker's DISHONESTY Is Not for Us."

Within a week, Joker launched a two-pronged counter-offensive. First he sent a "JOKER GETS IT DONE" postcard proclaiming, "MY OPPONENTS ARE ATTACKING ME BECAUSE I AM THE FRONTRUNNER!" with no evidence to support that farcical claim.

The longtime lobbyist for special interest groups whose campaign was dependent upon money from developers, property managers, investors, Realtors, lawyers, trade industry associations and the like hypocritically urged residents to "SEND A MESSAGE AGAINST NEGATIVE CAMPAIGNING. Vote for Experienced, Full-Time Leadership That Works for YOUR Interests, Not the Special Interests!"

Then Joker directly attacked Energy and Zelig, but omitted Anointed One, who also was endorsed by, and received large contributions from SEIU, apparently to avoid ruffling the feathers of the four sitting legislators who endorsed her.

Joker's notebook-paper-sized mailer screamed, "DO THE MATH! Out-of-Town Union Endorsements + Union Campaign Contributions = TWO BOUGHT AND PAID FOR DELEGATE CANDIDATES." Head shots of Energy and Zelig were below the accusation, with the caption: "THESE TWO ARE GUILTY of taking union cash and endorsements so they will do their bidding in Annapolis."

On the flip side, Joker asserted that SEIU and the two candidates were "the ones BEHIND the **vicious personal attacks, crude distortions** and **outright lies** about me and my record." Joker reiterated that he "became the frontrunner" and accused Energy and Zelig of taking "the low road" rather than challenging him on issues.

Joker was shoveling manure again. I can't say with certainty that Energy and Zelig had nothing to do with SEIU's anti-Joker mailer, but I highly doubt they did. Energy told me he had no role in it, and Zelig, the *real frontrunner*, would have no reason to attack an unpopular candidate. I believed Energy and Zelig possessed high integrity and ran scrupulously positive campaigns, and would not stoop to bomb-throwing. But it doesn't surprise me that a union would. Furthermore, SEIU's anti-Joker mailer included a disclaimer that stated, "This message has not been authorized or approved by any candidate."

Either Joker selectively chose to ignore that disclaimer, or he didn't believe it, and used the opportunity to make the preposterous, pulled-from-thin-air claim that the attack was made because he was the "frontrunner" and needed to be knocked down.

Besides, even if Joker wanted to parse SEIU's exact wording like the former lawyer he was, the essence of SEIU's message about Joker's illegitimate conduct was accurate and was taken from public record. The court in Joker's disbarment case concluded that Joker engaged in "forging the endorsements" on a check and "misappropriating the funds."

The District 12 campaign had proceeded civilly for a long time, but with Man of the People's criminal election law violation and the ugly back-and-forth battle between SEIU and Joker, with Energy and Zelig caught in the crosshairs, the gloves had come off and everything that makes a political campaign a car wreck—simultaneously sickening and compelling—was transpiring.

# June 18, 2014 – The Kingmaker

Game Over!

The primary was less than a week away, and my mailbox was overflowing with campaign mailers like a garbage bin on Hoarder's Cleanup Day. One of the mailers was from Zelig, where he put the final hammer down, fired the kill shot, inserted the "dagger!" as basketball announcers bellow when a sharpshooter makes a last-minute three-pointer to put a game away: a testimonial from the Rock God, who was a political Kingmaker. "Howard County Leaders Agree on Zelig" read the headline. Rock God's testimonial appeared with his head shot: "Zelig is a hard-working, dedicated community leader. His commitment to public service will ensure that District 12 is well represented in Annapolis, and he has the experience to hit the ground running to serve you on day one."

With Rock God publicly announcing his support of Zelig to voters, I knew Zelig couldn't be beat.

I felt disgusted to have a candidate from another district insert himself into another race, using his influence to try to sway the outcome. Can't politicians just focus on their own race? Isn't that enough? You know, like my kids' pre-school teachers astutely counseled their own brand of rascals, "Worry about yourself?" Just as I believed the three newcomer contenders for the open delegate seat in Rock God's District 13 should have run against each other independently rather than vie for the privilege of riding the coattails of powerful Team 13, I believed candidates in other contests should stick to their own districts and constituencies, and not attempt to influence voters in another district or meddle in the independent campaigns the candidates were admirably running in District 12. But that was wishful thinking. All is fair in politics, as long as it is legal. Those who have the power to influence use it as they wish to further their own goals and surround themselves with their hand-picked choices.

# June 19, 2014 – One Door Closes; Another Doesn't Open

I visited Door Number 1,307 at 7:15 p.m. The resident turned out to be James Bock, a former *Baltimore Sun* reporter whom I had met a few times while I was at *The Sun*. We talked for a half hour at his door about the newspaper business and our career paths since we left; long commutes; his new life in retirement; our kids; the political game and challenges my campaign faced; and the governor's race.

After my conversation with Bock, I decided his would be the last house I would visit. I liked the number 1307, both lucky and unlucky, my birth date followed by James Bond (well, almost, just missing one zero). I thought it would be good to close my door-to-door travails on the note of a wide-ranging conversation with someone I knew. While I knew other candidates would be redoubling their canvassing efforts over the next four days before primary day, I believed it would be spinning wheels and wasting time for me. I decided I would get more visibility from riding the Sachs for Delegate BikeMobile around the community. At Number 1307 on my 65th outing, Bock was my swan song.

# June 23, 2014, Election Eve – Volunteers? Uh...Yeah, by the Truckload

I rode the BikeMobile after work, running into the Gadfly campaign setting up signs at an elementary school polling site. As I approached the school parking lot, Pest, Gadfly's husband, was pulling out in his catering van. A large Gadfly banner hung on a rail. Pest stopped and got out to greet me.

"You've added a lot to the campaign, it was great having you in the race," Pest told me.

"Thanks. I've tried to stay true to the reasons I entered. It's been a big adventure."

"So who do you think has the best chances tomorrow," Pest asked.

"I haven't seen any polls, but Zelig and Anointed One definitely seem like the frontrunners, if I had to guess," I said. "I would say the third spot is up for grabs."

Pest agreed with me on Zelig and Anointed One. Then he rattled off his wife and two other candidates to round out his top five. I had a positive impression of Pest and it was nice to know he had talents as a prognosticator. But it probably would have behooved him to have more discretion than to tell me face-to-face that he thought I was a bottom-feeder, even if he believed that to the core of his being. It was like me naming my top five catering companies in the area and omitting his Dionysius Kitchen. It was tactless, but he was caught up in the moment.

"How many volunteers are you going to have working the polls tomorrow," Pest asked.

I considered for a moment whether I should tell the truth. Ah, screw it, I decided. Yes, I had to admit to myself, I was crossing the line toward becoming more like a politician, compromising my integrity that gay rights activist Steve Charing had recently applauded by fudging the truth—and even worse, rationalizing that I was only fudging the truth, because really I was outright lying—and I wasn't even in office.

"I think I'll have about 10 or 12," I lied, knowing I would only have a few.

"We're going to have about 100 volunteers," Pest boasted, making me feel impotent. "Good luck, see you around tomorrow," he said, and got back in his catering van to head off to the next polling site.

*Damn, if I knew Pest was going to go three figures, I would have jacked it up to 50! I was learning the art of prevarication, way too late, and obviously defaulting to too much modesty!*

At the school, I was served one more reminder of Zelig's tenacity, work ethic, dedication and comprehensiveness. By 7 p.m., he had posted 10 small Zelig signs and one large Zelig sign at this one polling place. I wondered: Could Zelig have blanketed each of the 62 polling precincts that way, 600 signs in all? I had to acknowledge: Probably so.

A Twitter tweet on primary election eve from Man of the People for Delegate confirmed that my assumption was probably accurate: "Congrats @ZeligMD for beating #TEAMMANOFTHE PEOPLE2014 in planting signs at the #HoCoMD precincts! We're joking the polls have been "#Zelig'd!"

Entering my home street, I passed a young man working the intersection as a "sign twirler" for Joker Gets It Done, just as I had leaving for work in the morning. I stopped to talk to Ballerina and her sister and daughter, who were posting signs at my home precinct. I pedaled home, nothing left but for Judgement Day.

# June 24, 2014 -- Judgement Day

Today would be my Olympics, not the 100-meters, but the marathon or the decathlon. The top three would ascend the medal stand, the winners' medals draped around their necks, and cry tears of happiness for the fruits of labor over the years leading up to the crucial moment. The fourth-place finisher could feel pride in coming close, the respectability and self-satisfaction that comes from having given the effort and fought the good fight, but would still be a loser just like the 10th place finisher—but probably even worse because of second-guessing what might have been if they had only done this or that—and would not be elevated to a loftier level of status and power, or even remembered, going home with nothing tangible.

At 7 a.m., I rode the BikeMobile to my home precinct, a retirement residence, and met my son. Retiring Delegate Drummer was there wearing an Anointed One shirt. There was a slow trickle of voters during rush hour, an indication of a low turnout. When I went in to vote around 7:20, the election volunteers outnumbered the voters; there was no line, not like when I came to the same poll in November 2008 to vote for Obama and had to wait in a line at mid-day that snaked out of the large meeting room and down a residential hallway. Passing out my literature outside, I met a Zelig volunteer, a manager of a physical therapy clinic, wearing the purple Zelig t-shirt. At 8:30, he was relieved by another Zelig volunteer—a well-oiled machine.

I drove to work at the tail end of the morning rush, passing two young men sign-twirling for Joker across the street from each other; they would still be out flipping and spinning when I returned at evening rush hour, assuring Joker the most style points of any campaign.

I flagrantly violated Election Day dogma by not running around to polls all day and greeting voters and passing out my literature. What kind of politician doesn't do this? It was positively blasphemy of Guidebook to Election Day 101. But I didn't do it, didn't think it would make a difference, in fact, thought it would be discouraging and disappointing, with a turnout more befitting a funeral viewing for a miserly old recluse than a One Direction concert. The dye was already cast, I believed.

After work, Amy and I went electioneering at Phelps Luck Elementary School, where my kids attended. I counted nine Zelig signs; he was hitting his 10 per site average. I talked to a Zelig volunteer, a recent college graduate who I had seen at numerous forums. She was stationed at Phelps Luck for the full 13-hour election shift. Zelig had me scratching my head again: How did he get that kind of dedication from a 22-year-old? Didn't she have Facebooking to do? Girlfriends to hang with at Starbucks? There were more campaign volunteers milling around, looking for something to do, than voters arriving at any given time.

The straggle of voters was a disheartening statement about American democracy. At the top of both the Democratic and Republican tickets, there were highly competitive races that would determine Maryland's next governor. That alone would seem enough reason to bring out voters, let alone the opportunity to influence the outcome of the District 12 delegate race that could determine all three politicians to represent them in the State House, potentially for decades. But it wasn't.

# THE MOMENT OF TRUTH

*"The truth does not change according*
*to our ability to stomach it."*

FLANNERY O'CONNOR, AUTHOR

The buzz at gubernatorial candidate Mizeur's outdoor "victory cel-ebration" party was starting to fizzle around 9:30 p.m., as the crowd had not been fed encouraging news, left literally in the dark. I told Amy to stop announcing the District 12 election results rolling in with early precinct returns after she read off the top three places, which didn't include me. But I gave in to temptation.

"Okay, what the hell, go ahead and read the rest." I braced for the truth.

When I heard Amy name Joker, the self-proclaimed "frontrunner," in front of me in eighth place, my heart sank. I was buried in ninth, right where all the traditional markers of political success—money, en-dorsements, volunteers and political connections—would have naturally placed me. I was wrong that I could beat the odds and outperform my relative (low) standing in money raised and influential connections. Predictably, the only candidate trailing me was Spare-A-Dime. I wanted a better showing, even if I didn't win, but all I could do was accept my fate and hope it changed as more precincts reported later in the evening.

We learned that the underdog candidate who I actually believed had a chance to pull an amazing upset also was not going to pull off the miracle, as Lieutenant Governor Brown was far outdistancing Mizeur. The air was draining as reality set in, though the candidate hadn't appeared to address the crowd yet. The party began to feel like a wake. I was surrounded by hopefuls, but suddenly felt alone.

"Should we hang around to hear Heather? Is there anything else you want to do?" I asked Amy.

"I've had enough, what about you?"

"No. I gave it my best. I'm done. Let's go home."

Nine months of work, planning, risks, challenges, tension, struggle, rejection, affirmation, drudgery, disappointment, excitement, adventure, surprises, learning, innovation, rising to the occasion, purpose and meaning, suddenly and emphatically over. There's nothing like a campaign to make you feel alive. But I instantly started feeling adrift, without the anchor that had added significance to my life. As much as I know I am *somebody* by my mere humanness and being—we're all told we're all God's children, right?—my ego still craved to be acknowledged as a *real somebody* by the outside world, to be awarded the external seal of approval. Instead, barring a miracle, I would wake up on June 25 feeling like Ray Liotta's Henry Hill of *Goodfellas* in the anonymous suburban monotony of his Mafia-free witness protection life, eating noodles with ketchup—*I'm an average nobody...get to live the rest of my life like a schnook.*

# EPILOGUE

*"You have to remember one thing about the*
*will of the people: it wasn't that long ago that*
*we were swept away by the Macarena."*

JON STEWART, FORMER HOST, COMEDY
CENTRAL'S THE *DAILY SHOW*

I wish I could say I awoke June 25 to a well-coiffed morning TV news anchor giving me the thrill of my life—that an unexpected change in voting patterns had vaulted me into a dead heat for third place. But I couldn't.

The previous night's early returns clearly set the pattern. Zelig and Anointed One dominated in Howard County, as expected, each earning more than 4,500 votes, far outpolling Energy, who was third with 2,870.

Gadfly proved her strength in the smaller Baltimore County side of District 12, perhaps stemming from her continuing advocacy against The Promenade at Catonsville mega-development, cruising by a wide margin to the highest vote count there with 2,135. Next Big Thing, Energy, Anointed One and Zelig followed, closely bunched within 26 votes of each other.

Zelig and Anointed One were so strong in Howard County that their solid performances in Baltimore County kept them far ahead of the pack, with Zelig placing first at 21.3 percent overall and Anointed One second with 20.5 percent. The dogfight for third came down to Gadfly, Energy and Next Big Thing.

As a "carpetbagger" with no real roots in either side of the district, Next Big Thing performed nearly equally well on both sides, garnering 1,558 votes in Baltimore County and 1,433 in Howard County. But Gadfly still outpolled Next Big Thing in Howard. The difference separating the three contenders may have been Energy's 33-year teaching career in Howard County, the majority of which occurred at the main high school serving District 12. Energy's performance in Howard County was too much for Gadfly and Next Big Thing to overcome. Energy placed third with 14.9 percent, followed by Gadfly at 12.8 percent and Next Big Thing at 10.1 percent.

Rounding out the bottom five, ahead of me and Spare-A-Dime, were Ballerina, Man of the People and Joker, at between 6.4 percent and 4.2 percent.

I captured 747 votes, for 2.5 percent. That seemed pathetic. And disappointing. But I tried to view the outcome positively. Seven hundred forty seven people who had the option to vote for any three of 10 candidates chose me and not at least seven others. Now that's looking at the glass one-tenth full!

And someone who knew a lot about politics and had followed the race closely, Jason Booms, the Spartan Considerations blogger and former political consultant, e-mailed me on the day after with a positive message that filled my cup to one-eighth.

"You ran a great, principled campaign," Booms wrote to me. "You came close to beating Joker among early voters; given the amount he spent on TV ads, that is no small feat. You clearly connected with a segment of the electorate."

In his wrap-up analysis in Spartan Considerations, Booms said Zelig and Anointed One were "virtual locks" and Energy benefitted from "serious institutional support" (particularly teachers' associations) and "a divided field." Next Big Thing's "relative newcomer status hurt his campaign" and his positioning as the "Pragmatic Choice" failed to capture enough hearts and minds, Booms said, before offering me a final prop:

"And a big thumbs-up to Adam Sachs for running with integrity and grit in the face of long odds. I was hoping he might fare a little better, but when the Mizeur numbers started coming in, it was clear that an upset would be extremely unlikely."

## A Value for the Money

But if statistics can be used to say anything, I could make them say I was the best candidate for the money to claim my hollow victory. I couldn't possibly beat Spare-A-Dime for that honor, since he spent nothing and received votes, so we'll eliminate him as an outlier. So on the measure of least money spent per vote, I absolutely crushed the rest of the field! *(See Appendix 3 on Shopping for Votes.)* I spent $3.36 per vote I received; Energy was a distant second, at $8.63. The top two finishers, Zelig and Anointed One, spent $16.93 and $17.39 per vote, respectively, about five times more than me.

The leader in most money spent per vote predictably was the profligate Joker, with a whopping $114.96. Second to Joker in that category was Next Big Thing, at $29.10. So maybe there's a non-scientific conclusion there: the "carpetbaggers" spent more money per vote than the rest of the field, and still did not come close to winning.

All told, the eight candidates who employed money-raising operations spent about $600,000 on the primary election, including three who spent more than $100,000—Joker, Anointed One and Zelig. When I consider that, all I can conclude is: What a colossal waste of money! There must be a better way than for candidates to immerse themselves in raising more and more money so they can endeavor to litter lawns with signs and deluge the market with endless self-promotions, almost all of which are meaningless drivel, empty rhetoric, simplistic sound bites and mean-spirited attacks.

We need our media companies and public broadcasting outlets to step up and provide a real public service by opening up the airwaves in some manner to more debates, forums, interview segments or advertising so those who are interested in participating in civic life and engaging in democracy truly have a chance to view and evaluate the candidates beyond which candidate has the most money to flood their mailboxes with postcards and neighborhoods' lawns with signs.

Overall turnout was pathetic, at about 20 percent in Howard County, nearly 25 percent in Baltimore County, and 22 percent in Maryland, a low for a Maryland gubernatorial primary, a figure that had fallen steadily from about 40 percent in 1994.

But it wasn't just Maryland experiencing apathy among the electorate in 2014. Less than a quarter of registered voters showed up in California's primary three weeks earlier, a new low for that state. Fewer than 10 percent of Republican and 4 percent of Democratic voters turned out for Texas's primary. And less than 1 in 6 registered their choices in primaries in Indiana, North Carolina and South Carolina.

# EVERYWHERE

On February 27, 2016, I was in a hotel room in Rehoboth Beach, Delaware, when I turned on the morning news on WBOC-TV 16 out of Salisbury on Maryland's Eastern Shore, home to the Perdue Farms chicken processing conglomerate. The anchor voiced-over footage of a rally in Annapolis featuring environmentalists and Eastern Shore residents advocating for the Poultry Litter Management Act, which would hold "Big Chicken" accountable for properly managing chicken manure. In the front row of a pan shot of rally-goers holding signs warning of the environmental dangers of poorly regulated "Chicken Poop" was a legislator in a crisp, dark suit I immediately recognized: Zelig, a primary sponsor of the bill protecting Maryland residents from chicken manure pollution. Everywhere, indeed.

# Tyler Benson: What It Takes

T he apathy of so many registered voters—citizens who faithfully fail to exercise the most fundamental right of democracy while citizens of other nations die fighting to earn it—stands in such sharp contrast to certain candidates. Tyler Benson was one of those.

I got on Benson's radar during the campaign, possibly because we have a mutual friend or maybe he just picked my name and e-mail up off a statewide candidates' list, and I followed his journey casually through his messages.

But one message in particular piqued my interest in his candidacy, and inspired me to get in touch with him. Benson dreamed up what I thought was a great publicity stunt to illustrate a huge constituent problem: horrendous traffic congestion in the suburbs just outside of Washington. Benson staged an evening rush-hour race with his campaign manager and treasurer. In Benson's "Great Race," Benson would start at a Metro subway station and ride a bike along a proposed subway route between two urban cores designed to relieve congestion across Montgomery County, Md.; his campaign manager would take the subway on an existing meandering route between the two subway sites; and his treasurer would drive.

Benson wanted it bad, and believed he could win. He was a highly ambitious and driven 28-year-old trying to bang down the General Assembly door in perhaps the most affluent and highly educated district in Montgomery County in one of the wealthiest, predominantly white-collar counties in the nation, much like my neighboring home county.

In one Bethesda ZIP Code in Benson's district, the median household income was $167,475, 83.5 percent were college graduates, and the median value of a house was nearly $900,000 in 2014.

Benson railed against the exorbitant cost of living in his home county, saying living there as a millennial was "almost like a tax on being young" and that he was "representing a generation that has not been well represented in government." Benson, who graduated from Vassar College and obtained a master's degree from the Johns Hopkins University Bloomberg School of Public Health, talked openly about the challenges of being a young adult, struggling to pay the basic costs of living and to find a job during the recession despite doing all the right things.

"It was my understanding there was some kind of American promise growing up, that if I did well in school, and got straight A's, and went to an Ivy League school, and went to the best school of public health in the United States, that maybe I would be able to find a job," Benson said in an interview in Montgomery County's *Gazette*. "It isn't that easy...Maybe our government needs to take a little bit greater care to understand that there is a whole generation of talent and energy and industriousness, filled with a desire for public service, and we are underutilized."

Benson took a leave of absence from his job to make a full-time, 18-month run for delegate in a district that had one open seat.

Impressed with Benson's imagination, determination and the issues he was raising, I arranged to meet him for lunch three weeks after the primary to see what drove him.

I discovered a young man with a voracious, all-consuming appetite for breaking into electoral politics and a hunger for the prerequisite campaigning—maybe too much hunger.

Benson told me he raised money from 800 donors by asking at their doorsteps; visited 10,000 doors himself, generating on-the-spot contributions from 1 of every 6; had volunteers knock on 5,000 more; tolerated innumerable rejections; recruited 50 volunteers; developed an e-mail marketing list of thousands; began his campaign before he even announced publicly; and worked morning to night engaging in phone calls, planning, strategy meetings and canvassing.

The author of the political blog The Seventh State, in his analysis of Benson's race, wrote that "Benson's campaign shows exceptional hustle," but added, "however…his well-meaning effort nonetheless sometimes strikes people as too hard-charging."

Similar to Zelig, Benson reinforced my own feelings that I was inadequate, ill-equipped, and insufficiently determined and committed as a candidate. Like in one of my endorsement interviews where the interviewers punched holes all over my one-man band, Chevy Smart Car-style campaign, Benson grilled me on how many doors I knocked, how much money I raised, how many volunteers I had, who had endorsed me and how many I had received, how long I had campaigned, and how far in advance I had decided to run.

But the dedication Benson devoted to his campaign took a huge toll on him, even as an energetic young man; as an unmarried man, it consumed his life. He lost weight, ate poorly, sometimes only one meal a day, and got minimal sleep.

Feeling downright guilty at how my effort paled in comparison to Benson's, I offered my pat excuses for why I didn't put in more time or have more resources or do better—a full-time job, kids and wife, a graduate school program. I suggested maybe it was easier to run as a single person.

"Well, yes and no," Benson said. "My time is my own, but at the end of the day, there's nobody around to offer support or talk to. Sometimes it would have been nice just to have someone just to make a meal after campaigning all day and hardly having time to eat."

The grind of the campaign and aggressive politics could be a lonely ordeal, said Benson, who had suffered from the emotional impacts, the rough times, petty slights, overwhelming disadvantages, seeming unfairness, rejections, disappointments and fatigue, with no one to build him back up.

And even after all his effort, Benson still finished far out of the running to advance to the general election, placing a distant fifth in a field of eight in which the top three advanced. Benson garnered 7.4 percent of the votes; the top three each scored more than 21 percent.

The two incumbents benefitted from all the advantages of incumbency to swamp him. The third-place finisher was an attorney in a prestigious Washington law firm and a former Capitol Hill staffer who already enjoyed Democratic Party insider status—he had previously turned down an opportunity to be appointed to the seat.

A glance at fundraising explained at least part of why Benson could only make a small dent in the outcome despite his prodigious effort. Entering 2014, the top three finishers each had more than $120,000 on hand, while Benson had $22,000. The fourth-place finisher, who doubled up Benson in votes, had $117,000, and had made $120,000 in personal loans to his campaign. Benson simply was overwhelmed by political power, connections and money.

Think of all the time Benson spent on the drudgery of campaigning, visiting 15,000 homes for 2,600 votes, about 1 vote per 6 houses. And think of how much worse he likely would have done without putting himself through all that rigmarole.

Benson said he was relieved that his campaign was over, but, like me to a much lesser degree, also felt lost without a campaign that had so encompassed his life, passion, purpose, desire and dream. When you live for a dream for so long and it's suddenly over, what do you do next? Benson said he was going to keep running until he made it. But if he's still in the same district and all the incumbents run for re-election, he would face another torturous, uphill battle.

Benson had been infected with the political bug. It was in his gut, and had spread to every fiber of his being. I could tell during that lunch that he was eager to keep running for office even though there was nothing to run for anymore. But there was the concept of staying on the radar—paying political dues—by immersing himself in community service activities, a la Zelig, and I had no doubt at the conclusion of our lunch meeting that Benson would do that for a few years until his time to re-emerge in campaign mode.

In February 2015, I received an e-mail from Benson announcing that he had campaigned for all the Democratic nominees for the general election in his district and had become a Democratic "area coordinator" to work on increasing voter turnout for the 2014 general election. Noting the low voter turnout, Benson announced that he had co-founded the Millennial Caucus of Montgomery County to inspire young adults to get more involved in the political process. He also announced he had launched an "entrepreneurial venture at the intersection of social media and political engagement."

He concluded, "Though I am shutting down [the 2014 Benson for Maryland] campaign...I am and will continue to be active in local politics."

Benson was true to his word. Since that campaign swan-song message, he became a representative to a downtown advisory committee and an advisory board member on the Washington Suburban Sanitation Commission, in addition to continuing membership on the Western Montgomery County Citizens Advisory Board.

Like Zelig, Benson went right to work building his political resume and network of future donors, supporters, word-spreaders and path-clearers to be ready when opportunity knocked. I am confident Benson's drive will land him in public office someday. My meeting with Benson, and learning about his enduring political pursuits and desires even after he lost his election convincingly, served as the curtain-call reminder to me of why I didn't precede him in acquiring my own high-backed chair, and why I will never join him when he breaks through.

## You Kill My Dog, I Kill Your Cat

With my campaign experience still fresh, I attended National Night Out, a community crime-fighting event, in my neighborhood. It was a magnet for November's general election political candidates, and I talked to Energy about the primary. Energy told me about a run-in he had with Joker at the high school precinct where Energy had taught math.

"My volunteers were telling me that Joker was badmouthing me and Zelig at my old high school," Energy said. "That wasn't right. He was telling voters we were 'union stooges' because we got endorsed by SEIU. I couldn't believe it. That was so obnoxious, really low. We were going at it."

In addition to endorsing Energy and Zelig, the Service Employees International Union (SEIU) was the organization that sent the anti-Joker mailer to voters that said "Joker Stole His Own Client's Money."

"Joker told me he was going to fight back against SEIU during the campaign," Energy said, "but he didn't say he was going to attack us by calling us pawns of the union and blame us for playing dirty politics against him. We had nothing to do with that."

Energy told me he took umbrage at Joker's mailer accusing him of being in the union's pocket and smearing his name, and Joker's condescending verbal comments to voters at the polls. He confronted Joker at the high school.

According to Energy, Joker leveled these fighting words against him: "You kill my dog, I'll kill your cat."

That line could only have come from a former General Assembly member or a lobbyist, and Joker was both. The dog-cat retribution reference is a colloquial Annapolis lawmakers' saying referring to the practice of one lawmaker getting even with a fellow legislator who has done something dastardly or underhanded such as working to defeat one's own bill.

Energy said he argued vociferously with Joker that he didn't coordinate with SEIU on the anti-Joker mailing and had no knowledge it was in the works, but he said Joker didn't buy it.

"I told him, 'I didn't kill your dog.' The union did the mailer on its own, but he didn't want to hear it. So he was calling me a liar *and* a 'union stooge,'" Energy said with exasperation, as if reliving the ugliness of the confrontation. "I'm not a liar or a stooge. That really ticked me off."

Energy's recounting of that exchange exhibited the fierce, ruthless and nasty side of politics of which I was always leery. Energy, I was convinced, was an honorable and genuinely nice man who did not believe in attacking or rolling over others, yet he got sucked into the muck. I'm sure if I had gotten as far as Energy, I would have had to swim through the mire also.

Energy, Anointed One and Zelig went on to form a District 12 team slate along with Career Pol and trounced their three Republican opponents in the general election, as expected in the predominantly Democratic district gerrymandered for just that sort of result.

As for me, I won't be killing someone's figurative dog or cat as an act of legislative retribution. I said after the first time that I'd never say never about running for office again, and that hedge was a good thing, because it allowed me to have an experience of a lifetime in a rollicking political campaign at the state level, dealing with significant national issues. But now you can write it into a veto-proof law; it has been passed, signed, shuffled across the desk and put in the books: *Hasta la vista, baby.* Never again.

# APPENDIX 1: ANATOMY OF A $100,000 FUNDRAISER

Maryland Senator Marcus Zeitzer, chairman of the Maryland Senate Judicial Proceedings Committee, raised $100,775 on October 9, 2014, less than a month before the 2014 Maryland general election. He generated the bounty even though he had no Republican opponent in the election. Zeitzer's fundraiser is emblematic of how incumbent politicians can leverage the desire of business interests, political action committees (PACs) and unions to stay in the good graces of, gain access to, and have influence with, elected officials in positions of power by donating large amounts compared to a typical grassroots voter. Zeitzer collected cash in big wads, with 69 of the 101 total contributions equaling $1,000 or more. The average contribution was $998, and only 17 of the 101 contributions was less than $500. Just 5.4 percent of Zeitzer's haul came from individuals without an identified affiliation with a business interest, PAC or union, according to Zeitzer's campaign finance report. Here is an anatomy of Zeitzer's $100,000 snatch, exemplifying the power of wealth in politics:

| Source | Contributions | Average Per Contribution | % of Total |
|---|---|---|---|
| Corporations/ LLCs/ Businesses/ Contractors | $21,250 | $966 | 21.1% |
| Unions/ PACs/ Funds | $9,150 | $704 | 9.1% |

| Legal/ Law Firms/ Lawyers | $13,500 | $844 | 13.4% |
|---|---|---|---|
| Financial/ Investment Firms | $6,275 | $1,046 | 6.2% |
| Alcohol | $1,000 | $1,000 | 1.0% |
| Automotive | $10,000 | $1,667 | 9.9% |
| Utility/Energy | $1,000 | $1,000 | 1.0% |
| Bail Bonds/ Insurance Services | $17,000 | $1,545 | 16.9% |
| Real Estate | $10,500 | $1,313 | 10.4% |
| Health Care/ Physicians | $5,700 | $713 | 5.7% |
| Individuals | $5,400 | $600 | 5.4% |
| **Total** | **$100,775** | **$998** | |

# Appendix 2: Lobbying: "Pay to Play" or an Expensive Method to Educate Lawmakers?

I n the six months from November 1, 2015 through April 30, 2016, including the three-month 2016 Maryland General Assembly session, industries spent nearly $20 million on lobbying the legislature, an increase of 18 percent over two years. The unanswerable question: How much does big spending on lobbying influence the outcome of policy and legislation, and thus an industry's profit-making potential, government support and ability to operate with limited government restriction? You can be sure the industries that spend heavily on lobbying believe they get a return on investment. Here are the 29 industry categories that spent at least $50,000 on lobbying during that six-month period.

| Industry | Spending on Lobbying, Nov. 1, 2015 – April 30, 2016 | Average Spending on Lobbying per Participating Organization |
|---|---|---|
| Health care | $4.53 million | $100,568 |
| Utility/Energy | $1.82 million | $139,934 |
| Builders/ Realtors | $1.65 million | $91,481 |
| Insurance | $1.2 million | $109,181 |

| | | |
|---|---|---|
| Business | $1.19 million | $85,027 |
| Other* | $1.15 million | $104,873 |
| Telecom | $784,614 | $112,088 |
| Gambling | $728,821 | $91,103 |
| Transportation | $664,952 | $83,119 |
| Automobile | $660,274 | $73,364 |
| Education | $516,583 | $172,194 |
| Religion | $493,567 | $123,392 |
| University | $464,267 | $154,756 |
| Social Justice | $463,424 | $92,685 |
| Retail | $436,290 | $62,327 |
| Union | $388,393 | $77,679 |
| Banking | $362,964 | $181,482 |
| Alcohol | $327,863 | $81,966 |
| Tobacco | $258,999 | $81,966 |
| Environment | $242,233 | $80.744 |
| Waste Management | $234,000 | $117,000 |
| Local Government | $229,179 | $76,391 |
| Defense | $222,651 | $111,825 |
| Bar Association (Law) | $203,206 | $101,603 |
| Institution (museum/zoo) | $123,834 | $61,917 |

| | | |
|---|---|---|
| Agriculture | $101,857 | $101,857 |
| Guns | $52,489 | $52,489 |
| **Total** | **$19.81 million** | |

*Other includes organizations and companies with unclear or various goals and interests.

**Source:** Common Cause Maryland, from data from the Maryland State Ethics Commission Lobby Report.

# Appendix 3: Shopping for Votes

S tudies have shown that the amount of money a candidate raises and spends is strongly correlated to votes and electoral success. Some candidates take the Bergdorf Goodman route, betting that the high-end, extravagant spending style of Prada, Gucci, Givenchy and Jimmy Choo will pay big dividends, while others adopt the bargain-basement approach of a Kmart, whether by philosophy or necessity. Here is how much the District 12 Maryland delegate candidates in my race raised and spent for the primary (remember, the primary winners still had to consider strategically budgeting for the general election four months later), and what it cost them to earn each vote.

| Candidate | Money Raised | Money Spent | Amount Spent Per Vote Received |
|:---:|:---:|:---:|:---:|
| Joker | $151,125 | $143,244 | $114.96 |
| Next Big Thing | $94,070 | $87,041 | $29.10 |
| Ballerina | $52,987 | $46,980 | $24.62 |
| Anointed One* | $110,966 | $105,336 | $17.39 |
| Zelig* | $121,784 | $106,785 | $16.93 |
| Man of the People | $23,863 | $23,808 | $15.11 |
| Gadfly | $36,443 | $36,751 | $9.72 |

| | | | |
|---|---|---|---|
| Energy* | $44,830 | $38,197 | $8.63 |
| Adam G. Sachs | $2,508 | $2,508 | $3.36 |
| Spare-A-Dime | $0 | $0 | $0 |
| **Total** | **$638,576** | **$590,650** | **$19.94** |

*Primary election winners
**Source:** Maryland campaign finance reports

# About the Author

**A**dam Gordon Sachs has garnered 2,277 votes in his two unsuccessful runs for public office, county council in 2006 and state delegate in 2014. He is a master's degree candidate in pastoral counseling at Loyola University-Maryland (2017 graduation) and has interned as a therapist at outpatient community mental health clinics. He has worked in public relations representing a health care profession, health insurer, developmental disability agency, public school reform organization and the American Lung Association. He has been a reporter for the *Baltimore Sun, Sarasota (FL) Herald-Tribune,* NFL Properties and health care trade publications. His first book, the novel *Three Yards and a Plate of Mullet,* also published by Sirenian Publishing, describes the travails of a rookie sportswriter in a backwater Florida town covering an intense season of high school football and going head-to-head against the ruthless, win-at-all-costs coach from the town's dynastic family. Sachs lives in Columbia, Maryland with his wife, Amy. He has two children, Rebecca and Daniel.

## Sirenian Publishing Titles and Blogs

*Three Yards and a Plate of Mullet*

*Don't Knock, He's Dead: A Longshot Candidate Gets Schooled in the Unseemly Underbelly of American Campaign Politics*

The Midlife Dude Blog: www.midlifedude.wordpress.com